DISCARDED

DISCARD

TUNDRA *passages*

Post-Communist Cultural Studies Series

*Thomas Cushman, General Editor*

# TUNDRA *passages*

history and gender in the RUSSIAN FAR EAST

*petra rethmann*

The Pennsylvania State University Press | University Park, Pennsylvania

Library of Congress Cataloging-in-Publication Data

Rethmann, Petra, 1964–
Tundra Passages : gender and history in the Russian Far East /
Petra Rethmann.
p.   cm. — (Post-communist cultural studies series)
Includes bibliographical references and index.
ISBN 0-271-02057-1 (cloth : alk. paper)
ISBN 0-271-02058-X (paper : alk. paper)
1. Koryaks—Social conditions.   2. Korëikskiæ avtonomnyæ
okrug (Russia)—Social conditions.   3. Korëikskiæ avtonomnyæ
okrug (Russia)—Social life and customs.   4. Man-woman
relationsips—Russia (Federation)—Korëikskiæ avtonomnyæ
okrug.   5. Post-communism—Russia (Federation)—Korëikskiæ
avtonomnyæ okrug.   I. Title.   II. Post-communist
cultural studies.

DK759.K6 R48   2000
306'.09577—dc21
00-027249

Copyright © 2001 The Pennsylvania State University
All rights reserved
Printed in the United States of America
Published by The Pennsylvania State University Press,
University Park, PA 16802-1003

It is the policy of The Pennsylvania State University Press to use
acid-free paper for the first printing of all clothbound books.
Publications on uncoated stock satisfy the minimum requirements
of American National Standard for Information
Sciences—Permanence of Paper for Printed Library Materials,
ANSI Z39.48–1992.

to | ▢ ▢ ▢

*Moite Uvarova*
*with gratitude and respect*

# contents □□□

The transliteration of Russian words in this book follows the Library of Congress system. I have recognized soft signs and hard signs from the Russian language by using one or two apostrophes, respectively. I have made general exceptions for accepted Western spelling of names such as *Olga*, rather than *Ol'ga*.

Throughout the text, I use the anglicized version of the names of important ethnographers of the Russian Far East. For example, instead of *Iokhel'son*, I use the more common *Jochelson*, instead of *Bogoraz*, *Bogoras*. I use anglicized plurals throughout to render indigenous names in a more readable fashion (for example, *Koriaks* instead of *Koriaki*).

In January 1992, when I arrived at the northeastern shore of Kamchatka peninsula in the Russian Far East, I expected to do a study on the process of sovietization as it existed until the middle of the 1980s among Koriak reindeer herders, an indigenous people who lived in the northern part of the peninsula. In particular, I was interested in the question of how Soviet state power and administrations had managed to seize dominion and institute authoritative rule in the peninsula. What means had the state deployed to implement its ideas? How had it policed political change? How had these processes affected Koriak everyday life? And how had reindeer herders coped with the historical changes that deeply transformed their existence in the tundra? These questions seemed pertinent for several reasons. During the Gorbachev-era of perestroika, little was known in the Western world about the life of northern indigenous peoples in Russia. How had they fared under the Soviet regime? How had they experienced Soviet power and dominion, and how had they dealt with these issues in their lives? Would the recent changes introduced by Gorbachev bring autonomy and economic betterment? As the outlines of the Soviet Union melted into thin air, nationality issues increasingly moved to the fore. At the same time, it became violently clear that Russia's epic journey of transition—from tsardom to the Soviet state to a democratic beginning—was not as straightforward as activists, scholars, and politicians might have thought. In fact, it was marred by social atrocities that surprised many observers.

By the beginning of the 1990s, media attention had increasingly turned to the much-troubled regions between the Black and Caspian Seas, the Baltic states, and the Central Asian countries in view of these areas' fervent demands for ethnic autonomy, their active assumption of cultural self-expression, and their insistence on international political support. Although in their struggle for autonomy—what some have even called life in the post-colony (Freidin 1994)—these regions received much attention (and for good reason), the northern fringes of the former empire did not. While post-Soviet society was wreaking havoc around them, indigenous peoples seemed to live encapsulated

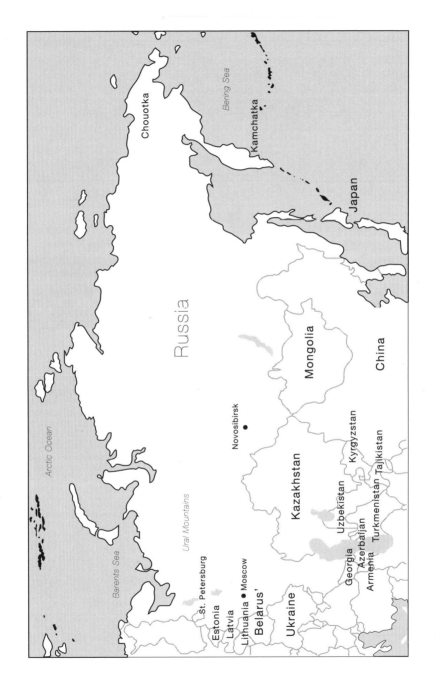

MAP 1 | Russia and the former Soviet Union

in their own ahistoric, uneventful world. Certainly by the beginning of the 1990s, some voices had protested the destruction of the tundra by state-induced animal overgrazing (under the Communist-plan economy) and oil plants and the depletion of other natural resources (for example, Murashko, Pika, and Bogoiavlenskii 1993; Klokov 1996; and a series of publications in the journal *Zhivaia Arktika*). But these protests were insufficient to ensure northern indigenous peoples a place on television screens. Such neglect enjoys a long-standing tradition and seems to flow from an urban imagination that described non-Western "primitive" cultures as "cold" (Lévi-Strauss 1966), that is, by implication, as unstimulating and drab. In the case of northern Russia's indigenous peoples, this metaphor has a particularly deplorable, if ironic, ring: Living in cold places is not newsworthy.

In the context of Russian-oriented and post-Soviet scholarship, the absence of a focus on indigenous issues suggests, I believe, a historical and political interest that has concentrated predominantly on urban centers and has avoided the periphery. Of course, until the very end of the 1980s, when perestroika was already well underway, access to ethnographic fieldwork for foreign researchers in, for example, the Russian Far East was greatly limited. Thus, on one hand, it can be said that scholarly neglect of the political and geographical periphery emerges only partially from a lack of interest in nonurban, out-of-the way localities. On the other hand, however, North American and European scholarship has long emphasized the contrast between democratic and state socialist notions of power and has frequently studied issues of nationalism and identity in relation to socialist notions of social improvement and nation building—with a heightened emphasis on political structures and state policies but little emphasis on local struggles for power and meaning. The possibilities for understanding the Soviet world were thus greatly limited by the categories of this conceptual division. As one consequence, there was only little room in earlier scholarship for examining historical and social issues of indigenous people living in nonurban, out-of-the-way places. But in the wake of the recent political processes and changes in the Russian Federation and new developments in both post-Soviet scholarship and in the social sciences in general, emerging alternatives have made it possible to think about issues of power, identity, and cultural difference in new ways (Rethmann 1997). For example, the Western vision of Russia, and by extension its people, as a political Other or "alien civilization" is breaking down. In lieu of stable political boundaries, arguments for dialogue and recognition of one another's problems have emerged.[1] It is hoped that this book contributes to the possibility and intellectual promise that lie in these openings.

Situated at the brink of a historical precipice, this book is both a reflection of the historical conditions that helped to change Koriak lives after the Soviet period and a chronicle of contemporary conditions of everyday life at Kamchatka's northeastern shore. Since the beginning of the 1990s, the social and economic predicaments of indigenous peoples in Russia have received increased attention in the writings of social scientists, as well as in newspapers and magazines (for example, *The New York Times* and the Toronto *Globe and Mail*). There have been reports on the unrelenting poverty in indigenous settlements, the torments of unemployment, the lack of monetary resources, starvation, the spread of diseases such as tuberculosis, cancer, and scurvy, and the insidious effects of drinking. In this context of social suffering, it is important to note that the social distress and economic desolation experienced by indigenous peoples in Russia greatly contribute to the current conditions of suffering and desolation.[2] Yet it seems equally important to note that an emphasis on social suffering places indigenous peoples in a discourse of endangerment that leaves only little room for recognizing their imaginative and creative efforts to forge new futures.

At the heart of this book is the refusal to represent and describe Koriak women and men as a culturally "dying Other," as many newspapers characterize indigenous people in the Russian Far East. This view ignores the creative ways in which, for example, Koriak women and men seek social possibilities and opportunities to create forms of dignity and respect. Their attempts to mitigate the harsh circumstances of their lives begin on the grounds of suffering, but they are not rooted in its acceptance. One goal of this book is to explore the creativity of local people in confronting and challenging past and present historical inequality. A second goal is to bring issues of gender, particularly issues faced by both Koriak women and men, into social sciences discussions examining the complexities and challenges of post-Soviet life. A third goal is to contribute to improving our understanding of the wider social and political issues faced by indigenous peoples in the Russian North.

## Research Connections

This book is based on two field trips to northern Kamchatka. My first trip spanned a period of ten months, from January to October 1992, and

□ □ □

my second trip a period of five months, from June to November 1994. During both stays, I lived in the villages of Tymlat and Ossora mainly with two Koriak families, both of whom invited and cared for me with extraordinary generosity and warmth. In living with these families, I was constantly reminded of the importance of social opportunities and limitations in lives other than my own. In recent years, excruciating poverty and various forms of social violence have begun to ravage Koriak families. Indeed, it is hard to fathom the depth of human suffering at Kamchatka's northeastern shore. Drinking, unemployment, loss of cultural autonomy and governance over Koriak lands, resettlement programs, barter with bottles of vodka or schnapps as currency, and atrocious depletion of natural resources such as sea animals and land by foreign corporations compounded Koriaks' sense of social depression and neglect. On several mornings while walking along the shore, Koriak friends and I found the pebbly strand littered with dead fish, bellies cut open and only the roe removed. While the cadavers wasted away on the land, covetous offenders traded the final product, caviar, for gainful prizes. Never-ending food shortages, drinking, and increasing unemployment gave life a particularly bitter twist. In the summer of 1994, there was barely anything to eat. Each day, villagers left their homes to collect berries and mushrooms in the tundra; they stayed for weeks at the beach to harvest mussels and catch fish for themselves and their kin. The economic uncertainties and political unpredictabilities that ravage the wider country also haunted—and increasingly so—Koriak existence at Kamchatka's northeastern shore.

Because of the conditions in which I lived and worked, the focus of my research began to shift. I discovered that the questions that mattered to me were not necessarily the questions that mattered to many of the Koriak women and men I knew. They too asked questions about history; they also expressed great interest in discussing how the recent circumstances of their living had been shaped. But, most of all, they were eager to discuss the current social and political calamities that devastated their lives. Thus I began to ask questions that I had previously not—and probably could not have—anticipated and imagined. Why was Koriak life so full of agony and despair? How were villagers affected by the deep changes in Russian political discourse and economic order? Why did I hear women frequently complain about the gendered disadvantages in regional political and community formations? And, given the ethnic complexities that existed in villages, how did people negotiate the tensions and multifaceted differences among themselves?

□ □ □

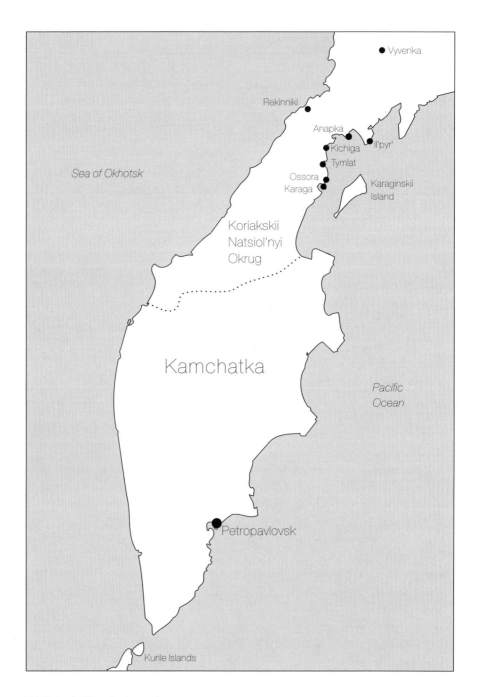

MAP 2 | Kamchatka region

As we lost our shyness with one another, people increasingly asked about the lives people led where I was from. At that point, I began to realize that the questions that women and men asked involved different subject matters and themes, revealing a good deal about their different concerns and the issues that were on their minds. Whereas men mostly posed questions about animal life in Germany and North America—questions I could not always answer to their satisfaction—women frequently wondered aloud about the relationships between women and men in the countries in which I lived. Did women in North America also want many children, they asked? Why did I not have any children? Were men always as preposterous and burdensome as they knew them? I thus began listening to the themes Koriak women and men thought worth talking about. My focus on history and gender in this book, then, forms my own answer to many discussions on issues of local change, state rule, and gender differentiation.

In our discussions, I attempted to answer each question as honestly as I could, discussing the issues openly. I talked to old and young; and I took notes—in apartments, in tents, in the snow, on trips, or in fishing camps. My open note taking often sparked questions; people wanted to know what I was jotting down. They rarely interrupted their talk, sometimes dictating to me *what* I should write down. Our communication also sparked discussions on issues, thus allowing me to ask questions on themes that would otherwise have been explored haphazardly at best. This kind of dialogue opened a space in which I could learn from Koriak women and men; these conversations made this ethnography possible.

Koriak women and men and I communicated with one another in Russian. Russian is the one language spoken by nearly everybody whom I knew at the northeastern shore. Koriak elders, however, frequently spoke no Russian, and, in any case, among one another they communicated in their respective Koriak dialects. In the late spring of 1992, when I lived for two months in a reindeer-herding camp, I acquired a rudimentary knowledge of the dialect of Rekinniki, enough to identify certain equipment and tools, but not enough to engage in conversation. Middle-aged and younger Koriak women and men often no longer spoke the language of their parents and grandparents. When they did, and when I knew people well, I often asked them to translate for me. For example, the narrative of Nina Ivanovna featured in Chapter 4 was told in the Koriak dialect of Anapka and was translated by her eldest daughter into Russian.

□ □ □

My choice to use names and other personal idiosyncrasies involves both a dilemma and a risk. I have, however, changed the names of all the people whose lives I discuss in this book, except for those in Chapter 4. This chapter presents the narratives of three Koriak women elders, each of whom explicitly expressed her wish to be named. Their stories, they implied, were their works; they were the authors. I have also tried to respect the wishes and demands of all the other people who appear in this book. Although I aim for accurate portrayals, I have changed to some extent details and personal circumstances to protect people from recognition lest their stories put them at risk. In villages at the northeastern shore, people frequently refer to one another by affinitive terms or nicknames, diminutive forms of their names. This kind of name-giving practice frequently engenders a sense of fondness and warmth. I have, however, chosen to use mostly Russian standard forms of names, even at the risk of being unable to convey something of the affinity that exists at the northeastern shore. In that way, I hope, I can give people even greater protection.

In the end, of course, my use of places and names is my choice, and thus my responsibility.

In writing this book, I faced another question. In which tense should ethnography be written? For Koriaks, I believe, the answer to this question has enormous political implications; for the discipline in which I work, it also has political (and intellectual) implications. On the one hand, the use of a perpetual "ethnographic presence" seems to suggest that cultures exist as homogenous, tradition-bound entities agelessly through time. The use of the ethnographic present runs the risk of removing time from history, thus turning cultural Others into timeless primitives and ancestral puppets of tradition (Fabian 1983). On the other hand, the use of the past, too, involves its own problem. In contrast to the ethnographic present, it seems to suggest that "primitives" are a breed of the past. It is only too easy then for urban readers to suspect an (unbridgeable?) abyss between the primitive and modern worlds. In this way, the use of the past does not suggest that indigenous peoples have a history, but rather that they are history. In this book, I use both the ethnographic present and past; I use them inconsistently. For example, in my chronicling of Koriak women's narratives of regional history, I use the ethnographic present to show that what can easily be relegated to the realm of history is still alive and thrives. But in my telling of one young Koriak woman's efforts to craft social possibilities in her life, I employ the past to show that the conditions of living in northern Kamchatka are rapidly changing.

□ □ □

## Research Issues

Whenever I visited people in their homes at the northeastern shore, I was greeted with both curiosity and respect. People were eager to hear about the world that I thought I knew best; I was afforded the prestige of a foreigner from whom one could learn. Yet my uneasy relation to foreignness surfaced in different ways. Generally I was allowed a great deal of movement, yet traveling to different places other than the villages in which I stayed became a problem. Local officials who had some power over my movements frequently refused me permission to travel along the northeastern shore. These forms of policing were sometimes combined, as, for example, the day I found out that Koriak friends received visits by local military personnel, asking questions about the questions I asked. Panic-stricken, I began to wonder whether I should abandon the project altogether. Friends told me that I should calm down; after all, they had dealt with such issues all their lives and knew how to answer such questions. There is little I can do here to match their generosity and their wit.

In this context of harassment and sometimes open threats, my presence at the northeastern shore was often a contested issue, and it was impossible for me to stay neutral on numerous occasions. Because I lived with two families, I was frequently drawn into local debates and asked to take a stance. This book, then, assumes a certain partiality on my part. Yet instead of dismissing such partiality as the failure to live up to the requirements of a professional objectivity and detached neutrality, it seems fair to ask about the particular shape of this partiality. Here I situate my argument within a story to explain my own positioning and to show how some of my choices to deal with issues of my research emerged.

*Kirill had guided the Russian merchant to Galina's house. Nobody knew him, but rumor spread that he was from the city, from Petropavlovsk, and that he wanted to start a tourist business based in Tymlat. He came to enlist my help. His idea, so he explained, was to provide hunting and fishing facilities, particularly for wealthy and foreign hunters. These people, he said, were willing to pay immense sums to shoot ram, wolf, and bear. While he was speaking, Galina invited him to sit down on one of the three chairs in the house, so that he could sit at the table. But in a jarring tone, this visitor told Galina that he preferred to talk to me in private, an unfriendly request.*

*Galina invited him into the kitchen where he sat down with an offended demeanor on one of the rickety chairs. Callously, his eyes wandered to the children and Galina's*

□ □ □

*grandmother, who later called him the "Fish-eyed Man." His attempts at a seemingly amiable but insincere smile remained unanswered. Galina shooed her two children out of the kitchen and continued pottering, listening along with Kirill, Grandmother, and me to what he had to say. He painted in bright colors his idea of starting a business with foreigners. The village would experience an enormous economic upswing, he said; nobody in the village would have to fear unemployment as work and money would be there in abundance; the times of financial worries would finally be over. His enterprise, he then explained, would employ at least half the village population, and with my support his plans would be easy to realize. He needed my help to guarantee coverage of his tourist business in newspapers and hunting magazines abroad. Yet he grew weary as pointed inquiries by Galina yielded more details.*

*He explained that he intended to build a small house, a cabin, not too far from the village: Koriak men would transport food, equipment, and other technical supplies to the place where the hunters stayed. The Koriaks were not to be seen, he clarified, because they were just too dirty and smelly, and the sight of them would act as a deterrent for any foreign sport hunter. I was stunned by his display of blatant racism and detestation. When I refused any assistance in supporting his plans, he reacted angrily. He would, so he announced, return within the next days and ask me again. If I would not change my mind, he threatened, he would take care that no one in the village, certainly no Koriak person, would still be prepared to help, whatever it was I wished to do.*

In the end, the Fish-eyed Man was unable to inflict harm, yet neither were his intimidations empty threats. On several occasions, he returned with ever more menacing remarks about my, and finally Galina's, safety. During both field trips, such issues surfaced in similar ways. Although this book does not deal explicitly with some of the challenges I confronted during my research, it also does not skirt them. Yet instead of engaging them from the perspective of purely self-reflexive writing, I have chosen to embed them in the text when I deemed it useful or necessary.

## Tundra Passages

The title of this book takes its cue from two different yet intersecting forms of knowledge that centered my project in important ways.[3] First, Koriak cultural practices of traveling are important here because they show forms of community and social understanding from a perspective of difference and flux. Second, in keeping in step with the travel perspectives on Koriak life, I use stories as passageways to show social processes from the perspective of idiosyncratic viewpoints and experiences of change.

Almost all the Koriak women and men I knew traveled extensively; Koriak lives are lives on the move. Sisters and brothers, aunts and uncles, parents and friends travel to see kin, confidantes, soul mates, and lovers. People travel to exchange news; they travel to visit places where family members once lived and where people have not stayed for a long time. In the arrangement of Koriak life, everybody travels: animals, humans, souls, and spirits. Manifold paths traverse space in numerous ways. Walking, riding, and boating transgress boundaries that are never stable but constantly shifting. Trails are seasonal: thaws transform frozen water streets into impassable rivers, and the wind closes passages by blowing snow and debris into the confines of clearings and thickets. Many Koriak women and men I met intimated, too, that traveling involves a culturally specific way of making a living. In the northern tundra, many Koriaks' understandings of themselves began with the understanding that they not only live off but also with the reindeer. Together with the reindeer, Koriaks say, they travel through the open, vast spaces of the northern Kamchatka landscape of tussock and bogs, contorted rivers, and unlocked plateaus. As reindeer herders, they take care of the animals that, in turn, take care of them.

In the beginning of my living at the northeastern shore, I felt confused by the amount of traveling I experienced and saw. I was irritated because almost all the ethnographies I had read on the region stressed the importance of bounded, territorial cultures and stable cultural styles. Yet when I visited Kamchatka's northeastern shore, I found a variety of styles but no homogeneity. The dominant framework for understanding indigenous cultures in the Russian North and the Russian Far East has been one of stability and cultural congruity, in which "culture" emerges from territory and localized communities. Yet in contrast to the "homogeneity" orientation of much scholarship, Koriak women and men positioned themselves differently in relation to community and tradition, regional hierarchies, and social change. I have thus come to think that Koriak "communities" are best understood in a context of mobility and fluctuation. Taking as my starting point the traveling practices of many Koriaks I knew, I can, in this book, speak to a variety of local contexts and dilemmas.

In this way, I have "borrowed" the organization of this book from the cultural practice of many Koriak women and men I knew. To *borrow* in this way

□ □ □

FIG. 1 | Traveling (photo: author 1994).

involves theoretical attention to the different perspectives, multistranded conversations, and shifting agendas that produced and shaped locally differentiated configurations of Koriak life at Kamchatka's northeastern shore (Bat'ianova 1995). To borrow in this way also involves an alertness to the idiosyncratic, divergent, and often mutually opposed ambitions, desires, and hopes that mold and frame individuals' projects of living. The variety of opinions and cultural strategies of many Koriak women and men I knew challenged me to build from such heterogeneity as a source of analytic creativity and promise. As one corollary, in my project readers will find no overarching explanatory framework in place. This book makes room for a welter of strategies, interpretations, stories, and ideas that commonly but variously engaged all the Koriak women and men I knew. One thing I learned in the process of writing this book was that scholarly theory cannot be abstracted from local dilemmas but is instead stimulated by them. No single theoretical frame can, in the

□ □ □

end, capture and explain the complexity and manifold involvements of life at Kamchatka's northeastern shore.

Yet a focus on traveling as an organizing metaphor in this book raises another challenge: how to sustain Koriak features of traveling while offering readers a sense of orientation and coherence. To avoid overwhelming readers with an overabundance of conceptual perspectives and movement, I chose to organize each chapter (except for Chapters 2, 3, and 5) around the perspectives of particular Koriak women and men and their stories. As a form of analysis, stories open up passages for understanding particular aspects of individuals' lives. They center on the specificity of social arrangements and points of view while focusing on broader social and historical contexts in individual particularities. As one consequence, the stories recounted in this book are not intended to uncover general cultural principles. Building from individuals' perspectives as a source of analysis and understanding, the chapters in this book attempt to draw readers simultaneously into discussions of regional history, social forms of gender differentiation, and regional to global relations.[4]

## Acknowledgments

In writing this book, I have garnered many debts. The creativity, concern, and effort of many people with whom I lived and worked have inspired this book. My greatest debt is to the Koriak women and men with whom I have lived and worked at Kamchatka's northeastern shore. Although they knew all along that my project would do little to aid their lives, they generously and with great hospitality allowed me to participate in their lives. For reasons of privacy I do not list their names here, but I want to thank them for their tolerance of my mistakes and the care they expressed in letting me be with them.

Many others, too, were essential to my research, thinking, and writing. The German Academic Exchange Service (DAAD) generously supported my research in 1992. In 1994, further research was supported by a Social Sciences and Humanities Council of Canada Research Grant (SSHRC) and the Center for Society, Technology, and Development at McGill University. I also wish to thank the Faculty for Graduate Studies at McGill University for granting me an Alma Mater Dissertation Fellowship and the McMaster Arts Research Board for making the completion of this book possible. The Russian and Eastern European Center of the University of Illinois at Urbana–Champaign generously supported and funded two week-long stays. Very special thanks

□ □ □

go to Helen Sullivan for her interest, patience, and expertise. I am indebted to the Discussion Group on Women in Slavic Cultures and Literatures, from whose discussions and ideas I greatly benefited.

Throughout the process of my research, John Galaty and Margaret Lock have shown unflagging support of my intellectual path and have challenged me to work a bit harder to develop some of my ideas. I want to thank them both. Warm thanks also go to David Koester and Vika Petrasheva, who helped to solve visa problems. In addition, Vika Petrasheva generously offered a place to stay and helped in forging various research connections in northern Kamchatka. Olga Murashko discussed at length with me the possibilities and intricacies of research in the Kamchatka peninsula, and the late Galina Gracheva offered great hospitality while I was "stranded" in Saint Petersburg. During my second stay in the northern Kamchatka peninsula, I spent one week with the late Aleksandr Pika; several months later, Sasha died in a boating accident while conducting research in Chukotka. This book reflects, in a sense, some of the conversations we had.

Throughout the writing process, I have benefited from the support and direction of my colleagues. I am deeply grateful to many who have read my work or discussed it with me. In particular, the readings and comments of Larissa Abriutina, Elena Bat'ianova, Julie Cruikshank, Galina D'iachkova, Harvey Feit, Andrea Kleinhuber, Igor Krupnik, Nancy Ries, Wendy Russell, Blair Rutherford, Peter Schweitzer, and Nikolai Vakhtin have helped to improve this book at various stages, in various forms.

The friendship of Patricia Foxen, Michelle George, Louis Greenspan, Katherina Gubler, Jasmin Habib, Hans-Georg Kraffzick, Heike Schimkat, Laurel Schultz, Andrea Suerbaum, and Tuula Tuisku has sustained me throughout the process of writing this book. I am deeply grateful for their laughter and support. In completing this project, I owe a unique debt to Robbyn Seller, soulmate and friend. There are others whom I need to thank for their friendship and support. They are too many to name here, but they know who they are, and I thank them all.

My students at McMaster University, many of whom are now good friends, nourished this book with their intellectual vivacity and enthusiasm. Special thanks also go to Rosita Jordan, Luce Lavigne, and Janis Weir for their help and good humor in coming to my administrative rescue on several accounts.

Finally, and above all, I want to thank David for his unfailing love. There are no words to fully express the depth of my gratitude for him.

□ □ □

1 | □ □ □

Departure

This book describes how, in the mid-1990s, an indigenous people in the northern Kamchatka peninsula in the Russian Far East experienced, interpreted, and struggled with the changing living conditions of post-Soviet Russia. It describes how Koriak women and men actively negotiated the manifold historical and social processes—from tsardom to the Soviet state to a democratic beginning—by protesting, accommodating, and reinterpreting the conditions by which their existence was continually made and remade. It also examines how Koriak women today creatively engage with—and fight—regional configurations of power to challenge and contest formations of social inequality and male domineering. This book is about both the present and the past. It is an ethnography in the sense that it stresses the specificity of local practices and discourses of history, gender, and agency. At the same time, it attempts to contribute to discussions about the predicaments and struggles of marginalized and indigenous people and the issues they face in broad contexts of regional to global relationships.

My interest in exploring issues of gender, history, and agency at Kamchatka's northeastern shore emerged when I found that I rarely had conversations about any of the topics I was interested in—rituals, traditions, tundra uses—without paying attention to the contexts of historical changes and regional and community differentiation. The most important source of insight for recognizing the significance of these aspects for Koriak lives was that the people themselves regularly brought up such topics: cultural idiosyncrasies and distinctions between Koriaks and Russians and among Koriaks; administrative power and divisions; regional economic inequalities; female-to-male social positionings—all were issues that made local culture worth talking about for them. As these issues were never entirely absent from our discussions, I found that Koriak women and men frequently connected them to extraregional historical and social developments. A starting point for the analyses in this book is the recognition that local meanings and interpretations are never entirely divorced from global processes and change.

A consequence of this recognition involves the reluctance to situate Koriak women and men in frameworks of either radical cultural difference or social assimilation. Koriaks were frequently described as primitives. They subsisted on reindeer herding, fishing, and hunting in extensive tundra lands. They lived in difficult, hardly accessible terrain, often several weeks' hike away from the coast or settlements. They recognized waters, animals, humans, and plants as parts of a closely interconnected world. In conjunction with these kinds of understandings, they asked spirits for help and brought their sick to shamans. These forms of existence and knowledge have invited sets of conventional imagery that described Koriaks as backward and ignorant, frequently in contrast to those who lived in urban centers. These understandings also incited forms of social policing intended to bring Koriak women and men as assimilated citizens under the sponsorship of the state.

Stereotyped understandings of cultural difference easily invite a set of imagery that positions subjects, communities, and cultures in categorical structures of "us" and "them." As both process and notion, assimilation allies different peoples under the umbrella of one homogenous, ethnicity-transcending identity, enshrouding them in an overarching category of personhood. Both understandings, difference and assimilation, leave only little room for recognizing the possibility of commonality and differentiation in the modern world. The Koriak women and men I knew did not think of themselves as a "cultural Other"; yet neither would they have agreed that they have become like the Russians and Ukrainians who had moved into the Kamchatka Peninsula. Together with anybody who reads this book, Koriak women and men share a world of expanding capitalism and natural resource depletion. Like many others, they contend with excruciating poverty, increasing social violence, and domestic abuse. As Koriak women and men, they may speak from vantage points that are distinct from those of, for example, urban or rural Russians and other citizens of the world. Instead of describing Koriak perspectives as a site of cultural difference or assimilation, it is challenging to place them within a wider web of local-global cultural politics and regional positions. By taking up this challenge, I hope to demonstrate that Koriak perspectives are not a site of cultural

□ □ □

difference or isolation but are continually forged in response to, and in dialogue with, various social and historical developments. In such a view, I believe, lies promise as well as social and political possibility for many of the Koriak women and men I know: The challenge is to appreciate difference not as routine lip service to diversity but as a creative intervention in a world we share.

## History

To describe Koriak women and men as primitive others across an abyss of space and time means to ignore their contemporary predicaments and the complex social issues with which they struggle. On the other hand, to describe them as conformist or assimilated citizens in the context of the Russian nation is to deny them the possibility of difference in the modern world. Between these two positions lies a terrain that addresses the questions mostly obscured by these classic contrasts—radical cultural difference, on the one side, and homogenous or assimilated identities, on the other side. History, I believe, is one such place. In breaking down the extreme categorical differentiations between difference and assimilation, it becomes possible to see how contemporary Koriak understandings of themselves are neither the result of cultural identities nor the *sum total* of cultural specificities and idiosyncrasies. For example, chronicling the encounter, the dialogue, among Koriak women and men, regional neighbors, and the state makes it possible to see how "Koriaks" were formed in the imagination of the state, regional majorities, and visiting anthropologists who learned to know "them." It makes it possible to see how such powerful discourses that form and authorize Koriak identities do not have an unquestioned hegemony. It makes it possible to show how Koriak women and men respond, reinterpret, and challenge them even as they accept and are shaped by these forms of knowledge.

In taking Koriak involvements and concerns with past events and the contemporary world as my starting point, I choose to write from a perspective that stands in contrast to that in nearly any ethnography of the region I have read. My reading of history as a complex assemblage of conflicting narratives and different voices—the recognition that different ways of telling spawn different kinds of truth—confronts the totalizing function (K. Clark 1981, ix–xii) of these texts. The narrative realism in the Soviet ethnographic record (approximately 1930–85) reveals highly self-conscious texts revolving around

□ □ □

master plots of socialist struggle, progress, and civilization. The texts produced from roughly 1930 to 1940 attest to the enthusiasm and unswerving zeal with which agents, teachers, and administrators set out to bring history and progress to those who presumably lacked it. In time, the ethnographic monograph replaced the many essays, columns, syndicated articles, and editorials that contained the bulk of ethnographic information. In the 1950s and 1960s, the ethnographic monograph finally emerged as the privileged genre of Soviet ethnography; its defining goal was no longer to show how history inevitably advances toward an end but to emphasize the achievements of socialism and revolution. This goal was usually achieved by splitting the monograph across a temporal divide before and after the Revolution. Each part consisted of thematically distinct sections—economics, kinship, social life, and so on. In the first section, the life of northern indigenous peoples was frozen in an ahistorical archaic frame of timeless tradition. In the second part, readers were treated to ethnographic data in the form of materialist, thus objective, descriptions, statistics, and graphs. In this sense, the making of the ethnographic record in northern Kamchatka involved the fervor and ambitious zeal of Soviet administrators and political activists while building on the strength of socialist narratives and tropes.

This commentary is not intended to criticize Soviet scholarship for disingenuousness and misrepresentation, nor do I mean to show disrespect for scholarly positions against which my own readings and interpretations are set. The aspects of Soviet ethnography that rest on stark, imaginative dualisms as organizing features are aspects with which I have long struggled in this ethnography. The particular question I faced was how to incorporate a body of literature shaped by a plethora of assumptions that are partisan toward certain kinds of truth and sometimes do injustice to Koriak women and men. Yet the problem of totalizing or homogenizing styles is not intrinsic to Soviet ethnography: In recent years, anthropologists have criticized homogenous representations of "other" peoples, initiated careful textual analysis of past and present ethnographic writings, and criticized theoretically problematic assumptions such as the separation between analysts and objects of study. The point of my commentary is not to exchange one theory for another or to argue for a theoretically more nuanced Western stance: My point is to specify the intellectual challenges at hand.

The works that I find most promising for examining Koriak points of view show how cultural understandings and self-understandings are made through history and how, in turn, historical processes and meanings are created and

□ □ □

shaped in the gap between divergent cultural positions (for example, Stoler 1985; Comaroff and Comaroff 1992). Such a perspective rejects the notion that culture is outside or parallel to history but is always and everywhere constructed in historical ways (Wolf 1982; Ginzburg 1983; Elias 1982). At the same time, such a view recognizes that history is shaped by and through the encounter of different people, value systems, and forms of knowledge. Culture cannot be placed in opposition to history; similarly, history cannot be understood as the linear, progressive motion of time but must be understood as the dynamic unfolding of particular sociopolitical circumstances and events *in* time. I am particularly concerned with the way in which the women and men I knew explained and commented on historical processes in the region and in the context of local dilemmas.

In this project, such a view prompts me to consider how the current social and political situation in Koriak communities at the northeastern shore has emerged from the complex processes of the past. The way in which Soviet ethnography produced highly self-conscious texts that bespeak a buoyant utopianism and an unswerving belief in the master narrative of progress has recently received much scrutiny[1] and has stimulated a number of important responses.[2] In North American and European scholarship, a frequent reaction has been to study issues of nationality and identity most commonly in relation to Soviet narratives of progress—with a heightened emphasis on political structures and state policies but with little emphasis on local struggles about power and meaning.[3] Together, these critiques have set the challenge of retaining a focus on the transformative politics of the state while looking for the interstices where state power seems most uncertain.

In this book I use the term *state* to refer to those aspects of national and Soviet policies that were experienced as external yet hegemonic forms of government by most Koriak women and men; I thus stress the homogenous and imposing character of the state. Koriak relations to state power were rarely absent from local discussions on history and identity. I heard Koriaks describe state policies and administrative practices as projects to which they answered either by frustrating, fulfilling, or ignoring them. For example, local elders expressed their identity rarely by accusing or condemning state authority, but more often by emphasizing how they could continue cultural and ritual practices they considered important for their identity. Young people often emphasized their ties to state rule by pointing out that government policies had opened up social possibilities, such as schooling and professional training, to them. The social tensions created in this gap—in which historical identities

□ □ □

were made and history was interpreted in cultural ways—is one feature I wish to explore in this book.

## Gender

In this project, I join many other scholars who are interested in the question of how formations of gender differentiation are central to our understanding of local issues and everyday conditions of living. Conversations and local dilemmas in which people were enmeshed reminded me that Koriak women and men brought distinct perspectives and strategies of negotiation to structures of local and regional inequality and production of social meanings. Raising the question of gender at Kamchatka's northeastern shore calls attention to the complexity and specificity of social and cultural intersections. In this book, I argue for situating local commentaries—such as those of different Koriak women—within wider negotiations of power and inequality while recognizing local identity formations, specificities, and stakes.

The critique of anthropology as part of a male-centered discourse (for example, Trinh 1989; Strathern 1987) has by now become well known in Western scholarship and has provoked significant responses. Feminist anthropologists have criticized the un-self-conscious obliteration of women from ethnographic texts (for example, Leacock 1981; Reiter 1975), initiated careful ethnographic analyses in the study of gender and culture (for example, Silverblatt 1987; Bell 1983; Boddy 1989), and explored how social and economic historical developments have influenced the meanings and lived realities of women in various societies (for example, G. Clark 1994; Cole 1991). However, a number of these important works retain one of the most problematic features of feminist discourse: theoretical and analytic conventions that frequently represent women as disempowered and maltreated, as "innocent" victims of global economic and technological developments. Such responses turn our attention to the ways in which intellectual traditions are built on categories and assumptions that cast gender—in conjunction with intersecting arrangements of race (for example, hooks 1990; Mani 1987; John 1996) or colonial status (for example, Spivak 1985; Mohanty 1984)—as sites of exclusion. On the whole, they tend to study gender as a segregated category— as a stable and clearly definable category of social life—thus ignoring the connections between wider configurations of meaning and power that are formed in tandem with social asymmetries of, for example at Kamchatka's

□ □ □

northeastern shore, inter- and intracommunity divisions, ethnic contrasts, and economic inequality.

In one response, a number of feminist and critical scholars, working from and across an array of academic disciplines, have opened up discussions about how gender cannot be a theoretically self-evident starting point for feminist analysis but requires critical engagement with its own foundations, constructions, and—following Foucault (1978)—the history of its own creation (deLauretis 1987). The most radical section of this discussion asks about the assumptions of intellectual trajectories that have given rise to cultural and socially specific productions of gender in the first place (Butler 1989; Flax 1990). Gender structures subjectivity and experience rather than describing a set of fixed relations (Grosz 1994; Morris 1995). As a consequence, scholars argue that issues of gender cannot be studied in isolation but intersect with, and are shaped by, the specific relations and conditions of women's lives. These works reject the notion that gender runs parallel to other social configurations—political status, economic and ethnic inequality—for these formations are themselves constructed and experienced in gendered ways.

By putting gender at the core of my analysis, I create an oppositional dialogue with familiar ethnographic imageries. One the one hand, questions of gender are still largely missing in the ethnographic record of the Russian Far East. Apart from the fact that gender has until now not been an important category in research on northern Russia, analysts have so far rarely asked their readers to attend to the many-sided differences between women and men as well as to those among women. On the other hand, there exists a welter of colonial panopticisms by which Koriak women have been described in largely depreciating terms. The exoticization and victimization of Koriak women come together in images of women as rebellious fighters for emancipation; slovenly primitives; and slaves of tradition and hierachization (L'vov 1932), in correspondence to the particular biases and gender assumptions of each author's political and historical viewpoint. The traveler Kennan saw them in 1871 as unashamed bluestockings and power-seeking emancipationists:

> Whatever may be the motive, it is certainly an infringement upon the generally recognized prerogatives of the sterner sex, and should be discounted by all Koriaks who favor masculine supremacy. Before they [Koriak men] know it, they will have a woman's suffrage association on their hands, and female lecturers will be going about from band to band advocating the substitution of hickory clubs and

slung-shots for the harmless willow switches, and protesting against
the tyranny which will not permit them to indulge in this interesting
diversion at least three times a week. (Kennan 1871, 202)

In 1927, the traveler Bergman described them as indigent and disheveled
mendicants:

> Some elderly women sat and scraped skins near the fireplace and
> put the scrapings into their mouths. They were so dreadfully dirty
> that my wife shuddered when she looked at them. . . . In the inner
> compartment [of the tent] we sat ourselves down on reindeer skins
> and awaited the inevitable tea. . . . We were glad that the Koriaks
> did not break bread with their tea, for what would it have looked
> like? . . . Russians, Kamchadals, and Lamuts had assured us that the
> Koriaks never wash themselves, from the cradle to the grave. Now we
> no longer doubted the truth of that assertion. (Bergman 1927, 220)

In 1932, the political activist Kuz'mina characterized them as the disfran-
chised victims of entrenched social injustice and oppression:

> It is morning. It is cold in the house. The fire went out a long time
> ago; some coal pieces still glow in the ashes. She does not want to
> crawl out from under her warm fur blankets; but today her husband
> has to travel far . . . and she has to hurry to make tea for him. The
> fire roars, sparks fly. Clouds of smoke emerge. The smoke hole is
> slightly open, and a stream of cold air creeps into the house. . . . The
> fire is heating up. The tent is filled with heavy smoke. The interiors
> of the tent are barely visible.
> The entire family still sleeps. Only the woman at the fire is busy
> with work. She has to take care of the water kettle; the spout may burst
> if the fire burns too hot. Only little ice has melted into water so far;
> but she also has to bring iukola [dried fish] and seal fat for breakfast;
> bake little griddlecakes, fetch sugar, get done with the boots that she
> did not manage to finish yesterday, and prepare food for the dogs.
> (Kuz'mina 1932, 94)

One concern of this book is to derail and reexamine the colonial heritage that
has shaped homogenous and hackneyed modes of gender representation and

□ □ □

to use analytical and textual strategies that work counter to the exoticizing techniques of earlier ethnographies.

In arguing that gender-differentiated responses to history and the contemporary conditions of living at Kamchatka's northeastern shore are instrumental in understanding Koriak agendas, strategies, and debates, I do not argue for the "addition" of women to classic ethnographies. Inserting female issues into ethnographic texts does not necessarily tap the unquestioned hegemony of male-oriented gazes; neither does it necessarily pay attention to myriad social, historical, and cultural forms in and through which gender is produced. In the context of dominant ethnographic representations that have been shaped by a welter of problematic assumptions, cultural analysts are challenged to reexamine intellectual suppositions and create new forms of description. In this book, breaking out of the framework of homogenous and conventional descriptions involves the creativity of making gender matter.

An example can illuminate the complexity and significance of this challenge. Given the pressing social dilemmas of living for Koriak women and men at Kamchatka's northeastern shore—as for other indigenous subjects in northern Russia—it is not surprising that in recent years the social and economic predicaments of indigenous peoples in the Russian North have received increased attention in the writings of social scientists and even in some newspapers and magazines. There are reports on the unrelenting social poverty in northern Russian settlements, the torments of unemployment, the lack of monetary resources, the starvation, the spread of diseases such as tuberculosis, cancer, and scurvy, and the insidious effects of drinking. Aleksandr Pika's (1993) research on violent death among indigenous peoples in the Russian North, for example, shows that suicide rates are sharply increasing. Dmitrii Bogoyavlensky (1997) examines how the current period of transition creates social anxiety and stress for northern and southern Kamchatka people. These studies bring attention to the forms and effects of social misery in northern Russia.

One problem with analyses of suffering in northern Russia, however, has been that they pay only little attention to the ways in which women and men experience the circumstances of social distress in different ways. With their focus on social hardship and in their humanitarian concern, northern research studies of suffering are also a site of the most general and unspecified theories of gender. They rarely ask how formations of social suffering and cultural inequality are gendered in and of themselves. Yet the Koriak women I knew expressed particular concerns. As they spoke about the domestic workday, the lack of male support in raising children, and the deference husbands frequently asked from their wives, they implied that women and men were differently implicated in the fabric of everyday life. Both women and men expressed much concern over the impoverished living conditions, yet women also argued that the sexual carelessness of men who father two or three children but refuse to assume responsibility for bringing up these children makes women's lives needlessly hard. The women who I knew said that male drinking (yet women also drink) brought them frightening experiences. (It is important to note that women also drink.) For example, in the summer of 1994 in Tymlat, six young men, four of whom had been married and had fathered children, were killed in a grisly car accident. Speeding along the dusty and frequently fog-obscured road from Ossora to Karaga, they crashed into a sideways-dug ridge. There was an awful silence as the news reached the community, yet the reactions of the young widows swung back and forth between dead calm and open rage. Why had their husbands been drinking? they asked. And how on earth could they be so foolish as to race along a barely visible road?

This is a kind of gender-specific response that has rarely been described in social science scholarship of the Russian North. In this book, I open up the orientation of northern Russian research to the ways in which conditions of social hardship and desolation are experienced in gendered ways and the ways in which gender is a source of both creativity and constraint.

## Being Koriak

The ethnography of Koriak life has been traced and profoundly shaped by the Russian ethnographer Waldemar [Vladimir] Il'ich Jochelson [Iokhel'son] (1855–1937). As a member of the populist and revolutionary political movement *Narodnaia Volia* (People's Will), Jochelson was forced to leave Russia in 1880; after he returned illegally in 1885, he was arrested and exiled for ten years to the Sakha District in Siberia.[4] Invited by Franz Boas to participate in the Jesup North Pacific Expedition (the ambitious project to investigate the origins of American Indians and to examine the physical and cultural relationships between the peoples of the Russian Far East–Siberia and the northwest coast of North America), he and his wife, the medical doctor Dina Jochelson-Brodskaia, arrived in the northern peninsula in 1900. The Jochelsons traveled among the Koriaks of Penzhenskii and Gizhiga Bays, along the Sea of Okhotsk, and in the Taigonos Peninsula. Under the scientific

□ □ □

guidance of Boas, they conducted comprehensive studies among the Koriak and Iukaghir, collected a considerable amount of ethnographic artifacts, and did much photographic work (see also Krupnik 1998). Although the material they collected during this time is certainly not beyond history and change, Waldemar Jochelson and Dina Jochelson-Brodskaia definitively staked out the ethnographic terrain.

At the turn of the century, when the Jochelsons arrived in the northern peninsula with sleds, dogs, and caravans of technical equipment, Russian, North American, and Japanese traders and entrepreneurs conducted trade in small posts in the tundra or traveled as itinerant salesmen along the shore. The Koriak women and men the Jochelsons met must have been widely traveling, widely trading people who recognized foreign trade as an important source of income and accommodated their own products to this trade.

According to a census undertaken by Jochelson with the help of the anthropologist Vladimir Bogoras, Koriaks at that time numbered between 7,500 and 7,600 people (Jochelson 1908, 445), and they engaged in a pastoral and fishing economy, supported by hunting. The dualistic Koriak economy has probably been the most frequently commented-on feature (see, for example, Jochelson 1908; Gurvich and Kuzakov 1960; Arutiunuov 1988; Ditmar 1855; Levin 1936). The *Nymylany,* a self-designation used by the groups usually described as Maritime Koriak, dwelled along the coastline and at the estuaries of rivers. Intense and complex trade relationships bound the Maritime Koriak and the Reindeer-herding Koriak groups that lived deep in the tundra in an intricate and reciprocal system of exchange. Fish, seal fat, and whale blubber exchanged hands for reindeer fat and fur.

Access to fishing sites and use of land in the Koriak tundra were not regulated by juridical decree. People claimed and renewed their claims to campsites by their annual use of these places. Koriaks at the northeastern shore chose which pastures to drive the reindeer to, where to establish summer fishing camps, and where to pitch their tents for the winter months. Past and concurrent use of such sites circumscribed the social context in which such choices could be made. Some elders to whom I talked decided to extend their campsites widely; others chose to visit and use the same place each year. But whatever choices people made, they valued their autonomy to travel and to form diverse affiliations in conjunction with this mobility.

Reindeer herding and fishing were two of the most obvious aspects of Koriak existence; in turn, they also shaped the architectural arrangements of living at the northeastern shore. Whereas reindeer-herding groups lived in easily removable, fur-covered tents erected on the ground with the help of malleable elder tree branches, Maritime Koriak lived in permanent semiunderground houses, solidly built with the help of poplar or aspen. Both forms of dwellings differed in size according to the number of inhabitants, yet it seems safe to assume that in general Maritime Koriak habitations accommodated a larger number of occupants.

One point of entry into Koriak understanding of sociality can be a glimpse into the social and architectural organization of living in the tundra. In the Reindeer Koriak universe, the quintessential unit of living was the *iaranga,* the tent. Tents consisted of canvases of reindeer fur, stretched over a supporting framework of wooden poles. They subsumed all the elements of age and relationship, gender and generation, person and property, from which arose the intricate structure of the *iaranga* as a social world. Schweitzer (1989) has described how the relationships were more than the base of the cultural polity; they also underpinned the social construction of the human world. These ties linked spiritual, gender, food, and ethnicity relationships to others in a community, forming the basis for cooperation and thus survival in an uncertain world. They shaped the invisible scaffold of the sociocultural order. Today, Koriak elders in particular fear that these understandings are marred beyond repair.

There was a great deal of regular contact between family members, especially as many activities occurred directly outside the living area and were part of the living area. While acknowledging that individuals belonging to one camp or house community would, in the course of their lives, frequently leave to form different associations, Koriaks nevertheless recognized camp or house communities as the principal unit through which sociality was enacted. In elders' narrations (see Chapter 4), it becomes clear that camp residents were proud of their autonomy; part of this autonomy was to associate freely with other camps, thus enhancing and creating new forms of sociality.

Camps were usually founded by a conjugal couple, but they could also be set up by a brother and a sister, a father and a daughter, a mother and a son. Camp communities enveloped a number of dependents who could not be part of another camp or were otherwise forced to live in impoverished circumstances: orphans, widowed mothers, divorced sisters, debilitated and inept men. Although Koriak women and men elders acknowledge that dependents usually worked for the economic prosperity of the camp leader (usually the person who controlled the largest amount of animals), they also emphasize that Koriaks did not encourage dependence. For their work

□ □ □

in another person's or group's camp, dependents were recompensed with animals. Dependents usually worked only until they had a reasonable number of reindeer; then they would found a camp of their own.

Much of the literature on Koriak forms of living stresses that the population was loosely divided into nine territorial groups, known as Nymylany, Chavchuveny, Aliutortsy, Palantsy, Kamentsy, Parentsy, Karagintsy, Apukintsy, and Kereki (Antropova 1971, 18–20). Although during my research it became increasingly clear that tensions existed between Koriak women and men as to whether such divisions had ever existed and, if so, whether they should still embrace such divisions today, it seems also fair to say that in particular for Koriak elders such community distinctions are still of significance. My research locates itself at the Aliutortsy level, that is, among the Koriak women and men who lived in or came from the villages of Tymlat, Kichiga, Anapka, and Rekinniki. Ethnographic sources (for example, Antropova 1971, 22; Gurvich and Kuzakov 1960, 73–75; Stebnitskii 1938) stress the fact that Aliutortsy Koriak were the only group that employed shifting patterns of economy, living off reindeer herding and fishing at the same time. The last All-Union Population Census, in 1989, determined the number of Koriaks to be between 9,200 and 9,300 (a total number of 9,242), but with no breakdowns into single subdivisions.

## Political Culture

In the last eight decades, Koriak women and men had been subjected to a spiral of local government authorities, district councils, regional assemblies, and bureaucratic discipline that have helped shape contemporary Koriak existence from village administration to the highest political level. Since approximately 1924, the year in which Soviet state administration assumed power in the peninsula, the state has argued for the implementation of certain government policies by implying that indigenous peoples would fare better under its sponsorship. In changing the conditions of living at Kamchatka's northeastern shore—building houses, creating settlements, introducing wage labor—government officials maintained that they created social progress and economic growth. In the context of government leadership decisions and Soviet nation building, Moscow became the center of political potency that extended its rule outward to the provincial areas and to what it considered the periphery. The northern peninsula was part of the periphery, if at the edge

□ □ □

of the periphery, of only small significance in national power rankings. In the geopolitical order of the state, a tremendous gap was thus created between "the government" (*vlast'*) and "the people" (*narod*). Koriaks had to look up to the governing bodies that looked down at them. For many Koriak men and women I knew, this structure posed a fundamental political dilemma, yet at the same time offered them the possibility to continue some of their own cultural practices. As peripheral subjects, they were simultaneously inside and outside the hold of the state.

Much of the literature on the political culture at Kamchatka's northeastern shore emphasizes how the state has worked to erase cultural mobility, associated with *disorder,* to promote cultural order and stability (for example, Gapanovich 1925; Sergeev 1955; Bat'ianova 1991). In the 1930s, since the consolidation of state power in the northern peninsula, one important means of achieving "stable communities" that could be managed by government officials was the creation of administrative districts. Today the northern Kamchatka peninsula is divided into four districts: Penzhenskii, with the village of Kamenskoe as its administrative center; Tigil'skii, with the village of Tigil' as its administrative head; Oliutorskii and the village of Tilichiki; and Karaginskii, with the village of Ossora. In building an administrative management system designed to bring a widely dispersed people under the unifying rule of the state, the state endeavored to create centered government units. But many of the Koriaks I knew argued that the creation of administrative nuclei involved a fundamental irony: Instead of bringing widely traveling people under the unifying authority of the state, Koriak women and men were forced to look in centrifugal directions. This, they imply, was not a project of stability but of destabilization. By creating administrative borders that divided Koriak families and kin by enclosing them in different districts, this administrative order disrupted socially meaningful ties. In the 1950s and 1960s, Koriak women and men say, they had to ask administrators for permission to visit relatives who lived in another territorial sector. In the present, Koriak elders deplore, their children and grandchildren have lost contact with their wider families.

In the Soviet political system, more locally experienced political disjunctions, too, helped to segregate Koriaks from one another, as well as from regional administrations. As in most areas of the country, government worked from the top down; governing officials were appointed from above at the regional (*oblast*), district (*raion*), and settlement (*poselok*) levels. Even village councils (*sel' soviet*) were not expected to be community representatives. In one of the villages in which I lived, the leading village administrator was

□ □ □

FIG. 2 | Northern Kamchatka settlement seen from a distance (photo: author 1994).

a Nenets man, born and raised in a reindeer-herding camp in the West Siberian region of Salekhard. But there were no bonds of cultural recognition or solidarity between him and the reindeer-herding Koriak men I knew. In contrast, this village administrator was considered part of the governing apparatus; he participated in and was considered a representative of the power that attempted to hold Koriak women and men under its sway. The split created in the governing system between indigenous peoples became evident in other contexts, too. In Tymlat, several Chukchi teachers from the region of Achaivaiam worked as teachers and schoolmasters in the local boarding school. As people who claimed to have maintained more of their traditions than had the Koriaks, they looked down on Koriaks, who, in turn, resented what they perceived as culturally based condescension. It is through cultural politics, then, that regional and cultural differentiations have been enforced and constructed.

Still another discourse of regional differentiation shapes how Koriak women and men have been integrated and treated by the state, that is, the discourse of ethnic and regional identity. In the context of the Soviet state, all citizens were expected to have an ethnic affiliation, which was printed in each person's passport. Although in the public rhetoric of the state ethnicity was presumably unimportant (as an integral part of, and route to, nationalism it was shunned), this ethnic discourse was not one of equality. In northern

Kamchatka, some ethnic groups were able to establish themselves in positions of decision-making power, using the possibility to enforce ethnic dominance in power centers.

## Conditions of Living

In my descriptions, I shift back and forth between two settlements, Tymlat and Ossora, at the northeastern shore. Although in the context of the municipal landscape at the northeastern shore these two villages are situated in proximity—they are about forty kilometers apart—they differ strongly in their local and ethnic configurations. Ossora is the administrative center of the Karaginskii district in northern Kamchatka and has almost cosmopolitan repute. It connects all other places in the district with the peninsula's urban center of Petropavlovsk-Kamchatskii in the south; it also accommodates the district's hospital and police stations. Of a population of approximately 4,000 villagers, only about 8 percent are Koriaks; the remaining 92 percent are mainly Russian and Ukrainian, with a small minority of Itelmen, Chukchi, and Armenian. To reach Ossora, travelers first take a Boeing aircraft to Petropavlovsk-Kamchatskii and then a smaller aircraft to Ossora's airport. If Tymlat's inhabitants must take care of bureaucratic concerns, are sick, or wish to travel out of the *raion,* they must go to Ossora. Yet traveling may be difficult: In summer, one can go from Tymlat to Ossora only by boat or helicopter, in winter, by snowmobile or dogsled.

In Ossora, the majority of Koriaks I knew lived in poorly constructed houses with no insulation against the cold, no water, and only little space. Wooden plank-supported houses clustered along two pebbly and potholed streets; the brick-walled sides of public and administrative buildings still featured slogans reminiscent of the revolutionary ethos that had once sustained the Soviet state ("War-Victory-Communism"; "Lenin Is the Father of All Soviet Children"). But the belief that had once promoted widespread trust in such proclamations was gone. As in numerous other places in Russia, feelings of hopelessness and a fair amount of cynicism prevailed.

In contrast to Ossora, Tymlat is a village of about 500 inhabitants of whom approximately 70 percent are Koriaks and the remainder are predominantly Russian and Ukrainian, although members of other nationalities—Nenets, Armenian—also live here. As a result of the increasing presence of Russian merchants and traders at the northeastern shore, Tymlat emerged in the mid-nineteenth century as a small settlement (Vdovin 1973, 54) in which Koriak women and men began to live permanently. On tundra soil, close to a rocky beach, it nestles in one of the manifold bays that skirt the northeastern shore. Today travelers can reach Tymlat by boat, helicopter, foot, or dogsled. Following the route from Ossora parallel to the shore, cliffs descend precipitously into the ocean and provide Tymlat with some protection against the harsh winds that frequently assault the village. Aircraft fly regularly only once a week between Ossora and Tymlat; they touch down at the northern end of Tymlat and stop on loosely arranged wooden boards that cover the muddy sands of the landing field. The arrival of any helicopter is an important event; the swirling sound of helicopter wings is easily audible at a distance, and residents rush to meet passengers.

But although Tymlat and Ossora differ greatly in their respective regional standings, a widespread sense of social abandonment haunted Koriak women and men in both settlements. Everyday conditions were gloomy and grim; poverty and unemployment created a phlegmatic atmosphere, pressing down on villages like the heavy, foggy clouds constantly hanging above the northeastern shore. Many workers had not received their salaries for five or six months, in some more serious cases, for ten or eleven months. People drunk with vodka or *samogon* (self-distilled schnapps) staggered along two sludgy roads. Children hid away from school: Their games mimicked adult predicaments. Jesting imitations turned angst into play, and boastful stories mirrored adults' veilings of discouraged selves. With the end of communism, dizzying inflation took hold (Lemon 1997), and prices for essential aliments such as tea, bread, and milk spiraled unimaginably high. One response to the ruinous effects of constantly rising prices was that liquors such as vodka and wheat- or potato-fermented home brew turned into a liquid hard currency (see also Pesmen 1995), being much more reliable and stable than money. In Tymlat and Ossora, anything, from a trip to Moscow to clothes to small packets of tea could be bought and sold for alcohol and had its inflation-proof vodka equivalent.

Along with the food shortages in the time of perestroika, the dissolution of the collective farm system exacerbated the economic situation. As elsewhere in the country, at the beginning of the 1990s, food stocks were rarely replenished, and shelves yawned. In the first months of 1992, sugar, flour, cigarettes, and matches were the only procurable goods, and from time to time deliveries of bread from Vladivostok arrived in village stores. Once shipments of bread were disembarked, the news spread like wildfire, and in a short time the

□ □ □

shop was bursting with people, while others were pushing before its entrance. Those able to procure some bread usually tried to snatch up more than three loaves—more than three loaves were not sold to one person—inviting the fury of others; yet they displayed indifference to others' reproaches and spells.

In this context of economic and social desolation, both young Koriak women and men and elders explained that living in settlements had exacerbated their sense of deterioration. Indeed, one important area in which Koriak women and men discussed issues of deterioration among themselves was the meaning of place. The problem with settlements, Koriak elders argued, is that they are no longer communal places of living. "[In houses] we are alone. We live for ourselves. That is how it is." Another sign of Koriak disconnections from meaningful forms of sociality is that "people have begun to steal." Elders explained that while they lived in the tundra, things were safe and were safeguarded by others in the absence of their owner. "You could leave your things with any person you wanted, and even ten years later things would still be there. Nothing would get away." Stealing occurs, people said, because nobody cares. Among the Koriak women and men I knew, their sense of deterioration was most frequently expressed in contrasting life in a settlement with life in the tundra. In Koriak eyes, settlement denotes both a space and a social relation to power.

To illuminate the significance and complexity of this point, it might be useful to introduce an example. In the late fall of 1994, several fatal accidents took the lives of young men. In particular, the death of one young man who died in tragic but locally unexceptional circumstances shook up communities at the northeastern shore. A twenty-seven-year-old herder had been found by one of his brothers at the fringe of the village, frostbitten to his knees. In a state of drunken stupor, he must have staggered out of the village and into the tundra. Taking him across his shoulders, his brother, Sasha, carried him back to the village and looked for a plane to take him to Petropavlovsk, where doctors might have saved his life. But in northern Kamchatka, it is mostly weather conditions, not timetables, that govern the departure of planes. For days, continuing snowfall impeded visibility; although Sasha begged several pilots, each refused to fly. Finally, Sasha's brother died at the airport. Relatives were quickly summoned; a funeral was arranged.

I remember that all the people were very silent, caught up in their own thoughts. Nobody spoke about the cause of death or openly sought an explanation. Later, after the funeral, when most relatives had already left to travel back to their homes, people began to comment that Sasha's brother must have felt uncomfortable and disrespected. He must have felt looked down on, they said. Yet what could he do? Wasn't life just one big offense, one person asked?

In particular, Koriak elders argue that living in settlements creates terrible conditions that frequently kill women and men before they reach their mid-forties. One of the biggest problems Koriak communities face today is how to avoid the violent deaths of young men, who die in accidents as a result of drinking or in the aftermath of drinking sprees.

In a way, it is problematic to single out drinking to describe Koriak women's and men's sense of loss and powerlessness. Yet I introduce this subject here to specify, not to abstract from it. Although alcohol consumption is a problem in Koriak settlements, it is equally a problem in the wider Russian society (White 1996). Some anthropologists have observed that there is no difference between native and Russian drinking. The problem with such a view, however, is that, for example, Koriak women and men as members of an indigenous (thus regionally marginalized) group are part of a prejudiced discourse in which whites easily view drinking as a serious sign of the loss of tradition and the inability of indigenous people to adapt to social change. Such a view is unproductive for understanding Koriak conditions of living at Kamchatka's northeastern shore. The following story is a case in point:

In one of my first days at the peninsula, I met a man who warned me not to travel too far along the northeastern shore, a warning that echoed other counsel I had received. There was nothing in the region for a foreigner like me. He was certain that I would be shocked, just as he had been, by the lack of moral sensibility, intelligence, and sanitation. He advised me to carry along several bottles of schnapps in case I was ever in need of help; otherwise, nobody would help me. Alcohol, he opined, was the all-powerful means to success at the shore.

The man who recommended alcohol as a strategy and research tool to secure the openness and protection I would need as a single woman traveler in northern Kamchatka had worked for several years as a salaried professional hunter for the state hunting enterprise (*gospromkhoz)* in the region. I call him "The Hunter" henceforth. He had traveled the peninsula up and down, from one shore to the next; he knew local people for what they were worth: bottles of vodka and schnapps. At the time I met him, he traded in furs and pelts. The Hunter "bought" reindeer and sealskin coats, boots, and hats by the bottle,

□ □ □

not in cash. The prices he paid were low: two or three bottles for a coat, one bottle for a pair of boots or a hat.

At the same time, The Hunter was prospering by selling these furs for U.S. dollars, paid to him in cash, mainly by American and German sport hunters. He said that he was doing business with them; "business" was one of his most frequently used words. His American friends, he explained, had sharpened his wits with a single key phrase: Time is Money, he said, and continued to offer ever more business maxims. In the villages I visited, he was known for glib double-talk. In the settlements along the shore, he argued for the selling of furs; the U.S. dollar, he claimed, would in the end benefit the region as a whole. For the present, Koriaks would have to make do with the schnapps he was able to give; later he would be able to afford payments in good dollar bills.

Like the Fish-Eyed Man who makes an entrance later in this chapter as a prejudiced and unsuccessful entrepreneur, The Hunter's clamorous argumentation hampered his doing any serious business with many Koriak women and men I knew. They were well aware that he addressed them as bumbling know-nothings and losers. He openly charged them with having little morals ("they drink so much it makes them blind"), implying that he had little morals himself.

In this context of double-talk and distortions, one Koriak woman I knew openly challenged The Hunter to prove his financial acumen. Why, she asked, had he not been able to pay for the furs in money instead of schnapps? Could it be that his commercial wit was second rate, unable to bring in the dollars he wanted? The challenge was posed comically, but it was a fair question, and The Hunter took it seriously. She had a point.

Such a commentary was an arena that many Koriak women and men I knew used to challenge and expose hierarchically structured expressions of regional disparity. As a means of challenge, such commentary may seem ineffective and frustratingly tame. It neither upsets the order of regional hierarchy nor directly displaces the Hunter's power. Nevertheless, such commentary challenges an assumed superiority by maneuvering in the spaces that reveal the vulnerability of power without disarranging the challenger's life. The comment's implicit wit taps the self-assumed importance of The Hunter and allows two different but related views of life in the settlements at the northeastern shore. One describes Koriak existence as harsh and in need of improvement, the other as downbeat but not devoid of wit and hope.

□ □ □

## Regional Relations

At Kamchatka's northeastern shore, Russian and Ukrainian administrators predominantly held regional dominance in the villages in which I lived. Although the presence of white traders and small entrepreneurs was increasingly palpable in the northern peninsula since the mid-nineteenth century (Vdovin 1973), the majority of Russian and Ukrainian "newcomers" (*priezhie*) arrived in the mid-1950s. At that time, government programs encouraged a form of economic development that invited the increased presence of Russian and Ukrainian workers and their families at the northeastern shore. The majority of whites, as Koriak women and men usually call the newcomers in the region, worked in the flourishing fish industry. The incentives were attractive: The wages were three times higher than on the mainland; the family of every worker received a well-equipped apartment (in the Soviet Union, apartments were not privately rented out by property owners but were distributed and run under the auspices of the state. Usually a person had to apply to the local authorities to qualify as eligible. The waiting lists were very long, including waiting periods of several years); and many families received and were able to afford a car.

A consequence of the political turmoil that followed the breakup of the Soviet Union was that Russian and Ukrainian administrators, teachers, and workers in Ossora wanted to return to their respective hometowns in Russia and the Ukraine. With the end of communism, state subsidies in northern Kamchatka had begun to dry up. The Yeltsin government had neither the money nor the interest in financially assisting workers and an industry—fishing—that was hazardous and hard to control. In the context of economic instability and political uncertainty that followed Russia's privatization program, a great number of Ossora's white residents began to put up their apartments, refrigerators, television sets, and furniture for sale. It was far too expensive, they explained, to ship appliances and tools from northern Kamchatka to their homes. Because they imagined a difficult start once they returned, they put high prices on their apartments, frequently the equivalent of six or seven years of a herder's salary.

This regional inequality provoked many of the Koriak women and men I knew into caustic commentary, albeit they did not embrace hostile or antagonistic actions. Indeed, in the autumn of 1992, when one young Koriak man began to rally against the whites who lived in Tymlat by encouraging fellow villagers to take up a struggle in arms ("Let's take our rifles! Let's

□ □ □

kick the Russians out! If they don't want to go, we shoot them. Get out of the village, Russians"), he was publicly exhorted by Koriak elders to refrain from expressing his anger. Hostility, they said, only created more hostility and conflict. Most villagers wanted no part of it.

Social relations between Tymlat and Ossora were unstable and uneasy. In they eyes of many Koriak who live in Ossora, the existence of their kin in Tymlat seemed marked by backwardness and slovenliness. They frequently contrasted their "cultured" manners with the "not-cultured" (*nekul'turnye*) manners of Koriak women and men who lived in Tymlat. Even visits by relatives were short. Many Koriak women and men in Tymlat I knew frequently felt insulted by their more cosmopolitan kin. It is obvious that after a couple of days most Ossorians wanted to leave; rushing through the village, they inquired about transportation possibilities. Usually their relatives in Tymlat observed this behavior with a stoic expression and deep silence. They were aware that their more metropolitan relatives looked at them with pitiful eyes and that they could not match the prosperity that life in Ossora— comparatively speaking—seemed to offer.

All these discourses have helped to shape my understanding of the significance of history and gender at Kamchatka's northeastern shore.

## Travel Guide

This book is divided into nine chapters and speaks to issues of gender and history. In this chapter, I have begun to set out the theoretical framework and ethnographic orientation for my further examination. In the second chapter, "History of the Periphery," I show how ethnographic imagery and historic developments have defined forms of Koriak existence at Kamchatka's northeastern shore. In the third chapter, "Dissecting Histories," I explore some responses of Koriak women and men to key sites of regional authority and domination in dialogues with ethnographic descriptions and political justifications. The fourth chapter, "Distant Voices, Still Lives," takes on the project of gender specification by treating Koriak women elders as individual commentators on culture and history.

Chapter 5, "Research Connections," situates my exploration of contemporary Koriak dilemmas at the northeastern shore within the social entanglements of gender, regional inequality, and community differentiation; it also looks at some conditions, as well as ramifications, of my own research. In the

□ □ □

sixth chapter, "Agency in Dire Straits," I tell the stories of two Koriak women who called my attention to the importance of gendered opportunities and constraints in Koriak women's present struggles against economic hardship and desolation. In a very different context, the care with which Koriak women work animal skins and furs has helped to move my thinking toward the pleasures women may take in work and in intimate relationships. This process is explored in Chapter 7, "Skins of Desire." Throughout my stay at the northeastern shore, one Koriak woman helped me understand the importance of creativity in challenging power disparities and in searching for innovative, albeit unusual, solutions for cultural survival. Chapter 8, "And Tradition," is dedicated to her.

I have described the significance of travel in Koriak women's and men's lives. In keeping with this orientation, there is no ordinary conclusion in the final chapter, "Arrival"? The passages through historical configurations of political and social authority, gender divisions, and community differentiations arrive at no received wisdom but relate other points of departure, leading travelers into novel fields.

□ □ □

# 2 | □□□

## History of the Periphery

I stayed in the hospital of Petropavlovsk; you
know, most people there are from the city. I
walked with this woman through the garden, and
she asked me where I was from. From the North,
I said, from Kamchatka. Oh, she said, that's
where primitive people walk just like bears.

—*Svetlana Uvarova, Ossora, March 1992*

The dichotomously paired tropes of isolation or tradition, progress or modernity, have been instrumental in shaping images of indigenous peoples in the
Russian Far East. Having its roots in urban consciousness and the civilized
imagination, such commentary is frequently heard at Kamchatka's northeastern shore. In this particular comment, Koriaks are associated with the brute
and wild, stripped of their humanity. The insidious insult of this remark lies
not in the metaphorical twinning of humans with such powerful animals as
bears. Most Koriaks I knew would consider this analogy rather flattering.
From the perspective of people in the tundra, bears are akin to humans.
Like Koriaks, bears are experts of the tundra: They are competent hunters;
they travel long distances in search of food; they are omnivorous eaters; and
stripped of their fur, their bodies resemble those of humans. However, the way
in which human nature and bestiality are threaded together in one insidious
metaphor offends and hurts: The bear's nature is characterized as perverted
and wild, belonging to the threatening realm of unconfined nature. Koriaks

are defined by the image of the nature by which they are surrounded and in which they live.

The lumping together of Koriaks with untamed beasts is only one of many means by which Koriaks have been frequently imagined and described. This and the following section trace some of the names and tropes that have been used to label and mark Koriak women and men as archaic and primitive know-nothings. Throughout history, Koriaks have been called many names: some derisive, some spiteful, some more merited and fair-minded. Some of these names were given to them by their regional neighbors, some by ethnographers, others by the state. In the following section, I begin with the exploration of regional and ethnographic labels and move on to those of the state.

## Naming

In spite of long-standing etymological and semantic disputes, by and large ethnographers seem to agree that the term *Koriak* has not been chosen by Koriaks themselves but denotes a linguistic hybrid, merged from culturally different idioms. *Koriak* emerges in the anthropological literature approxi-mately at the end of the seventeenth century (Vdovin 1973, 51) and can be traced to the etymon *kor,* meaning reindeer (Jochelson 1908, 406). Most ethnographers assume that the Koriaks' respective regional neighbors to the north, the Chukchi, or to the south, the Itelmen, used this or a similar-sounding ethnonym to name the reindeer herders, whalers, and hunters who lived in the rocky and sparse lands of Kamchatka's North. Either the Cossacks (Steller 1974 [1774], 240) or the local Russians (Jochelson 1908, 406) then put the term to widespread use.

In the beginning of my reading on northern Kamchatka, I found it hard to appreciate the label *Koriak;* it seemed awkward and contrived. Especially in light of Koriaks' claims that they are a group of people with different idiosyncratic features, the name did not convey a sense of the multiplicity and significance of community distinctions. However, although I try to describe my fieldwork without any false homogeneities, I use *Koriak* throughout the book. Currently, Koriak women and men have begun to use this ethnic label as a matter of pride in the face of increasing social and, as some argue, cultural deterioration. Confronting regional injustice and the self-centered interests of the nation-state, the ethnographic challenge may well be to show

□ □ □

the rightfulness of political class, not to tamper with the academically most authentic term for a people. In using *Koriak*, I then take a position with limitations as well as strengths.

These considerations aside, although most northern ethnographers saw fit to find and use the most authentic term for those they met in the northern tundra, the Soviet state saw an even greater need to mark and categorize the subjects who lived at the northern peripheries of its constitutional borders. Reports, statistics, and ethnographic descriptions from the seventeenth century through the beginning of the 1930s had encouraged a view of Koriak life as hopelessly stuck in tradition-bound and ahistorical forms of living. From the vantage point of the Soviet state, these peoples were in dire need of help. Indeed, the political term conjured up to designate them bespeaks government notions of paternalism and domination. As part of the state's nomenclature for the "Small Peoples of the North," Koriaks were called a *narodnost'* (people): politically too insignificant to be offered constitutional influence and weight, numerically too small to be called a nation.[1]

Small, by implication, meant to be labeled as insignificant, pitiful, low grade. It meant to be in need of administrative structures and institutions that would create economic progress, education, and ordered places of living— all of which should soon spread a dense layer across the northern peninsula. From the perspective of the Soviet state, Koriak women and men lived in misguided and ill-informed ways; their social structure was reminiscent of the evolutionary uncivilized stage called the "stone age" (Bilibin 1933d, 95). Koriaks were labeled primitive and by analogy small because they were people out of touch with history. Such a perspective, of course, proved expedient in legitimizing the particular shape of state authority and interventions that were to become so formative in and for Koriaks' lives. In the paternal view of the Soviet state, small peoples were insufficient and could not rule themselves; small peoples would benefit from the state's helping hand.

In the contemporary Koriak struggle for identity and cultural sovereignty in the Russian Far East, however, such language and argument are rightly condemned as pejorative and depreciating (for example, Korobova et al. 1991). Indigenous leaders argue that such terms make it hard for them to contend for Koriaks' autonomy and title to the land. They insist on Koriaks' rights to become equal to other nations. The following section as well testifies to a belittling attitude with regard to popular and administrative imaginations. This attitude is situated between the cardinal frameworks of either timeless tradition or political dominance.

□ □ □

## Tropes and Songs

> Koriak Dance
> [A] Koriak dance—
> [is] the sister of joy,
> I could rejoice in you
> Until the morning.
> Out of magnificent songs,
> Woven into gracious designs,
> I heard and saw,
> Brought to the door
> [the] peaceful silence of the tundra—
> Magnificent mountains,
> [the] buzzing of birds,
> and the movements of game,
> [A] Koriak dance—
> [is] the sister of joy
> I could rejoice in you
> Until the morning.
> The magic forces,
> You, palpably, own,
> That is why you are beloved by everybody,
> We dance—[as] homage.
>
> (Kosygin 1990)

This poem introduces an important means by which Koriaks have been often imagined and described. Lyric verse like this is frequently found in local newspapers and regional brochures. In contrast to the negative stereotyping of indigenous cultural life from the perspective of the state, here Koriaks are introduced as unswerving traditionalists and active practitioners of folklore. The poem suggests that their world was one of magic and lore, one of exoticism and enchanting tales. Such imagery bespeaks a positive image of the Koriak universe and existence. Yet despite its appreciative content and tone, there exists only an insubstantial contradiction to the language of the state. Both define Koriak through frameworks of archaic structure and prehistoric time. Dance is but one feature that accommodates such confining vision. It can be celebrated because it is harmless tradition, harmless because it does not

□ □ □

challenge the state authority and rule but rather defines the limits of custom and tradition.

The poem is charming because it makes free use of magic power metaphors and tradition-bound portrayals. It is insincere because it discounts different styles of Koriak dance to achieve cultural homogeneity. It is certainly true that in their dances and songs Koriaks have always imitated and invoked the movement of game, sea mammals, and birds. Women's and men's choreographic arrangements and body motions emphasize the keen eye and exceptional attention that Koriaks pay to the animals and to the land. But among the Koriak women and men that I knew, dance and song were as much a matter of personal taste and style as a matter of tradition-influenced configurations of steps, shoulder turns, hand movements, and head nods. Individual styles were so important, indeed, that the memory of a dead person was frequently invoked by the performance of her or his own compositions. A person's dramatic art showed her or his own sense of refinement and grace.

Actually, almost everybody that I knew liked and appreciated a wide array of music styles: classical, choral, disco, and rock. In particular, younger women and men were eager to learn about the kinds of music to which people listened in the part of the world from which I came. They had a fine knowledge of recent record hits, and they knew talent for what it was. In Tymlat, they called one of their neighbors Beethoven because he could flip the keys of an accordion so quickly up and down that you could not follow with your eyes. Beethoven played hits and Russian songs; in the village, he was considered an artist because he played beautifully at festivities and in the presence of his wife.

Yet apart from engaging the romantic vision of tradition, another function of poetry in the Soviet context was to leaven politics with imagination. Indeed, poems were a welcome means to lay claim to indigenous peoples' membership in the wider community of the state. The following rhyme exhorts this significance by identifying people as joyous and willing participators in supranational political projects transcending communal borders.

The nocturnal sun
Sparkles over the tundra.
The Native folks, children of the North,
Fisherman and hunters:
We are comrades, we are joyful.
Every toiler
Is dear to us, is our brother.

□ □ □

We are Tungus, Ostiaks, and Iukaghirs,
We are Kamchadals, Giliaks, and Koriaks.
We are the Small Peoples in a vast family,
We are reindeer herders and children of the gun.

(Stebnitskii 1931, 56)

This poem was written at the beginning of the 1930s, and as such it reflects an important dictum of its time: extranational community making. It honors and affirms the importance of indigenous ways of livelihood, yet it also pleads a cosmopolitan stance toward a widely extended intercommunal family. Every worker is a brother; everybody gains a new family. Kinship bonds are produced by and manifest through economic and not blood relationships. Here and for the most part in the eyes of local administrations, kinship is not a matter of lineage and descent but of class-consciousness and affiliation. Indeed, kinship idioms connect disparate communities unknown to one another by establishing one common category of belonging. By bringing communities under one order and law, the state becomes an extension of related communities. The ideas here are not those of different constituencies of cultural subjects (B. Anderson 1983), but those of the state.

The revolutionary style of this poem infantilizes Koriaks as "native Others." They are marked by an absence, afflicted by childishness and a lack of qualities, which excludes them from the ideals, from the ranks of European civilization. Gender is also part of the discourse of community making: international unity is engendered through the idiom of brotherhood. Class may be the defining, universal category; but here it depends on a masculinist construction. This is a key clue for understanding the process of community making; multinational associations of the revolution are communities of men. The themes of both poems may diverge, yet their vision of the indigenous world does not. A consistent and uniform narrative of cultural homogeneity identifies both poems as of one kind: A monologic voice cordons off the perspectives of Koriak women and men. They start to emerge in the following parts of the book.

The way in which I contrast some of the metaphors and tropes that sustained the master narratives of politics and tradition shows that these spheres were treated in separate ways, both of them subject to static imaginations. But there were also attempts to combine these two themes in one image, simultaneously ancestral and futuristic. In a final poem, development substitutes for politics.

□ □ □

Ocean and tundra,
Winter and summer,
Reindeer and motor vehicles—
This creates the everlasting poetry of Koriak life.
> (*60 Let Koriakskomu Avtonomnomu Okrugu* [60
> Years of the Koriak Autonomous Region] 1990, 33)

The poetry of the poem is the poetry of life. Is there a more powerful way to define people than through such stark and contrapuntal imaginations?

## History Positions

So far I have described how Koriaks have been merely defined from the outside, be it by ethnography, poetry, or the state. In this section, I begin to shift the scenes of my inquiry to show how Koriaks' own understandings of history in northern Kamchatka put a different twist on images of either tradition or advancement. In displacing the perspective from the outside that I exposed above, here I chronicle regional history, from the vantage points of both the tundra and the state. I envision history as an exchange of alternating points of view, jostling with one another, answering back and forth. It becomes clear that for all players matters of history are matters of perspective. Both Koriak women and men and the state have different stories to tell about the conditions and contexts of their changing existence.

In breaking up the calendar of history into two main periods—prerevolutionary and Soviet state era—I follow in part the conventions of ethnographic and historiographic writings on the Russian Far East. In this section, I choose such an arrangement because it offers the advantage of showing the making of local history from an encompassing vision. However, instead of following the monological tedium of a linear narrative, told from the view of administrations and the state, I aim to disrupt its unbroken progression. One problem with the chronicling of history in northern Kamchatka is that the historical record is fairly scant, lacking detail and telling information. I believe that despite such drawbacks a full picture will emerge.

Much like other indigenous peoples in Siberia and the Russian Far East, Koriaks have long been subjected to state exploitation. Ethnographic chronicles show that in the seventeenth century Koriaks first entered the historical record (Gurvich and Kuzakov 1960, 37) and began to pay *iasak,*

□ □ □

a native tax, to the tsarist government in furs. In particular, sable fur and the brilliantly prismatic pelt of wolverine were favored for coats and caps by the Tsarist court and the nobility across Europe. The Koriak inhabitants of northern Kamchatka were able to deliver both, yet they were often reluctant to do so. The mobility of reindeer herders presented a severe obstacle in the collection of *iasak*. Koriaks would simply break their camps to escape the taxing grip of government extortionists and move on to more remote, more unknown, more inaccessible places, but they could not entirely escape the clutches of governments and states.

The increasing demand for *iasak* and fur helped to open the way for the Russian Orthodox Church in the interior of northern Kamchatka. First reports about baptism and church services emerged in the eighteenth century. Many preachers of the gospel, however, seemed to express no desire to stay for very long to establish well-run and organized missions. Northern Kamchatka was an extremely cold and frightening place, and its indigenous population not very much inclined to embrace the faith of the Christian god. Indeed, most Koriaks seem to have taken umbrage at the missionaries' attempts and regarded them as a zealous step by the government to drive them ever more under the tutelage of the tsarist state (Vdovin 1979, 86–87). In the northern peninsula, it was not until the second half of the nineteenth century that the missionaries were able to extend their sphere of influence by building churches and running religious schools.

Records chronicling the history of the mission in the region are scant. They contain only a few detailed accounts of the doings of the evangelists, yet even so they sketch a tense situation of jarring views. Instead of quickly embracing the new faith, Koriaks confronted missionaries with their own way of looking at the world. Why should they embrace the new faith? Their arguments pointed to the fact that none of the animals by which they lived, which they hunted, and for which they arranged festivities throughout the year would appreciate or, for that matter, even recognize the Christian, thus alien, God. The questions they asked were very much to the point. How did the missionaries and the God they brought, neither of whom had any skills in reindeer herding and only little experience with the hunting of animals, know what dances, songs, prayers, gods, and sacrifices animals really need (Vdovin 1979, 96–108)? They were right, of course. At that time, the Koriaks' reindeer herds were suffering from inflamed festerings and purulent boils (Slepzova 1912, 2). As it turned out, God did not know what to do.

□ □ □

We know relatively little about the efforts of missionaries in northern Kamchatka, and we know even less about indigenous reactions toward them. There seem to be indications, however, that the more determined the missionaries were, the more unnerved the Koriaks became. In response to the increasing encroachment by foreign preachers on their lands, they began to create spiritual movements of their own. Some Koriak elders tell of one spiritual movement that filtered through the northern peninsula (see also Gurvich and Kuzakov 1960, 64). The uninvited efforts of the mission and the grueling wasting away of reindeer must have sparked, and affirmed, apprehensions of an apocalyptic breakdown of the Koriaks' world. They were, again, right. Elders explain that a powerful supernatural being was poised to travel out of the deep North into the more southerly located reindeer pastures. He would freely give healthy reindeer and rich lands to everybody who unconditionally followed him. In some encampments, Koriaks began to burn tents, furs, and stored food; they killed all the herds; they ceased to fish and hunt; and they ruled out catching and killing seals and whales. Thus bereft of anything worthwhile, they moved closer to the shore where they stood on rocks, naked and starving, raising their arms high into the sky in imitation of the cries of seagulls and other seabirds. The supernatural being failed to come; all his followers died.

This story that elders tell offers an important element in the writing of local history from a Koriak point of view. It brings into focus the irritations and concerns that Koriak hunters and herders must have felt toward increasing missionization and the sharply decreasing size of reindeer herds. For diminish they did. The increasing presence of missionaries, Russian, American, and Japanese traders, and government officials in northern Kamchatka encouraged the spread of epidemics among humans and animals. Meningitis, smallpox, measles, influenza, gonorrhea, ulcers, and venereal diseases like syphilis (Gurvich and Kuzakov 1960, 67) began to take their toll. It is remarkable that no official ethnographic source acknowledges a direct connection between these corporeal afflictions and the growing intensity of Koriak-white relationships. There are, however, indications in earlier travelers' reports that, in a highly critical way, link this expansive moment to the escalation of contagious diseases (for example, Bonch-Osmolovskii 1925, 80). Yet for Koriaks, what counted was their helplessness and despairing struggle in the face of these unknowns. For all that they knew, these afflictions brought death.

In fact, Koriaks seem to have had their own explanations for why, in the increasing embrace of whites coming from the West, animals and humans began to die. The ethnographer Bogoras (1930, 60), for one, reported that northern reindeer herders credited evil-minded and death-bringing spirits, all of which arrived from the West, with the epidemics and violent deaths that ravaged their camps. What barely anybody was willing to admit, Koriaks clearly grasped.

The disconcerting expansion of epidemics and infectious diseases, however, prevented neither Koriaks nor extraregional traders from expanding trade relations. At the end of the nineteenth century, when they came to increasingly sojourn in the region, most Russian, Japanese, or American small entrepreneurs built small posts along the shore or traveled as itinerant salesmen into the interior to visit distant camps. A loose congeries of practical items such as pots and knives, kettles and spears, scissors and buttons, needles and glass beads (see Burch 1988, 235; Gurvich and Kuzakov 1960, 65), as well as tobacco, sugar, and tea changed hands for reindeer meat, fish, and fur. Steel and flint of Chinese origin (Jochelson 1908, 565) also entered into the bargain. The currencies of exchange—chiefly rubles, furs, meat, and beads—probably fluctuated from time to time and place to place. One observer (Slepzova 1912, 22), for example, reported that by the end of the nineteenth century *mukhamors* (*Amanita muscaria,* known in North America as fly agaric), collected in the regions east of the Okhotsk Sea, functioned as a widely accepted medium of exchange in this trade. In recalling their own parents' stories, elders today affirm such reports. They explain that the fungi from the tundras east of the Okhotsk Sea were famous for their potency and strength, indeed more effective than the ones growing locally.[2] The effect of locally grown *mukhamors,* however, must have been impressive enough to the Koriaks' northern neighbors (Jochelson 1908, 582). They were a highly prized item in the intraregional trade between Koriak and Chukchi herders.

In 1994, these intercontinental and extensive regional trade relationships were still a great source of pride for many Koriak elders I knew. Koriak women elders wore and showed proudly their "American" beads. They were telling evidence of the widespread contacts and connections Koriaks once enjoyed, which, after the breakup of the Soviet Union, they so eagerly try to rebuild. It would be easy to describe the trade in and payment with beads as fraudulent and exploitive. But the pleasure and satisfaction Koriak elders take in these possessions suggest something different. They consider these beads as a source of living history and wealth; they are markers of social distinction that identify them as wide-trading people. Instead of being inept bunglers, these beads help them to identify themselves as cosmopolitan peoples who once enjoyed far-reaching economic and cultural relationships. The same is

□ □ □

true for the stories they tell about Korean and Japanese fishing boats that sailed along the northeastern shore. Koriak women and men listened to the beautiful singing of these fishermen; they were so impressed by the beauty of these tunes that they incorporated some of them into their own composing.

Yet as foreign trade and economic offshore relationships expanded, the Koriaks' camps and shoreline hamlets also became the sites of a growing trade in vodka and schnapps. The historical record has little to say about how intense and widespread the use of alcohol was, yet the frequent mention of intoxication suggests that alcoholic drink was not a sporadic but a regularly exchanged product. With regard to the Koriaks' use of alcoholic drink, ethnographers are not sparing in their opinions. Again and again, they condemn the Koriaks for hard drinking. There is not much subtlety in their descriptions, but occasionally one finds a recognition of the way in which mercantile and profit-making interests turn alcohol into "the foremost product of civilization, and [always] the first to arrive" (Bogoras 1917, 2). The traveler Beretti (1929, 25), however, did not share the fine irony of Bogoras but regarded the natives' use of alcohol with ambivalent feelings. He found fault with Koriak men for "very much liking" vodka and schnapps, yet at the same time he pointed to Russian and Japanese merchants who took advantage of the trade. Such tendencies still persist: The traffic in alcohol continues to trouble the Koriaks' lives today.

In the following section, I discuss a new era, a new form of state administration. Yet the transition from one political system to another was not as abrupt as indicated here. Before the Bolsheviks were ready to embark with the Koriaks on the long journey from the realm of barbarism to the enlightened stage of development, they first had to introduce the Koriaks to a new order not of their making.

## Soviet Outreach

In venturing into the period of Soviet outreach and encroachment on indigenous northern lands, I am fortunate to be able to draw from a substantial body of scholarship on history and political culture in the Russian Far East. Both Western and Russian scholars have paid meticulous attention to the development processes and politically centralizing ways in which state models of economic and cultural transformation were put in place in the Russian North.[3] In particular, Soviet scholarship has been criticized for obliterating

□ □ □

notions of cultural difference by invoking a master narrative of headway motion and steady progress. Even though such a critique is timely, it does have its own problems (for example, it begs the careful examination of the possibilities and conditions of ethnographic production in the former Soviet Union) and dispenses with this kind of scholarship too easily. Read slightly against the grain, Soviet sources and texts offer insights into the workings and particular shapes of history in the Russian Far East. Indeed, such readings have recently been taken up by scholars who argue that the logic of Soviet state rule fostered not a universal history but specific forms of national identity (for example, Koester 1997; Schindler 1991; Kerttula 1997). They argue that the standards of collective identity making have, ironically, enabled the maintenance of culturally idiosyncratic identities both in and against the state (Grant 1995).

A considerable part of Western literature on indigenous peoples in northern Russia is interested in the ways in which the state was able to implement administrative programs and to control its policies (for example, Weiser 1989; Kuoljok 1985; Humphrey 1983). Iuri Slezkine (1994) offers an encompassing and detailed reading of Russian sources that chronicle and reflect the development of Soviet rule in the northern regions of the state. In identifying the strategies, logic, and campaigns that were necessary to radically transform entire indigenous regions in the North into subjected territories, much of whose existence served to mirror the power of the state, he demonstrates that administrative interventions were formative in the creation of a subordinate citizenry of the state. Such works and the frameworks in which they are set make it possible to think about the ways in which the Soviet state helped to create and endorse the making of subordinate histories.

Very early in northern Kamchatka, the Soviet state used slogans, watchwords, and signs to win over the indigenous citizenry living in camps and along the shore.[4] One of the most immediate problems with which the state was faced was how to reach the masses, the herders and hunters, the whalers and fishermen who were to be placed under Soviet administrative authority. One major concern was the question of how to transform the Koriaks' universe, their values, in such a way that they came to see, and eventually to adopt, the messages and ideals of the state. In this cultural fight, a serious obstacle was certainly the supposed ignorance of those whom the state claimed to represent. As we have seen before, belittling and ingenious language was one means to achieve these aims. The use of traditional meeting and trading places such as fairs (Antropova 1971, 120) was another.

□ □ □

The Soviets called Koriak autonomy and mobility "primitive" or "underdeveloped" and looked at it as a cultural trait that needed to be effaced (Kantorovich 1931). A plethora of economic and political innovations was designed and put in place to manage the penetrating changes that were to unmake the Koriaks' way of life. In their efforts, the Soviets were keenly aware of the significance of culture, that motley of language, rituals, economy, styles, and tastes that would not easily crumble to historic dust. Their ideas thus needed a particularly effective form of accommodation, one that was to be found through the establishment of specific places of propaganda. In the 1920s, one of the most visible activities in the Koriak tundra was the building of *kul'tbazy* (culture stations). These socialist-oriented, public and political houses were, in the northern tundras, a microcosm of what was going on in the wider country. They were a primary means to gain access to, and change, public opinion. Propagandist movies, newspapers, and socialism in the form of entertainment were here presented to indigenous people. Under the sponsorship of the state, they all spoke one message with an unswerving voice.

Culture was an important arena in which indigenous cultures were to be changed, but without a homogenizing framework that would set a uniform infrastructure in place it was impossible to gain control over the Koriaks' autonomy and mobility. An important step in the taming of ungoverned mobility was the creation of administrative centers. Even though Koriak villages and hamlets lay along the shore and played an important role in economic trafficking between Koriaks and extraregional merchants, the tundra offered no bounded areas of bureaucratic management. Following from such reasoning, the tundra became the site of administrative divisions. The subtle irony of this process, of course, lay in the fact that increasing centralization engendered increasing decentralization. The way in which centralized polities controlled movement among Koriaks (passport system) and access to the means of production and resources created separations and facilitated inequalities among different Koriak groups.

Already in 1928, the village of Tigil', which was located at the southeastern shore of the Okhotsk Sea and harbored government institutions important for the southern peninsula, was able to extend administrative offices and jurisdiction to the northern and eastern parts of Kamchatka. Two more regional political boundaries emerged: To the west, the Penzhenskii (or *Zapadno-Koriakskii* [western Koriak]) district was found; to the east, the Karaginskii (or *Vostochno-Koriakskii* [eastern Koriak]) district was created. While these administrative divisions separated Koriaks from one another

□ □ □

by assigning them to different local authorities, the government laced up a regional administrative frame to prevent too much microdifferentiation. The *Koriakskii natsional'nyi okrug* (Koriak Autonomous Region) was founded in 1930 and included all the Koriaks of the area. In 1935, the Karaginskii district with its eclectic and hard-to-control population of Oliutorskii Koriaks split into two units: The northern part of the district was now called Oliutorskii district. Throughout this process of division making and differentiation, the culture station in Penzhenskii district, and Tigil', lost its significance. Palana at the western shore became the politically centripetal village of the province.

The political subordination of Koriak herders in such an administrative process of centralization sapped not only their own polities and social institutions but cut through the economic sphere. In the wider context of restraining Koriak mobility to focal sites, collectivization is probably one of the most commented-on features of Soviet policy making. Turning Koriak "property," primarily reindeer herds, into a resource managed under state-ownership was an effective step in bringing domesticated animals, as means of production, under state control. Yet in their own commentary on collectivization, Koriaks emphasize equally the violence of the state and the ambitions of northern neighbors.

Many Koriaks I knew interpreted the making of collectivization in the context of their own experiences with their Chukchi neighbors. To their minds, collectivization presented an especially malevolent form of theft. They began to draw comparisons between different cultural styles of lying and stealing. They remarked that Chukchi herders had always raided Koriak reindeer herds. They came as visitors during the day to find out how many well-kept reindeer there were in a camp. They returned in the night, pilfering the number of reindeer they saw as fit or could take. But they never took an alarming number. Just like their northern neighbors, the state took reindeer, but in contrast to them the state took in grand style. The Koriaks that I knew looked at the collectivization of reindeer as grand larceny and large-scale fraud. While administrators busied themselves with drawing fine distinctions between "unmixed" (pure reindeer herding) and "mixed" (combining reindeer herding and fishing) collective economies in the region (Antropova 1971, 128), Koriaks themselves noted the unmaking of their world.

In the broader scheme of socialist history and progress, collectivization, however, was only a beginning. Bolshevik agents expressed much fervor and zeal in introducing the enchantments of reason to Koriak settlements and camps. From the perspective of the Revolution, indigenous religion

□ □ □

and shamanistic beliefs, which were derided as "idol-worship" and boastful quackery (Bauerman 1934), presented a perfidious form of cunning and exploitation. According to elders, small but frightfully armed revolutionary units traveled from camp to camp, searching from tent to tent for spirit effigies, superhuman figurines, and other spiritual paraphernalia. Many women and men began to hide their drums, burying them in fur heaps or digging them under the earth. Some of them rest there today; others are still in use.

Apart from issues of supposed charlatanism and superstition, what was even more important in the state's eyes was that the practice of primitive religion had a politically injurious side to it. Its performance hardened conservatism in the face of challenge and change (Bogoras 1932). Confronted with an administrative logic of its own, the Koriaks, deeply perturbed, began to react in a terrified way. Fears that one might get imprisoned or killed when wearing one's *annapel* (a spirit manifest in a small stone) spread throughout the region. These protectors were a vital principle in the Koriaks' universe of animated beings (Jochelson 1908, 32–46; Vdovin 1973, 95), performing functions in keeping humans and animals well. They chaperoned the hearth, the essential life principle of the Koriak home; they sustained a person's body and health; they empowered a person's own spirit; and they helped restore the equilibrium between humans and the land. *Annapels* traced and upheld the world in its central foundations. Many Koriaks I knew wore or carried their guards with them even to the present day.

As so often in other areas, euphoric rhymes accompany the allegorical burning of shamanism at the stake. Here is one of them:

> We do not need any further
> This trickery!
> We stop serving
> The priest and the shaman!
> Old beliefs–
> Vanish like smoke!
> On a broad and shining path
> Walks the youth!
>                     (Stebnitskii 1931, 58)

In this context of violent intimidation and desecration, threats of pogroms began to haunt not only the northeastern shore. By the mid-thirties, rumors of government kidnappings and killings had spread throughout the region.

□ □ □

Koriak herders who commanded a considerable number of reindeer were in particularly great danger of being accused by the state. The Soviet world was a world of stark contrasts, and the principal categories of economy and production separated the Koriaks—again, not only them—into two absolute classes: exploiter and exploited, rich and poor. It did not matter that these were not meaningful categories for those who lived in tundra encampments and along the shore. The Koriaks rapidly began to feel the painful and at times deadly seriousness of these ideas. The "richness" of any Koriak *kulak* (here, a wealthy reindeer herder who "owned" a considerable number of animals and thus, by extension, the means of production) was libeled as an affront to all workers. The doings of such wealthy people were said to sabotage the buildup of a fair and egalitarian state. How exactly a rich reindeer owner is defined never emerges clearly from the record—but that question does not matter to the Koriaks today. What matters to them is that the then common practice of imprisonment left a legacy of grief at the northeastern shore. Many of the Koriak women and men I met mourn the death or unexplained disappearance of their fathers or grandfathers. Men, deported or jailed because they owned too many reindeer, played the drum too often, left too many offerings in the tundra's sacred sites. All of them may have acted in accordance with the ways in which they had been brought up, but all of them acted against the revolutionary ethos of the state. Everybody in Ossora and Tymlat knew that the accusations were ill-minded and wrong. Some of the men I met showed great compassion when their fathers were told that they were sentenced to several years of prison; often they went in lieu of them. One of these men explained to me that his father had been too old for such "nonsense"; he, like others, spent two or three years in jail. It is here that many of them learned to speak in the Russian tongue.

Some of these men felt that their knowledge of the Russian language served them well when regional authorities tried with increasing force to intervene in collective rituals, performances, and feasts. The way in which I was told the story of one *khololo* (the feast in which the spirits of seals and sea mammals are carried into "the other world") in the northern tundra bespoke the brazenness and wit with which Koriak men were able to stand up to the authority of the state. For Koriaks, rituals were, and still are, an especially affirming way to acknowledge the power and importance of animals.[5] *Khololo* is one of the most salient animal rituals today. Taking place in the fall, usually in November, Koriak women and men congregate in the house of a successful hunter to celebrate both his prowess and skill and the animal's munificence.

□ □ □

Skilled hunters know that it is not solely their knowledge and skill that allow them to make the kill: their excellence borrows from the unselfishness of the animal that allows itself to be killed. Animals and humans are joined in a circle of give and take, of perpetual reciprocity. Through the celebration of *khololo,* Koriak women and men give expression to their gratitude and respect.

Many years earlier, a young boy in the village of Rekinniki had killed his first seal, and in the following autumn a *khololo* was arranged to celebrate both the animal and the boy. The Koriak men to whom I talked told with excited voices of the feast: the impressive number of people that attended the feast; how strong the mushrooms had been; how many drum players were there; how women danced with verve and grace; and how flaring the sounds had been that they cried in imitation of the seal. The festivity must have been well on its way when a local policeman entered the room. They should be quiet, he said. They should stop these celebrations, he said. Loud singing and drum playing were no longer allowed, he explained. Russian and Ukrainian village residents wanted to sleep. The Koriaks understood that now they were outsiders, foreigners in their own land.

Men spoke up. This was their village and their feast, they said. This was what they had always done. Where did the policeman get his food, they asked, if not from the animals he now so scornfully dismissed? An argument ensued, but the policeman would have nothing of it. He threatened to report all the Koriak women and men present when two boys crawled up behind him and pulled his legs away. A pistol flew through the room. A Koriak man grabbed it to tuck it away. Nobody was quite clear about explaining who picked the ensuing fight, but it was rather clear that the policeman left the house beaten up. Non-Koriak local residents threatened Koriak villagers that they would issue a report about the event to the district administration in Ossora, yet they never did. Such a report also involved the testimony of the policeman. Yet how should he explain the loss of his gun? He was too embarrassed to retell the series of events in an official setting. In the end, he asked the Koriak men for the return of his weapon. They refused. They advised him not to disturb their celebrations anymore; they expressed their hopes that then policemen, administrators, and they might actually get along.

Their hopes were thwarted again: From their perspective, the state was never much interested in getting along. In fact, more decrees were issued; more troubles were to come. In the 1950s, the villages along the northeastern shore became the site of a further number of economic changes that were to change the face of the region in a fatal way. The Second World War may have

□ □ □

interrupted the efforts of state administrators to bring light into the darkness of the Koriaks' world, but the ambitious endeavors of the socialist world were quickly resumed. A considerable number of the few "private" reindeer that until then Koriaks had been allowed to "own" were slaughtered; at the same time, smaller herds were amalgamated into bigger ones. This, for Koriaks, cataclysmic deed was accompanied by another, maybe even more insidious one. As animals were again "centralized" into larger herds, so were humans, to rehash the tone of records, brought under the central authority of a few settlements. In concrete terms, this meant that villages located too far away from the shore were deemed "economically nonviable" and became the sites of forceful abandonment, of "closing." A series of relocations dislodged Koriak families, relatives, and their neighbors from their homes and moved them to newly expanded village centers. Each village population moved several times. The following catalog itemizes the number, dates, and frequency of relocations at the northeastern shore.

The village of Kichiga, situated between Tymlat and Anapka, was one of the first settlements to be closed at the northeastern shore. In 1956, it closed forever, and its inhabitants were resettled to either Tymlat or Ossora. In the same year, the old village of Karaga, until then the administrative center of the Karaginskii district, lost much of its political significance. This status was now given to Ossora, located more conveniently at the juncture between Tymlat and Karaga. In 1970, the entire populace of the latter was moved to the new Karaga, again directly located on the northeastern Pacific coast. In 1974, it was decided that the village of Anapka should be closed. The water, it was said, was too shallow during the tide; freighters and other cargo ships could not anchor in Anapka's harbor. Production was not efficient in such a place. Its population, women and men, families and children, had lived here for approximately twenty years when they were relocated to the respective villages of Il'pyr', Tymlat, or Ossora. Their first dislocation had taken place in 1952 when the old village of Anapka was looked at as economically nonviable, because it was too far from the shore. The people of Rekinniki were relocated more often than anybody else in the region, namely on three occasions. Until 1947, their village was located in the northwestern tundra near the river Pustoe. The population still lived in tents; transport was difficult; and goods needed to be carried to and from the shore across the land. In that year, villagers were resettled to a newly built Rekinniki, again close to the river Pustoe but this time only twelve kilometers from the ocean. Ten years later, in 1957, the villagers were moved again, now to a location directly on the

□ □ □

coast. This village was closed in 1980; everybody was moved to either Tymlat or Ossora.

Such sober listing of relocation and violent moves, of course, does not capture the agony and distress that followed on the heels of such measures. Many elders died; many tried to return. Koriak reactions to this series of relocations become clearer in Chapter 4 when women tell their own stories. Suffice it here to say that not everybody was willing to abandon home and everyday livelihood practices. In nearly each "closed" village, erased from maps when they ceased to be meaningful places of living in the state's eyes, elders continue to make a living. They have neither the resources nor means to continue reindeer herding, but they fish and hunt.

In the summer months, seasonal and extraregional fishermen who live along the northeastern shore to make quick money by harvesting fish frequently deride these women and men as half-crazy. Why would anyone, they wonder aloud, want to live in rickety houses, in penury and insufficient conditions? Without running water and electric light? In abodes with earthen floors and hard, wooden planks for sleeping? Their questions miss the point. In these elders' eyes, these domiciles were not decrepit houses. They were home.

The story I have chronicled so far provides the necessary backdrop for the following chapters I am about to tell. In this chapter, I have begun to weave together two contrapuntal narratives; I shall increasingly continue to do so. Such ways of questioning show how different versions of history and ethnography tap each other.

## History Today

History, of course, does not end here but continues to confront the Koriaks in surprising ways. Rumors of more destruction, of more closings—hearsay had it that the village of Il'pyr' might be the next target—pervaded the villages at the northeastern shore. Once again, people were afraid to lose their homes, their neighbors, the places they knew because the existence of one village was deemed unprofitable, not lucrative, unproductive. In March 1992, the collective farm shop that had for sixty years provided each inhabitant of Tymlat with food, clothes, technical equipment, and miscellaneous practical things shut its doors forever. The havoc that followed was unbelievable. It seemed that with the shop an entire village, indeed an entire country, was falling apart. The illusion of progress was in shambles before the world's eyes.

□ □ □

FIG. 3 | Approaching Tymlat from the frozen ocean (photo: author 1992).

As everybody in the village lined up for the last time to redeem the food ration cards that had been in service in Tymlat for three years, there was a sense of gloomy premonition about impending hunger and starvation. Accompanied by two or three relatives, most families had sent their dogsled teams to transport the heavy sacks of rice, buckwheat, oats, and a few other grains, and other miscellaneous goods that were left in the store, back to their houses. As dog teams got entangled in a muddle of cords, as teamsters yelled and hardly anything could be heard in the confusion of barks and voices, an ominous foreboding burst through the crowd. Had not elders always warned about the coming of a time in which the earth would turn so cold that nothing would grow, that even in summer people would starve, and many would die of hunger? Was this the time? The heightened sense of panic and agitation held almost everybody in the throes of the terror of entrenched poverty and fear.

□ □ □

In May 1992, the first privatized shop opened in Tymlat. A wave of relief ran through the village, only to be thwarted by the sight of the wares that were now put on display, waiting to be sold. In lieu of bread, milk, tea, and grains, the new shopkeepers stocked fancy American-made footwear and color television sets that nobody wanted to buy, or at least could not afford. People had not seen salaries for months; the bank was empty. There were no further food transports coming from the centers; there were many rumors but little news. When I returned to Tymlat in June 1994, the situation—bad has had it been before—had worsened. Many families resorted to collecting, fishing, and hunting activities. This was not only the consequence of a newly awakened interest in tradition and time-honored modes of economy; this was also due to the fact that barely anybody could afford to buy the expensive foreign goods now available in village shops. In that summer, a friend and I hiked every day through the tundra to collect berries, elder tree seeds, and roots as food. We were not the only ones; almost everybody else did the same. Finally, the premonitions of elders had turned into a sort of reality. The world in northern Kamchatka was a destitute place.

Since that summer, Tymlat has seen many versions of shops. The most recent variant sells pirated videotapes, French liquors, watches, tobaccos, plastic dolls, and Reebok sport shoes at outrageous prices. Letters that arrive from the northeastern shore bespeak a general sense of hopelessness and sadness as most Koriaks I know look into an uncertain future.

But there are also signs of hope. In the last years, the wish to leave Tymlat to return to the place from where they came became so strong that a group of Koriak women and men from Rekinniki began to rebuild their "old" village. Indeed, their project has become a model of resolution and vigor in so impressive a way that other Koriak groups have started to discuss similar endeavors. The harshest problems with which they are faced are acquiring the financial means and construction materials needed to rebuild the village from which they were once expelled. It will, most certainly, be a long and difficult way for them to realize their vision; their efforts demand patience. Nobody can quite foretell what will happen. Yet these are indications that history is about to change, as Koriaks begin to insist on and argue for their rights.

□ □ □

# 3 | □ □ □

## Dissecting Histories

Chronicling the broad outlines of historical processes at Kamchatka's north-eastern shore offers the advantage of showing how events are connected with one another in time but allows only a sketchy reading of key events in that history. In this chapter, I seek to explore some of the pivotal themes—collectivization, education, shamanism, and love—in the encounter among Koriak reindeer herders, white travelers, and political agents as well as in Koriak women's and men's struggle for cultural meaning and survival. In highlighting those aspects most eclipsed by ethnographic descriptions of the region, I move back and forth between these accounts and the responses of Koriak women and men. I thus explore the alignments and personal stakes of Koriak herders in matters of regional hierarchies, official administrative interpretations, and tradition in dialogue with the "facts" of Koriak back-wardness and underdevelopment. The exploration of each theme contains its own destabilizing critique.

### Collectivization

The introduction of collectivization is probably the most frequently com-mented-on feature in northern Kamchatka ethnography since the 1930s. Among Koriak herders at the northeastern shore, collectivization involved turning reindeer herds, traditionally run under the management of experi-enced herders and elders, into collective state property. Part of the legitimiza-tion of this process was the concept of class struggle, that is, the dream and the idea that the elimination of entrenched social and economic antagonisms would result in political and economic justice (Bilibin 1993a, 1934). Stated in rigidly contrasting terms—poor reindeer herders facing rich, the exploited fighting the exploiters—the ethnographic record covering the years from approximately 1930 to 1935 is replete with scenarios of an imagined class struggle among Koriak reindeer herders and (a hoped for) social revolution. At the northeastern shore, class struggle was not a trivial issue; the record indicates that at that time it was the defining issue from which the Koriak world was made. In turning perceived nonegalitarian reindeer herders into an egalitarian-based citizenry of the state, the question of value—private or collective, poor or rich—was itself at stake. To create Koriak reindeer herders in the image of a perceived egalitarian nation, Soviet officials first had to recreate the economic realm.

Koriak herders did not stand idly by as their "property" was confiscated and given into the hands of the state. They indicated in several ways that the state's understanding of justice and social emancipation was by no means self-evident or shared by them. Ironically, what state representatives deemed as necessary and progressive steps in the building of an unprejudiced and fair-minded future involved fundamental injustice and violation of rights from a perspective in the tundra. At variance with the idea that the world was to be understood in terms of class distinction or exploitation, terms of little meaning to the Koriak herders, they confronted state administrators and officials with a philosophy of their own. The writings of the agent Bilibin (1933b, 1933c) allow some insight into the articulation of cultural struggle in the northern peninsula during the period of collectivization.

In his vivid description of a meeting in November 1930 in the Penshenskii district near the river Tikhloe, Bilibin himself attested to the socialist agents' and Koriak reindeer herders' dissonant perspectives of value and justice. At first, the gathering in the tundra took the usual course: The issues discussed here were discussed everywhere. Collective farms were to be formed, and new forms of legislation were to be introduced; in short, the restructuring of Koriak existence in the tundra had begun. One problem, however, was that Bilibin's arguments sounded obscure to the Koriaks. They forthrightly explained that Bilibin's talk did not make much sense to them. As far as they were concerned, there were no exploiters—wealthy reindeer herders who drained the last blood from their "servants"—among them. Not only were they incapable of understanding the sense of Bilibin's logic; they confronted him with a powerful argument of their own.

In the closing minutes of the meeting, Bilibin asked two "poor" reindeer herders, Um'e and Liuliu, to openly denounce their "master," Inylo, as an

□ □ □

oppressive exploiter. To his dismay, the men refused, arguing that they were encountering such reasoning for the first time. And they went on to explain: "We [are] so afraid as if you would send us to fight a bear."

Fight a bear? What is happening here? How and why do the reindeer herders link issues of collectivization to human-animal relationships? How does the bear enter the sphere of economic relationships, and why do Koriak herders invoke the bear in their argument against collectivization? Bilibin felt irritated and disoriented by Um'e's and Liuliu's argument, as his abrupt silence, followed by a quick change of issues and themes, attests. What was he supposed to do with such a nature-bound theory of economic relations? In the end, he decided to dismiss the Koriaks' reasoning as senseless and absurd. Yet the Koriaks' comments can scarcely be attributed to the childlike desires and attitudes Bilibin attributes to them. What, then, accounts for this unexpected appearance of the bear?

The herders' argument, I suggest, is drawn from a deep appreciation of an affinity between humans and bears.[1] Although I had read numerous anthropological works that point to the extraordinary significance of the bear in northern indigenous contexts (McClellan 1970; Hallowell 1926; Darnell 1977; Chichlo 1985; Kreinovich 1969; Vasilevich 1971; Zolotarev 1937), an important insight for my understanding came from stories that Koriak elders told me. Like other northern peoples (McClellan 1970, 6), Koriaks tell of a time when there were little differences between animals and humans. "There was a time when people talked like animals. Animals and humans could understand each other and could talk. Most animals were good, but not all. Then the humans became bad. That's why their tongues are so long today. People lost the ability to speak [with animals]." Humans were never more significant than bears. The uncertain power balance embedded in human-animal relationships is a useful way to think about the power of the bear.

The stories Koriak herders tell about bears show that bears are akin to humans in many ways. The power that brings humans and bears together is embedded in the match of bodily features, diet, courage, dexterity, and styles of consumption that these two beings share. Like humans, bears have the ability to walk upright, to eat herbs, plants, meat, and fish. They do not gulp or swallow their food but devour it with relatively slow motions. And they are skilled hunters when it comes to preying on a fair-sized meal. In northern Kamchatka, they are the only animals that are as dangerous as humans. A bear can kill a human and dismember the body. The ultimate demonstration of similarity lies in physical signs: Stripped of its fur, a bear resembles a human in striking

□ □ □

ways. This was nowhere more visible than in the tundra. There, herders advise never to pride oneself on killing a bear. The bear will hear and return. One should never believe that one is stronger than a bear. A bear will come and kill.

These understandings show the importance and strength of bears. Yet perhaps of greater significance for my own understanding of the significance of bears was my witnessing of an event that condensed many cultural features I had already heard about.

It was with Kirill that I first learned to appreciate and see tundra animals as related beings. Where I at first saw only game and beasts of prey, he taught me how to read the animals' sounds and movements socially. Where I saw only physically differentiated animal bodies and forms, he told me how fights and liaisons among them earlier on had brought force to the shapes they assume today. By way of preparing ritual offerings for the animals he killed, he showed me how to acknowledge their munificence. The knowledgeable hunter knows that it is not only his skill that brings an animal down. To believe this would be foolish and absurd, an extraordinary exaggeration, the negation of the intrinsic bond between humans and animals. He pointed to the ways in which animals make themselves known—partridges by rustling, geese by crying, hares by quick running and the force of their speed, foxes by their easily distinguishable reddish pelt, and elks by their dark-brown fur and their roar. What seems to the popular Euro-American imagination insignificant, and thus irrelevant, animal features, for Koriaks mark a behavior that endows each animal with an idiosyncrasy that demands special attention. No animal is the same.

It was a fine morning that Kirill chose to embark on a hunting trip for a bear, inviting me to travel with him. It was early spring, and the bears had just finished their hibernation. They were hungry and looking for food. Earlier, some bears had been spotted in the vicinity of the camp. They were expected to attack some of the newborn reindeer calves. As we prepared foods and hunting gear for several days in the tundra, Kirill grew excited at the prospect of spending time away from the camp. But before we were ready to do so, Kirill decided to travel once more to the food base, a food supply depot about twenty miles away from our camp, and shared by four other neighboring encampments. Such bunker-like storage bases are spread widely across the northern peninsula. They hold usually nonperishable foodstuffs such as flour and grains.

Leaving the camp to fetch some of this sustenance for the big hunting trip ahead, Kirill was not about to return for quite a while. The camp inhabitants slowly grew uneasy. Kirill had long been expected to return. Had something

□ □ □

FIG. 4 | A killed bear in the camp. Eyes, nose, and ears are closed with white hare fur (photo: author 1992).

happened to him? Had he encountered problems, unknown challenges that involved dangers he could not master, skills he did not have? From the distance of the camp, we could only guess at what might have gone wrong. But each of us was surprised when we found out what had prevented his return. When Kirill proudly entered the camp, with a dead bear tied to the sled that was supposed to carry the cargo from the food base, everybody gathered to greet this hunter with both humbleness and respect. What followed was remarkable.

When Kirill arrived in the camp, everybody came out to greet him and the bear. People spoke in excited voices and danced while approaching the animal's body. Women kissed the bear on its eyes and snout. Men offered greetings by pecking its cheek. The bear's fur, out of which the animal had been peeled at the place of its death, was carried into Kirill's tent. As women and men began to dismember the cadaver, storing the meat under large-sized

□ □ □

black resin sheets so that government air patrols could not detect it, the bear's paws were cooked in a deep cooking vessel over the open fire. When the meat was done, everybody received a piece.

In the meantime, the bear's eyes, ears, and snout that, after the killing, had been covered with white hare fleece so that the animal could not see, hear, or smell to find out who the successful hunter had been, were unplugged. Together with the fur, the head was placed beside the fireplace in the tent. Sitting near the warmest place in the tent, the bear was regaled as an honored guest. A cup filled with strong tea was placed in front of the bear. Reindeer meat and seal fat were brought for the animal to feast on. Riddles and stories were told to entertain the visitor; songs were sung, and one woman played the drum. When the bear, as well as its hosts, appeared tired enough to fall asleep, the fire was quenched. Only a few chips continued to glow in the dark.

The next morning, the bear's fur was removed, made ready for its tanning. Kirill's mother buried the animal's head in her arms while another woman sang and played the drum. Dancing to the tunes of the latter's song, Kirill's mother moved around the open fireplace and the tent. When she began to tremble and fall, everybody knew that the bear had accepted the herders' gifts and was willing to depart to "the other world." In discussions with Koriak women and men, I learned that the "other world" is a spongy layer of worlds, connecting the living with the dead, people, waters, animals, and plants in an all-embracing universe. The spiritual forces range from the familial forces of the household, to the residual Supreme Being located far away, to the dead, who may choose to return. This circle traces the major lineaments of the universe, underscoring in particular the fluidity between all beings. The notion of the "other world" is not related to "heaven" but marks the realm into which humans and animals, indeed all beings, go to renew themselves, only to return to this world.

As all this suggests, the bear is the site of a plethora of practices and meanings that tie Koriak women and men to animals; these practices do not assume a mastery over animals, but put humans in their realm. A bear was killed—but somehow the killing is beside the point. What is important is that the Koriaks have to humble themselves, to treat the bear as an important visitor, a noteworthy guest that graces their camp through its presence. No wonder then that the agent Bilibin was helpless when confronted with an economic argument invoking the bear. His and the Koriaks' cultural orientations took their power from two dissonant spheres of values, one

□ □ □

rational and European, the other no less rational but belonging, assumedly, in the realm of the primitive and naive. Bilibin came from a world of human, political agency, a world defined by the rhetoric of progress and the utopia of economic reform. The Koriaks on whom these issues were so forcefully thrown also inhabited a universe of agency, but in contrast to the universe Bilibin knew theirs was, to a large extent, defined by proper and moral relationships between animals and humans. What to Bilibin appeared to be an insignificant feature of nature was for Koriaks a defining aspect of their lives. At the heart of the problem that emerged in the meeting at the river Tikhloe lay a matter of misrecognition, a matter of cultural translation. This was Bilibin's problem. The argument that seems fantastic or bizarre from the perspective of European reasoning is, from a vantage point in the tundra, not so. But then, Bilibin was not interested in interpretation. He was interested in change.

By way of this analysis, however, I do not wish to suggest that the introduction of collectivization was just a matter of different systems of dissonant values or cultural orders of signification. Another problem that emerged for the Koriak reindeer herders was the idea that clan structures should be established to hold groups of widely dispersed people through a centralized body of authority. But the Koriak men and women elders that I knew argued that "we did not know clans." They explained that in the tundra decisions were made by people with experience and with herding expertise. But the ethnographic record indicates that "clan" leaders were chosen in keeping with politically, not culturally, important values. "Pauperized" Koriak herders or young men who had a sufficient command of the Russian language so that they could read and write held office as leaders; traditional leadership by elders was overturned. Yet many young men seem to have denied the role that was sought for them by the state; they and many other Koriaks continued to seek the advice and follow the decisions of elders.

## Education

> We do not bow
> To former exploiters!
> We do not need any vodka
> Give us books!
> Knowledge in the North

Is like the falcon in summer!
The sun of science
Shines over the tundra!
    (Stebnitskii 1931, 60)

Here I invert the stream of my inquiry to ask about the consequences of scientific thought and reason in the tundra and not about cultural imaginings and tropes. Indeed, the exulting promise of science aside, this poem implies that education was an important means in the fight against exploitation. The unfailing self-assurance of the poem leaves no room for ambiguity. Since the mid-1920s, science traveled wide, and it traveled fast.

Even though the unshakable infallibility of the lyric's lines bespeaks success and certainty, in the beginning it must have been hard for tutors to introduce the teachings of modern science in the northern tundra. In their efforts to carry reason and the intellectual achievements of civilization into the remote villages and camps at the northeastern shore, these agents found themselves confronted, always and again, with another logic. Animals, once more, play an important role. For example, when the teacher Stebnitskii (1932, 42), author of the poem above, lectured in the village of Kichiga to Koriak students on the topic of the roundness of the globe, the students presented him with a powerful argument. Did he truly not know that the northern peninsula was a tremendous crab (here loosely defined as "Grandmother") and that all Koriaks lived and fed at her breast, his pupils asked? When angered, she begins to quiver so hard that the earth itself might tremble and fall apart. From their perspective, of course, they were right. Earthquakes ravage the peninsula from time to time; outpourings of water and soil spill into opening clefts.

In any case, the logic of such argument was so incomprehensible and so disconcerted the teacher Stebnitskii that he began to pay close attention to the manner in which Koriak women and men raise their children. Like the observations offered by his colleague Bilibin, Stebnitskii's descriptions are frequently colored by the derisive and impudent tone that marks the majority of the early ethnographic record. Stebnitskii in particular liked to intersperse his own accounts on issues of schooling and education with ethnographic observations on child psychology and play. In one essay (1933) that is remarkably free of seditious language, he describes the way in which, and the fervor with which, Koriak parents enjoy and dote on their children. But he also describes the tasks and hard work that children have to carry out, beginning at a very early age. In summary, according to Stebnitskii,

□ □ □

children perform the same tasks as adults (1933, 44–45), in accordance with the gendered division of labor. For example, boys around the age of ten begin to work as herders, no matter what the food and weather conditions are. They hunt, collect firewood, and may drive for two or three days on their own to trading posts, to exchange furs for nonregional produce. Together with boys, young girls help female relatives to catch and prepare fish for preservation through drying. And just like their aunts, mothers, and grandmothers, they tan and sew hides to fashion clothes. These were labor performances that supported autonomy and early self-sufficiency, and Stebnitskii was certainly impressed by them. Today Koriaks argue that it was precisely this autarchy and independence that was taken away from them.

Cultural and political transformations designed to turn savvy and well-skilled children into a dependent citizenry of the state do not come all at once. The making of such profound cultural change involves extensive political transformations that reach deep into the heart of a people and their way of looking at life. In northern Kamchatka—as elsewhere in the Russian North—the process of turning autarchic and self-reliant subjects into a dependent and politically unequal populace was, above all, made possible by introducing an education system that alienated children from their families, people from the land. The insidious effects of the boarding-school (*internat*) system have recently been the focus of much attention (Bloch 1996). Here I focus on the Koriaks' response.

The term *boarding school* has, without doubt, its own problems and can be misleading in a number of ways. In the educational context of the Russian Far East, the phrase refers to a type of residential school, structurally similar to the residential school system for indigenous peoples in Australia, Alaska, and northern Canada. In northern Kamchatka—again, as elsewhere in the Russian North—children were forcibly removed from their parents and families to grow up in educational environments of state-endorsed models of ideology. Dependence was encouraged, autonomy discouraged. Housing, clothing, and education were free for indigenous northern peoples, yet at the same time they experienced alienation from prior generations and their ways of life. There was much outrage and concern among Koriak herders when this educational structure was put in place; resistance mounted. Koriak elders to whom I talked reported that they did not want to let their children go. They would not learn how to tend reindeer; they would not learn how to hunt for seal. They would not learn how to tan, and they would never gain the kind of knowledge one needs when alone in the tundra for days without end. Such

□ □ □

anxieties and considerations stand in awkward contrast to the upbeat tone of ethnographic texts in praise of the quick success of government education in the most remote places of the tundra (Sergeev 1934). The historical record offers statistics and tables in abundance, each of which indexes and supports the narrative of steady educational advance. Such enumerations may contain much accurate detail, but many Koriaks I knew filled such numbers with descriptions of pain. In the end, it is life itself that pushes through.

While I was living at the northeastern shore, I found it impossible to shake off the intensity of torment and misuse that seeped through many schooling stories I heard. In these days, most Koriak women and men I knew pressed similar charges against the state: All of them told stories of how they had been cut off from family members and friends; how they had been refused the right to talk to one another in their own tongue; and how the eating of "their" food, for example, *iukola* and seal fat, was outlawed. The Koriak women and men I knew described the school's regime as punitive and rigid. As one Koriak woman put it: "The bell rang for us to get up, the bell rang for us to eat, the bell always rang." Many pointed to the ways in which they had learned distrust and cheating. One story sticks out as I write on the effects of boarding-school education.

It must have been in the late 1940s in northern Kamchatka. One Koriak girl, in her teens, was asked by the school's administrative board to sign for the receipt of a camel-hair blanket. Such blankets were outlandish material in Kamchatka, and the girl explained that she would surely have remembered such an exotic thing if she had seen it. But she had not, and so she refused to sign the paper. The school's officials read her demurral as a sign of possible insurrection. The girl was detained in a special room for days, left with nothing but sips of water and one piece of dry bread. Fortunately, in one way or another, the members of the district's school board began to hear rumors about the incident. They intervened. As the result of a thorough investigation, it turned out that the school's administration had for years hoarded supplies intended for students. A trial took place. The janitor was sentenced to several years of prison; the others went free. Yet in spite of proof of her innocence, the girl was not allowed to return to this school. At the end of the trial, her father brought her to another institution. She said that her parents never questioned her actions. Quietly she finished her classes to move on to a career as an administrator. She said that she learned corruption but not trust.

As an inevitable consequence, many Koriak women and men I knew taxed the sort of science that may have once brightened the tundra with

□ □ □

the detriment and harm of dimming generational relationships. Elders in particular argued that the sort of education their children received drives them and their children and grandchildren apart. They are caught in a vicious circle: Children speak Russian quickly; elders cannot respond. Children do not understand the language of their parents; elders cannot give advice. This is a painful situation, yet it is certainly not everywhere the case. On the one hand—in spite of the fact that Koriak language lessons were removed from regional school curricula in the 1960s (Vakhtin 1994, 19)—many young Koriak women and men had a good command of the language. They spoke the language because they had still been able to spend the summer months with their parents in encampments in the tundra. On the other hand, there is also no doubt that many Koriak children refused to learn the language of their parents and, in turn, were supported by their parents in these decisions. In the national context, the Russian language was awarded such prestige that it was clearly the language one needed to speak to get ahead. The twisted situation endures.

At the end of this section, there is no particular story to tell, no particular morality to offer. There is much pain, and there are shaky truths. There is no special sense of justice being served, no special retribution system in place. Thus far the wrongs have only been noted, by ethnographers as well as by political activists. Questions remain open.

Today there is really no way of clearly seeing how things will develop. There are hopeful attempts by indigenous peoples to take educational matters into their own hands, yet there are also indications that the situation will sharpen. When I visited Tymlat in the summer of 1994, the applications of several Koriak single mothers for their children's admission to the local boarding school were turned down by its board. These women did not know how and with what means to raise their children. They felt helpless in the face of growing unemployment and sharply decreasing financial means. These mothers themselves had been brought up in a boarding school. They knew, as one tutor meanly implied, "that we will feed and dress their children." As I mentioned before, residence used to be free, but as a result of the financial crisis in Russia Koriak parents now must pay. Yet only a few single mothers could afford to do so. Those who could not were advised to keep their children at home. But from where, these mothers asked, should they take the money to feed and dress their children? Was there no justice in the fact that they had been brought up there, turned into helpless women? The irony was, as a woman implied, that once you ask the state for help, it turns against you.

□ □ □

## Marriage

Thus far I have dealt with the realms of economics and education as important sites in the political struggle that was to transform backward-living reindeer herders into politically self-conscious subjects. Education and collectivization were important means in achieving the perceived state of equality, but other, more moral but equally demanding tasks lay ahead. Government agents took much umbrage at Koriak men's custom of marrying the widows of their (usually) older brothers, that is, the levirate. They argued that such multiple conjugal arrangements were indefensible in the eyes of the state (Gurvich and Kuzakov 1960, 84) and had to disappear.[2] But although ethnographers describe the polygamous household as the quintessential Koriak domestic unit in the northern peninsula, these unions were reserved for well-off and powerful herders. Only they could sustain and entertain more than one wife at a time.

Instead of following the monogamous logic of official explanations, I examine the significance of leviratic arrangements for the persons involved. What was the experience of women sharing a husband? What could it mean for a man to be obliged to marry his brother's wife? In answering these questions, I bring together two stories separated in time but not in theme. Both accounts bring to the fore the erotic and social complexities of the issue. Both tell a story of rivalry and love, with the predicament of jealousy as their theme. This is an important step back from the themes of monogamy and sexual propriety met in regional ethnographies.

In one version of Ememquut's marriage to three wives—Marmot-Woman, Sphagnum-Woman, and Mold-Woman—Koriaks tell a story of envy and love. In this story, Ememquut, a supernatural being and son of Raven,[3] walks through a Koriak camp when he begins to notice bright sparks springing from the earth. It is Marmot-Woman who seeks to seize his attention. She succeeds; Ememquut marries her. The following day, he meets Sphagnum-Woman and marries her as well. But wedded to two women at the same time, he arouses the envy of another supernatural being, Envious-One. Fights ensue in which Envious-One does not succeed in killing Ememquut but in sending him to the lower world.

Feeling desolate, Ememquut walks through the bleak camps of the lower world. Ememquut meets Mold-Woman. She is sullen and coarse looking; wrapped in dirty and torn rags, she is also covered with a heavy layer of mold.

□ □ □

She smells fetid and foul. But to Ememquut's surprise, the soft and tender voice in which she addresses him lets him forget her unpleasant appearance. Ememquut is glad to have found a tender and sympathetic being in the lower world. He suggests marriage. Mold-Woman agrees, and they begin living as husband and wife. Ememquut discovers soon that Mold-Woman is the daughter of Sun-Man. Sun-Man hides his daughter in the lower world and dresses her in shabby clothes so that her softness and beauty do not tempt those who live on earth.

Soon Marmot-Woman and Sphagnum-Woman reach the lower world where they meet Mold-Woman. They introduce themselves as Ememquut's wives, whereupon Mold-Woman tells them that she is also married to him. His first and second wives advise Mold-Woman not to let Ememquut know that they have arrived. He might, they explain, then leave her because she is not pleasant to look at. But Mold-Woman is not offended by such bluntness. In contrast, she is very friendly and visits them regularly, bringing food and other delicacies.

When Ememquut begins to notice the frequent absences of his wife, he decides to follow her. From afar, he sees how generously and kindly Mold-Woman treats his two other wives. He jumps out of his hiding place with such a splash that he so frightens Mold-Woman that she falls down dead. Her coating cracks, and brilliant Sun-Woman appears, lighting everybody and everything around her with her grace and charm. Ememquut keeps all three wives, but the last one is more beautiful, and the two former ones feel abandoned and rejected.

In this story, the Koriaks feature several elements that political agents found excessive and worthy of rejection. They speak of polygyny, and they comment on the dangers of multiple sex. Yet the story's overall composition, structuring, and ending do not suggest the Koriaks' own preoccupations with such concerns. This story provides a window onto their perspectives. Their own emphasis is on the painful emotions and difficult romantic situations such arrangements carry with them. They remark on the tensions and arduous negotiations between marriage partners, and they highlight feelings of jealousy and envy. From their perspective, it is not the scandal of polygyny but its complexity that defines multiple marriage arrangements. At issue for them is not the problem of propriety but of jealousy.

These stories are one arena in which the Koriaks seek to express their own concerns. Ethnographic descriptions that mention polygyny frequently

□ □ □

focus on male prerogatives. Women's concerns are not recognized because their concerns are not considered socially relevant. But what happens when cultural actors turn these stories into life? What happens when Koriak men feel enslaved by the burden of obligation and women experience jealousy and disapprobation?

When I lived at the northeastern shore, the Koriak women in Tymlat told the story of a man who had left his wife, to whom he had been married in levirate, for a second wife of his own choosing. For reasons of concealment, I changed all names; but in accordance with local practices of naming, I decided to call the protagonists here Ningvit, the husband, Sits-on-a-Stone, his first wife, and Yellow Grass, his second wife. The following story had been told to me by a woman who herself had been in love with Ningvit for a long time, when his youth was still strong and he was known as a courageous man. She repeated the story in bits and pieces, never as a whole, and always hesitant to reach its end. Others who knew or had lived with Ningvit, Sits-on-a-Stone, and Yellow Grass filled in details; in particular, young women highlighted the end. But in their telling, the people's tone was never disparaging or mean. To them, it was not an outlandish story but an example of local moral norms and standards.

The older brother of the man I call Ningvit had died, leaving a wife and six children without a father. Fulfilling his obligation as younger brother, Ningvit married his brother's wife. He took care of her and fathered her children well. But even though his new wife and foster children never complained, sometimes he seemed burdened by keeping up his obligations. Rumors had it that in the night he would turn away from Sits-on-a-Stone.

The rumor, however, was a rumor and proved not to be entirely true for he and Sits-on-a-Stone parented five children of their own. He treated all children under his care with equal attention; in the village, he was known as a loving and doting father. He showered his daughters and sons with attention, and he taught them the appropriate things. The years passed. He and his wife continued to live as herders in a camp. Their children were growing up in the boarding school, spending the summers with their parents in the tundra. When all of them reached an age where they could carry responsibility and take care of their own, Ningvit, however, left. This time, he really turned his back on Sits-on-a-Stone.

Ningvit was probably in his fifties when he married Yellow Grass. His second wife matched his age, and she had eleven children of her own. Yellow

□ □ □

Grass's husband had died several years earlier. In the village, he had been known as a difficult and gruff man. Yellow Grass was pleased, more so because her children got along well with their new father. Wishing to be close to their children, Ningvit and Yellow Grass took up their residence in a rickety apartment. Sits-on-a-Stone also now lived in the village; she was furious, badly hurt. She would pass by Ningvit's apartment, waiting at the door, asking for his compassion or issuing angry threats. But neither Ningvit nor Yellow Grass would listen, let alone allow her to enter. As neither of them responded to her requests, she threatened to break the windows with stones. And so she did.

At this point, villagers would lower their voices. They pointed to Sits-on-a-Stone's jealousy as a form of misbehavior that was difficult to excuse or justify. How could she express her rage in such a way? Why did she attack her former husband and his new wife so viciously, embarrassing herself and putting her children at unease? I was bewildered and surprised. Was there not some justice in Sits-on-a-Stone's actions? Was it not understandable that she felt pained and unwanted, indeed obsolete, because of Ningvit's actions? What could she do? But everybody to whom I expressed my own concern pointed in an unexpected direction.

Among the villagers, there was a consensus that at the time of his brother's death Ningvit had done what was expected of him. He had married Sits-on-a-Stone without demur. He had been a good and faithful husband, as well as a caring father. Then he had not had the chance to find a wife of his own choosing. Now his children were grown, leading lives of their own. He had fulfilled his obligations. Did he not have the right to pursue his own desires, his own life? Not only Sits-on-a-Stone but also he had suffered and had been hurt. Now that he had done his duty, was it not just for him to take his own wife?

The stream of events that shape Ningivit's story reminded me of the first story I featured above. Like the characters in that story, these actors were entangled in a web of jealousy. The marriage arrangement that was regarded as so repulsive by government agents and ethnographers was in life an unstable alignment of unexpected twists, one that involved obligations, responsibility, and pain.

## Spirituality

Shamanism is probably one of the most frequently described yet notorious and disreputable features of indigenous life in northern Kamchatka.[4] Descriptions

□ □ □

authored by ethnographers who traveled across the peninsula in the first decades of the twentieth century particularly reveal how travelers then gazed with greatly depreciating eyes at such heathen cults. This contempt must have seemed to them so proper and right that they considered it barely worth the effort of disguising. In their world, shamans, Koriak women and men who enjoyed particularly close connections with the supernatural world, were made out as cunning deceivers (Beretti 1929, 25), their swindling so cheap that any discerning eye would easily detect their foul play or tawdry guile. In their own witnessing of shamanic performances, observers likened what they experienced and saw to "hysterical fits . . . of wild paroxysm" (Jochelson 1908, 47), "inconceivable stupidity" (Beretti 1929, 25), or just a subtle form of animal mimicry (Jochelson 1908, 49). Here I can only speculate that the association of shamanic possession with the diseased discourses of European models of hysteria or "drunkenness" (Beretti 1929, 25) is one of the key reasons that there are so few lengthy descriptions in ethnographic texts on the region. Shamanic performances are often mentioned, yet barely described in a detailed way.[5]

In a similar way, but for different reasons, political activists and Soviet agents met the practice in question with disdain. To them, the healing performances and future-predicting skills of shamans seemed like a particularly insidious form of exploitation (Kuz'mina 1932), deemed as "counter-revolutionary activity" (Bogoras 1932, 144) that clearly belonged in the realm of "magic" (ibid., 145) or superstition. What was even worse, this illusionism and feeble wonder working posed a serious threat to "socialist buildup" (ibid., 151) by keeping its practitioners—except, of course, for the shaman herself or himself—in dire dependence and fear. Measured by the revolutionary standards of the socialist vision, shamanism was an institution of the powerful, of exploitation, sui generis. It was anathema to all enlightenment, consciousness raising, and reason–inducing goals that Soviet agents, and by extension the state, had set for themselves. Shamanism had to disappear.

Amid all this disdain that ravaged their practices and beliefs, Koriak women and men, of course, had their own views. At the northeastern shore, the meaning of the term *shamanism* was contested terrain. In particular, Koriak women and men elders took issue with the term. They told me that shamanism described a world that had arrived with the Russians (a Koriak woman elder actually said that shamanism was a Russian invention). They had their own name, *anangnapel. Anangnapel* are individuals who are able to transcend the boundaries of the body to travel to other worlds. *Anangnapel* are people

□ □ □

gifted with the ability to restore, maintain, and increase people's emotional and physical health and well-being; they work to cure ailing bodies and suffering souls and minds. The ideas of shamanism I gathered at Kamchatka's northeastern shore begin with the understanding that humans, animals, and other beings such as plants, rocks, water, and the land are intertwined in an intricate set of mutually dependent and socially enriching relationships. This understanding of the world recognizes and values the creative and productive links that connect humans and nonhumans, through practices and spiritual ideas of co-dependence, not isolation. This is not religion as a distinctive set of rituals and beliefs; it rather involves one's own basic relationships to other beings and social knowledge. Many of the Koriaks I knew identified themselves through such an understanding.

An important feature of Koriak women's and men's spiritual under-standing was the careful control of bodily boundaries through protection spells, amulets, and bodily regimes. Shamanic practices of curing and health maintenance involved many styles, from managing night-long ceremonies in which a shaman chanted and danced to the accompaniment of a drum, to the use of magic potions and spells, to killing dogs (see, in particular, Jochelson 1908) and wild animals, and to the use of divination techniques. Indeed, protecting the body from weakness and enhancing its invulnerability to sorcery are important concerns among Koriaks today. One Koriak woman elder I knew was not shy to openly display in her apartment incarnations of the spirit guardians with whom she worked in close relationship. This is a rare practice and not endorsed by many of the Koriaks I knew, who spoke of the terrible dangers associated with such methods and routines. Of equal concern is the power of animal-human body relationships.

On a fine morning in early May, the father of a female friend, Valerii, set out for a seal hunt, which had been prevented by the raging storms of the last weeks. Asking his wife Lera to neither clean the house nor wash herself or the children, he left the house to meet his fellow hunters at the beach. The hunters remained for a long time on the sea; their boats were not visible from the shore, and my friend began to worry for her father's secure return. Together we waited at the beach. The sun had already set when they arrived back onshore, safe but angry about their ardent but ultimately unsuccessful hunt. On our way back to their home, Valerii told us that they had seen many seals, but that the animals had tricked them the entire day. Relaxing lazily on massive rocks, rubbing their freckled heads with their fins, they waited until the last minute to dive into the sea; nobody could catch them. Entering the house, Valerii immediately asked Lera if she had washed herself or the children. "Of course," she replied. Did he think that she would let the children go dirty? She told us that she had even washed their hair. Valerii was incensed. Had he not told her not to clean the house?, he angrily called. "Why, for heaven's sake, could she not listen for once?" Lera seemed unimpressed. Calmly she took the two younger children and walked back into the kitchen, starting to prepare some reindeer loins. To Valerii, things seemed clear. Throughout the day, the seals had imitated his wife's activities at home. Through mimicry, they had escaped the hunters' will.

Later in the evening, I asked Lera if she had known that her behavior would interfere with the hunt's success. "Of course," was her unflinching answer, causing me to loudly wonder if she did not wish success and luck for her husband's hunt. "Of course," she confirmed again, but only to continue to say: "Today is not the only day he will go and hunt. Together with others, he will go hunting seal all summer. What shall I do with the meat? Where shall I store it? I have to take care that there will not be too much."

To understand something about the relationships between humans and animals and to travel to other worlds, however, people must make their bodies "ready" so that they can visit other places and beings. *Mukhamors,* "magic mushrooms," which have made an entrance in the previous chapter as a valuable currency in local trade, are key in achieving spiritual mastery. *Mukhamors* are a spiritual empowerment of the body; they are an important means of travel to other worlds (another is traveling through the smoke of an open fire); they motivate metaphorical travels to distant places as a way to understand complex issues and difficult situations and to get advice. They are equally important in gaining the potency an individual needs to perceive and comprehend the information, signals, and advice she or he is about to receive. In one village in which I lived, a Koriak woman elder had lost seven of her nine sons by drowning. Determined to help keep her other two sons alive, she asked *mukhamors* what to do. They told her to play the drum every evening as well as she could, while visiting other families. For what it is worth, her sons are still alive. Every evening, she continued this routine.

In much of my insight about *mukhamors,* I rely on the wisdom and expertise of one of my most prudent hosts and teachers while I lived at the northeastern shore. The woman I call here and throughout the book Grandmother is not related to me by lineage or blood. I came to call

□ □ □

FIG. 5 | Eating mukhamors (fly agaric) (photo: author 1994).

Grandmother by this name for two reasons. First, in the villages in which I lived, elders are commonly referred to by affinal kinship terms, and I was also offered participation in this custom. Second, Grandmother was the grandmother of the woman with whom I lived. Galina's mother died when she was young, and Grandmother moved from the tundra to the village to take care of her granddaughter and her two brothers. When I came to live in this household, Grandmother also offered me the recognition of near-parentage and steprelation.

Nobody in the village called Grandmother *anangnapel,* yet she was acknowledged as an authority in spiritual matters and, if less so, as a healer. Grandmother healed not by applying ointments or medication but by the force of her presence. Indeed, her powers to heal simply through her presence were so widely known that nearly every day people would drop by, spending some time sitting beside her while she continued with the activities in which she was engaged: sewing, cleaning, or keeping an eye on her grandson. When

□ □ □

FIG. 6 |
Aleksandra Chechulina
playing the drum (photo:
author 1994).

I prepared to travel into the western tundra for some months, Grandmother took no chances on my safety. Rolling small pieces of dried reindeer and fish meat, sedge grass, tobacco, and beads in stripes of shriveled newspaper, then tying the bundle with a hard knot, she instructed me to leave these parcels in regular intervals on my way. Nobody, she explained, will attack you.

In hindsight, I think, Grandmother had her own way of drawing me into her own agendas. There were several things she considered worthwhile for me to know. But ethnography, the way I knew and had learned about it, was not an important category of knowledge for her. Learning, she implied, lies in one's willingness to open oneself to new experiences in the world; learning lies in the direct practice of things, not in reading and writing about them. This was made especially clear to me one afternoon, when one of Grandmother's nieces had just returned from a long trip in the tundra, carrying with her an enormous bag filled with *mukhamors.* These were not just the mushrooms from

□ □ □

the immediate surroundings of the village. These were strong ones from the north. Grandmother insisted that I should learn firsthand about *mukhamors.* She would sit at the kitchen table and wait until I came home. She had already prepared two cups of tea, placing three mushrooms beside her cup and three beside mine. Both of us ate.

The effects of eating, or traveling with, *mukhamors* can be diverse. They make you feel warm ("They are our heating system," elders joked). Eating *mukhamors* is also helpful in the summer, when people in the tundra are busy traveling with the reindeer and rarely stay at one place for more than two or three days. "*Mukhamors* make you strong," several reindeer herders I knew explained. "You can walk and walk, and you don't have to sleep." Eating the mushrooms can involve all-night ceremonies where people chant and dance to the accompaniment of a drum. And, most important, they do not make a person feel drunk. Grandmother always laughed at and dismissed comments from both Koriak and Russian neighbors that suggested that the upshot of alcohol and mushrooms might be the same. These people obviously did not know what they were talking about. *Mukhamors* expand knowledge and put one at ease, but alcohol makes a person violent and introduces the terror of aggression and fear.

In the course of my living at the northeastern shore, I learned that eating *mukhamors* involves forms of knowledge that were not mentioned in the ethnographies I knew. Of special importance seemed how to eat them; the specific part of the *mukhamor* that is eaten generates particular effects. For example, one should never eat only one stem but always two at the same time. Also, a person needs to think carefully whether she or he really wants to eat the *mukhamor* cap. On the one hand, not eating it might cause a sensation as if a person has lost her head; on the other hand, eating it might mean that one gains an additional head and "then you can be in trouble because both heads tell you different things to do." Other things are more a matter of taste: fried, cooked, mixed with berries. Jochelson (1908, 583) described how Koriak women used to drink the urine of a person intoxicated with mushrooms. I asked Grandmother about this. She replied that she was not sure about that, but preferred her mushrooms steeped in tea.

Many Koriak elders I knew tried to pass on knowledge about *mukhamors.* Grandmother, for example, taught all her great-grandchildren how to collect and eat them. And nobody I knew thought it odd that another Koriak elder dictated a long list of different kinds of *mukhamors,* including places to collect them and how to eat them, to his grandson.

□ □ □

4 | □□□

# Distant Voices, Still Lives

Ethnographies have been created by a host of problematic influences; the political issues reflected in their modes of representations vary by areas of the world, areas of history, conflicted genres, and agendas. In most writing about the Russian North, female voices are conspicuous by their absence. In this chapter, I show that Koriak women elders have their own stories to tell. Yet their narratives are not additions to the received categories of conventional histories or ethnographies (Joan Scott 1988). Instead, they are cultural and historical articulations from the perspective of experience and distinctive knowledge. Because each woman formulated her own story, these narratives do not offer generalizing explanations. No homogenous woman's voice is found today or in the past.

Recently, life stories have become an important means in anthropological research to express and document both historical events and personal lives from the perspective of gender. This is a major step in recognizing women's own experiences of particular historical contexts and involvement and concerns in the production of history. Yet life stories pose their own problems. An ample body of works on life histories and gender, for example, tends to treat narratives and stories as openings for understanding the "real" experience of women and indigenous peoples (for example, Behar 1993). Against such a view, the historian Joan Scott (1992) issues a caution. She argues that experience is never an unproblematic given in a person's life; rather, experience is always mediated and shaped by social structures that are already in place. In this vein, the anthropologist Julie Cruikshank (1990), for example, has shown that stories are never an uncomplicated means of understanding the lives, traditions, agendas, and thoughts of their tellings. She asks us to pay attention to specific, culturally situated frameworks through and in which the stories take place. In northern Kamchatka, such frameworks involve the importance of travel and everyday practices of living; stories are interwoven with these frameworks.

The disruptive edge of the women's stories I am about to tell lies in the possibility of their breaking up the flow of homogenous representations.[1] When women first began to tell me their stories, I assumed that I could use state-endorsed authoritative versions as a foil against which to paint oral versions of history. I assumed that women's stories would complement and expand the scope of official frameworks by bringing into focus their own interpretations of history and change in the region. Much of what I was told, indeed, indexed ever more reference points by which one could look at official narratives as disfigurements of history from a vantage point of the tundra. The stories that women told me, however, involved much more than confutation and critique. In telling their stories, women were writing their own histories centered on issues of cosmology, child rearing, political involvement, gossip, and love affairs. The narratives that I feature in the following sections clash and overlap. In putting the stress on their own ambitions, affiliations, and ideas, women's narratives confront one another's stories and the story of the state.

Attention to stories demands attention to the particular circumstances of their telling. None of the Koriak women I knew took the time to specifically pass on stories, circumstances, and events that had given shape to their own understanding of human existence. They continued to tan, collect berries, or put diapers on grandchildren as they told stories about the things that were important to them. Story telling was an integral part of everyday life; everyday life was formed and not disrupted by stories. Sometimes narratives traveled back and forth, from one woman to another, as each connected and put me in touch with another. Because each woman was an accomplished traveler, each story was told to me in pieces and parts, at different places, in different circumstances, at different times. In keeping with the spirit of these travels, I present the stories as a series of fragments; each break indicating a stop. I tried to maintain the style and originality of their telling as much as possible in my arranging and editing.

Storytelling in northern Kamchatka points to certain issues. Many Koriaks I knew reported negative experiences with census takers and bureaucratic administrators. Thus, none of the stories was taped; I jotted them down after the telling, recollected from memory or scribbled notes. At times, no matter what the circumstances or the setting, each woman began the telling of her

□ □ □

story with the date of her birth. At first I thought this an awkward beginning; yet I came to realize the significance of story time stated in terms of day, month, and year. It is here, in the broader frame of European time—and surely they were talking to a European anthropologist—that one's own story begins.

## Nina Ivanovna Uvarova

Nina Ivanovna was one of the first women elders I met at the northeastern shore. She lived with two daughters and one son in a small two-room apartment in Ossora. Like many elders, she felt isolated and alone. "My grandchildren don't come to visit me," she explained. "And here I have nobody to whom I can talk." Sometimes Nina Ivanovna would telephone Grandmother, who lived in Tymlat. In their respective dialects, both women would talk for hours with each other on the phone. Nina Ivanovna said it made her feel better.

When I met her, Nina Ivanovna suffered from high blood pressure and dizzy spells. She attributed her disease to the oppressive atmosphere in the village, a life she experienced as boring and dull. In Ossora, there was never enough air to breathe, she said, and there was nothing for her to do. Throughout the year, she looked forward to the summer months. That was the time in which she left the village to move to a nearby lagoon at the sea. There she lived with one daughter in a fine, self-made hut with a wood-burning stove and enough air to breathe. Every day, she went out to collect stunted elder tree branches and driftwood that had flooded onto the shore. Every day, she went out to gather berries, find roots and herbs, and check the fishing nets. And every day, she went to see whether the hill of whose sacral powers she knew was covered with mist. A beclouded peak meant storms and rain. The longer the hilltop stayed mist free, the longer she could stay at the lagoon.

It was at the lagoon, in this place of landlocked water and berry-yielding bogs, that Nina Ivanovna told me most of her story. Frequently we sat around the rickety table in the hut when she told me about her life. She spoke in Koriak. As her daughter translated her mother's story for me, she learned about emotions and events she had not known of. And thus she had questions of her own. A dialogue between mother and daughter developed, a conversation that drew them closer, gaining its own life in the daughter's recording of her mother's story. Here is Nina Ivanovna's story.

□ □ □

**I was born on the twentieth of August 1914. I was born in the tundra close to the river Anapka. The administrators decided that this was my birthday. Koriaks did not have such dates. My father told me that I was born in the year when there was much snow.**

Under the ordering eye of the state, the calendar of chronologically referenced time was introduced.

**I am the eldest surviving daughter of my parents. My father was a reindeer herder; we had many reindeer, and we never starved. From an early age on, my father taught me how to take care of reindeer.**

Women as well as men could become knowledgeable and skilled herders.

**My mother died early. She was a very good seamstress. I am not as good as she. Good sewing means to know how to cut patterns, how to tan the furs very soft, how to stitch as small as possible. In the old days, many fairs were held. My mother sewed fur coats and other things for the fairs in the north. My father took these wares and exchanged them for pots, rifles, knives, and other things. He traded with the Russians. Americans were also there. One year, my mother sewed a long coat out of sealskins. My father traded it for two rifles and some money. Neither my mother nor I ever went with him.**

Regional fairs drew all trade into wider, extraregional relations. They were important sites of exchange—gossip, wares, and information. By creating items of value and high price, women participated, in their own way, in trade and fairs.

**My mother died early. My father married her younger sister, Anna. She gave birth to a daughter, Mariia. My mother had never shown me how to tan and sew. I was too young. Anna only taught her own daughter how to tan and sew. My mother had spent most of her time with my father tending the animals. She had spent all her time with men. She wanted to teach me how to tan and sew later. But then she died, and I had to teach myself.**

Sororate and levirate existed simultaneously. A man would marry his wife's sister, usually after his wife's death. Nina Ivanovna's father married her mother's younger sister, but she refused to take care of her sister's daughter the way she should. Competition and rivalry were often implicated in obligatory, conjugal relationships. Tanning and sewing were important skills that expressed the artistic mastery of a woman. An unskillful seamstress was rarely

□ □ □

FIG. 7 | Nina Uvarova weaving a rope (photo: author 1994).

up to the demands of important festivities and trade. Mothers and aunts would usually begin to teach these techniques to girls at an early age. Nina Ivanovna's mother was frequently absent from the tent. She had no time to teach her daughter. But Nina Ivanovna managed.

**My mother married very late. When she married, her father gave her a very big herd. When I married, my father also gave me many reindeer.**

Women had their own property. When a daughter left her parents' camp, her share of reindeer was given to her. Frequently, Koriak girls married when they were thirteen or fourteen years old. To say that Nina Ivanovna's mother married late probably meant that she was in her late teens.

**Often my father and I would go out hunting or looking after the reindeer. He took me and tied me to his back. He did this to stay**

□ □ □

**strong. In the olden days, men did this. They were strong, not weak like today. Sometimes they tied us with our faces down to the sled and pulled us when we traveled. Soon I was able to drive a reindeer sled myself, catch the reindeer with a lasso, and join in sled races. I enjoyed fast and reckless races. I liked measuring my strength with the strength of men.**

In the old days, men built up their strength by carrying or pulling heavy things. Today women elders frequently express their discontent with young men who are not up to such exercise. Women and men used different means of romantic appeal, of creating beauty and attraction. A skillful seamstress enchanted men. A man bedazzled people by his skills and strength. Yet women matched the competence and recklessness of men. Like men, they sought challenges to prove their strength.

**At the age of ten, my husband-to-be was brought into our camp. He worked three years for me before the elders allowed him to marry me.**

Frequently men had to work in their future wife's father's camp before they were allowed to marry. Women's tone and manner of expression suggest that they experienced the young man's working for the bride as a source of pride. A young man's endurance, patience, and strength were tested before he was allowed to marry his bride. Even though matches were arranged, women were usually asked whether they agreed to join their husbands in marriage. Nina Ivanovna was asked for her consent.

Some accounts (Antropova 1971; Gurvich and Kuzakov 1960) indicate that there were other, more austere ways to subject the groom to a test. In these reports, a girl was not given in marriage before the groom had put down his bride in a fight. The bride-to-be was wrapped in furs, held together by tight knots. While she was running through the camp, the groom had to catch her, unfasten the hides, and touch her genitalia. In the meantime, all the women in the camp were trying to disrupt his attempts as much as possible. Biting, kicking, and pulling—everything was allowed. If the groom did not manage to catch and touch her, the marriage was called off.

It is unclear how factual these reports were. Women elders at the northeastern shore neither confirmed nor mentioned such reports, but they spoke of other conspicuous performances. They described how young men were sometimes given a piece of meat on which the parents of the bride had urinated. "Our laws were strict," women said. If he was not able to swallow the meat, the arrangement was canceled.

□ □ □

**As the end of this time neared, my father divided the reindeer and gave me my share.**

Nina Ivanovna married when she was thirteen. Like her mother, Nina Ivanovna received her share when she left her father's camp.

**My husband and I moved westward, into the direction of Rekinniki. We found a good pasture. The reindeer were doing well when we lived in the tundra. Later, when the Soviets gave us passports, they said that my husband was two years older than me.**

Most young couples left their parents' camps to find pastures of their own.

**We had already lived together for some time before I experienced my first menstruation. I did not know what was happening. And I was afraid to die. One woman showed me how to use moss and fur like wad. Men were not allowed to see menstruation blood. We secretly washed out the fur with water. Men would not see us. But of course men knew that women menstruate.**

Nobody had told Nina Ivanovna about menstruation, but other women elders say that they told their daughters about menses. They also explain that Koriak women knew several proscriptive rules that centered on menstruation. For example, a woman was not allowed to go fishing during the period of menstruation.

**We lived for six years in the Rekinniki tundra. I did not like the dialect people spoke in Rekinniki. I grew up with the dialect in Anapka, and I could not understand what people were asking or saying. I felt alone. In Rekinniki, I saw for the first time in my life wooden houses with a roof. Frightened by the warmth of the houses, I ran out. I began to participate in reindeer sled races. In Rekinniki, I also learned how to drive a dogsled. It was hard in the beginning.**

Like every traveler, Nina Ivanovna faced new and unexpected challenges when she moved from the Anapka tundra to the Rekinniki region.

**Then we moved to the pastures closer to the villages of Anapka and Kichiga.**

This must have been in the mid-1930s.

**While we lived in Rekinniki, I gave birth to a child, a son. It did not survive the winter, but soon afterward I was pregnant again. That child also died. We decided to move back to Anapka where I knew more people. In Anapka, I gave birth to three children. None of them made it through the winter and the disease. There was a**

□ □ □

**big disease in Anapka at that time. No child survived, and many
adults died.**

There are no ethnographic records that mention an atrocious, widely
prevalent pandemic at the northeastern shore in the end of the 1930s. Koriaks
themselves refer to the spread of this contagious disease as the "big disease,"
indicating its severity and the harm it wrought.

**In 1937, my husband received a letter. We could not read. We did
not know what was written in it. He was told to travel with this letter
to Tilichiki. My husband drove all the way to Tilichiki by dogsled. I
was very nervous and afraid because my husband did not return. We
did not know where he was. He returned after two years. He had
spent two years in prison. Then he told us that they also incarcerated
women. He saw how they worked in their traditional clothes.**

In the course of Stalinist purges, Nina Ivanovna's husband was identified
as an enemy of the state. The violence of the state even pursued corruption
where it had previously seen only primitiveness and ignorance. Women were
as maligned as men.

**Then, in 1942, my son Maksim was born. He was the first of my
children who survived. I was very happy. But in 1972, he drowned.
He had three children with his first wife, Lena, and three children
with his second wife, Ekaterina. I do not see my grandchildren very
often. They do not come and visit me. It makes me sad. After
Maksim, I gave birth to a daughter, but she died. In 1948, Luisa
was born. Then I gave birth to three other children, but all of them
died. Zina was born in 1958, Ivan in 1960, Aniuta in 1963. They all
survived. Later I still had one miscarriage.**

Other women elders tell similar stories. Child mortality in northern
Kamchatka was high. Drowning has always been, and is still today, a very
common form of death. On the eastern sea, winds are unpredictable and fast.
A boat is easily overturned.

**Ivan killed his first seal when he was ten years old. We were all
very proud. In November, my husband arranged for a big *khololo*.
That is how proud he was.**

At the northeastern shore, the killing of a seal usually established a boy as
a hunter. The event was widely celebrated—for the boy and the seal.

**In Anapka, I was working in the chicken farm. At first, I was
working in the collective farm atelier, tanning furs, and then in the**

□ □ □

**chicken farm. We collected mussels and then crushed them to feed the chickens.**

In the 1950s, one of the most ambitious state programs in Kamchatka's subarctic North involved the creation of poultry and cow farms. The project did not completely fail, yet it also never succeeded. In the winter, the interiors of animal buildings were strongly heated, but electric fires burned down barns and farms several times. Some Koriak women I knew kept the chickens during the winter in their own rooms where they foraged alongside chairs, tables, and beds for crumbs of fish and potato peel from the floor.

**In the village, the relationships with the Russians were not bad, but they thought that the life in the tundra was bad for our children. They thought we fought in the tundra, and they did not understand how we could sleep on fur.**

The Koriaks' practice of sleeping on fur seemed particularly offensive to the whites. It was an often-quoted example of their never-ending backwardness in many conversations I heard. But in the tundra, furs are useful items when one is on the move. Their versatility—they can be used as blankets and mattresses and transformed into clothes—marks them as significant, indispensable items in a world of movement and flux.

**Our food was looked at as bad. Even harmful. They took our children away and locked them into the boarding schools. It was very hard. Children are very capricious and need much attention. They took them away, and we could not look after them.**

The state's style of education removes children from their parents and families. The lacuna between the generations begins.

**When we moved into the village, my husband began to drink. Not much, but still, he drank. He often asked me to drink with him, but I refused. I said: "If I drink, I will drink much and you will not find me at home. You will only find me in those families where people drink a lot." I was responsible for the children. They were small, and somebody had to take care of them.**

Many elders take the stance that their own as well as their children's problems with toxic drinking began with life in the village, not in the tundra. The temptations of liquor lure everybody, but one's own sense of responsibility and meaningful involvement with others can help in staying clear of drink.

**There was a shop in Anapka. Koriak women collected blueberries and other kinds of berries and brought them to the shop. They**

□ □ □

**paid us money, and we bought needles and thread to sew. Sometimes in winter we even bought what we had collected in the summer. The island where we collected berries in the summer was sacred, and we offered beads, needles, and beautiful dishes. Men offered ammunition and knives. During the war, a group of Russians came, and they took everything from the island away. They took everything that lay on the ground or hung on the branches of elder tree bushes. Then they went to Tymlat and exchanged it for tobacco and tea and flour. Later all of them drowned. They were punished. Our gifts were offerings to thank the animals and the land. No one can take them away.**

The principle of reciprocity binds humans not only to animals but also to the land. From the perspective of these Russian travelers, Koriak offerings of sacrifices and gifts are signs of backwardness and primitive religion. These practices support the notion that the tundra is an ahistorical, undifferentiated space, offering no historical points of orientation. But Koriaks speak of their lands as imbued with a history of spiritual events and human use. Beings benevolent and evil inhabit rocks, rivers, and bays; sacrifices and continuous use create attachments to places. For example, in the summer, fishing places are not arbitrarily chosen; each family travels to certain places on the river or bays and thereby invokes a long genealogy of use by passed-away kin. Personal identities are expressed and affirmed in relation to the history of such places. A tragedy of resettlement is the premise is that people live in neutral places. But in the tundra, no place is like another.

Settlements are places of absurdity and puzzling twists. For example, foods are collected and sold; strangely, they then need to be bought again. This is the irony of settlement economy. The government can offer only what it has extracted before. Exchange is part reality and part illusion; exchange means movement and stasis at the same time.

**When they told us that they would close the village, we did not believe them. We told them that we would not go, but they did not care and just took us. They just came and ordered us. They said: "Go and pack everything up. From now on you will live in Tymlat." Two days later, they came again and said: "Go and pack everything up. From now on you will live in Ossora." They just took the clothes of people who did not want to go and threw them into the helicopter. I still remember the brother of Ivan. They took his baggage and brought it to the helicopter, and he took it and carried**

□ □ □

**it back. They took it again and he carried it back. This went on for a while, but eventually he had to give up.**

In the face of senseless destruction, even the most obdurate faltered.

**Today it makes me sad that I cannot talk with some of my children and grandchildren. They don't understand our language anymore, and they tell me things I don't understand. They never ask me anything. They don't listen to what I have to say. Today people say it is the government's fault, but I am not sure. I believe it is up to the parents, my daughters, to tell their children about our way of life.**

Initially I saw Nina Ivanovna's statement as one of resignation; it reminded me of other arguments I heard in the northern tundra. The state took everything away without adding anything meaningful. I have also invoked this argument from time to time. But Nina Ivanovna refused to put the blame on governments and administrative notions of progress and order. Culture, she said, is to take responsibility for one's own existence and actions.

This was the way in which our conversations usually broke off. Nina Ivanovna had lived her own life as one of many responsibilities. Now it was up to her children and younger neighbors to continue the Koriaks' way of life, albeit in different and renewed ways.

## Ekaterina Ivanovna Chechulina

Ekaterina Ivanovna was a neighbor of Nina Uvarova. Like the latter, she had been resettled from Anapka to Ossora, where she lived in one of two decrepit houses at the fringes of the village, named *Anapkanskie doma*. In the 1970s, these homes were specially built for resettled Koriaks from the village of Anapka and had been called after them ever since. None of these houses offered running water, washing facilities, or insulation against the winter's biting cold. The two-room apartments were small; usually more than four or five individuals lived in the narrow space. Tensions were high.

In 1994, Ekaterina Ivanovna lived with a daughter, a son, and two granddaughters, eight months and two years old, in one flat. In spite of its confinement and limited household facilities, she used one of the two rooms as her atelier for tanning, stitching, mending, and sewing. Ekaterina Ivanovna spent most of her time here. In this room, she kept reindeer, seal, and dog furs, needles, beads, and the long, wooden boards used for tanning. Both rooms

□ □ □

were imbued with the pungent smell of hair, fell, and dung. The apartment offered no other place to stow such things away. In the region, Ekaterina was known as a skilled and excellent seamstress. Sporadically she was able to enhance the sparse government pension she received by working on stitchery requested by Russian townspeople.

Her fame as a beautiful seamstress, as well as a skilled singer and orator, had even traveled outside the region. Musicians had come to visit her and produced tape recordings of her voice. One ethnographer recorded a whole list of riddles and moral tales; to another anthropologist, she dictated in three days of hard work the complete catalogue of remedial plants in the tundra. Ekaterina Ivanovna explained that this was part of the knowledge she knew best, yet she was also familiar with the demands of a more rational, European-influenced form of ethnography and science. She was at a crossroad of knowledge.

The stories that Ekaterina told me were stories told while we were out collecting berries or roots or in her sewing atelier. A sense of greatness and importance characterized her telling and her stories. She mixed events, spiritual knowledge, personal insights, and warnings together as she formulated the true story of her life. Local wisdom to her was not a matter of fact and realistic vision; local wisdom involved the courage to live one's own life as a form of power. Only a person bold enough to dare will experience and grow. When all is said and done, Ekaterina agreed with Nina Ivanovna that stories and life are matters of one's own responsibility.

Like many elders, Ekaterina liked to leave the village in the summer. Unlike Nina Ivanovna, she stayed not for long weeks alone in the tundra but took day-trips with her granddaughters: collecting berries, catching fish, and having fun. Together with Nina Ivanovna, Ekaterina had a bleak view of Koriak life in the village. She too complained about dizzy spells and the fact that there was never enough air to breathe. Yet in pointing to elders' weariness and feelings of fatigue, Ekaterina was not satisfied with mere indications; she issued a serious charge. The air that crept and stayed in the village was fetid, she said; it reeked. To live in a village meant to invite death; or worse, life in the village was death. It is to this question of death that Ekaterina speaks in the end.

**I was born in the year 1938. I grew up in the tundra with my grandmother, my father, and five sisters. I had only sisters. No brothers. My mother died when I was very young. We were a big**

□ □ □

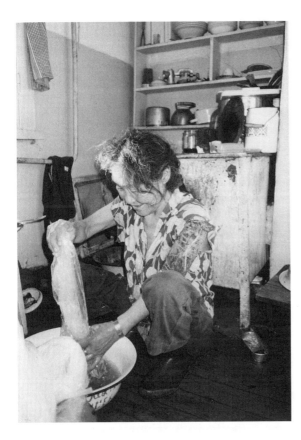

FIG. 8 |
Ekaterina Chechulina
washing bags to put to
further use (photo:
author 1994).

family. Our grandmother taught us how to tan and sew when we
were very young. That is why I know so much about it.

Long experience helped her to achieve artistic mastery.

When I grew up in the tundra, we held many celebrations. Our
celebrations were for the reindeer. One of them was in December.
We called it *mengirnang*. People who lived in other camps came
to visit. Many people came. They drove reindeer sleds, and we
celebrated together. We played the drum, we played games, and
people raced to show off the strength of their reindeer. My mother
and the other women made *asaetirking*. You remember? You have
eaten it yourself when you were in the tundra. It is this blend of
reindeer fat and seal fat. We mixed it so long until the fat became soft
and very white. The reindeer began to speak with one another. They

□ □ □

said: "This family holds a celebration for us. The next year we will grow and stay well." Celebrating the reindeer helps them to grow, to stay healthy, and to be fertile. At the end of May, we celebrated the birth of reindeer calves. My mother made *asaertirking* again. We played the drum and danced. We asked the calves to become strong animals and to be fertile.

A sense of reciprocity is endorsed in festivities and through entertainment. Animals recognize and appreciate human endeavors.

Today the biggest celebration is *khololo*. But *khololo* is a feast for the animals of the sea. When I was little, I did not know what *khololo* was.

In the context of changing forms of living, the meaning and significance of rituals also change. Ekaterina Ivanovna grew up in the tundra, not at the shore. But today, as a consequence of settlement policy, nearly everybody lives at the shore.

When I was small, we migrated with the herds to the coast to exchange meat and fur. I ate mussels and crab. I smelled the ocean. I felt dizzy. I did not like the smell. I felt sick, and I was afraid of the crabs. I thought, what kind of strange animal is this? I did not know. All I knew was reindeer.

Every journey brings new changes. Every journey expands knowledge.

Then they said I had to attend school. I went for five years to school, but I still don't know how to read and write well. In the spring, my father came and took me back with him to the tundra. He had to leave the herd in the care of others.

Schooling stood in the way of learning truly important things. It was also ineffective.

Then we had to live in the village. We lived constantly at the shore. We had boots made out of sealskin. But in the 1950s, they did not know such things anymore. Everything disappeared. I still have beads from the time when the Americans were here. We traded with the Americans. Then a new life started. Today none of this exists any more.

Trade was a source of knowledge and pride. It enriched by forging local to extralocal connections. The termination of such relationships brings tedium and staleness. This is the first time that Ekaterina speaks about social death.

When I lived in the tundra, everybody prayed. At sunrise, we started working. We knelt in the tundra and bowed our heads to the

□ □ □

earth. We crossed ourselves. After we finished our prayers, we kissed the earth. The earth cares for us. The earth gives health. We prayed every day. Today things are different. Today Koriaks have lost their faith. Our children don't believe in God anymore. But belief and faith are important.

Even after the mission left, Christian elements continued to thrive in the tundra, albeit in more syncretistic, culturally hybrid forms. As Koriaks put their own spin on missionary teachings, both the earth and God became important, mutually overlapping spiritual principles.

I know my protector, The Bear. I received my protector from my mother. She received it from her mother. The Bear is always with me. When I eat, so does The Bear. You cannot see him, but he is there. I feed him and talk to him.

The kinship between humans and animals, humans and their animal-spirit protectors, expresses itself in mimesis—in the simultaneity and imitation of signs, presence, and gestures.

When I was still small, I had a dream. A Human came and asked me if I wanted to see the Other World. I agreed, and the Human showed me a tiny hole. I looked through it and saw the Other World. It was very beautiful. Everything grew. I wanted to live there. Then the Human said: "Later you can go there. For now you still have to live here. At first, you have to live your life here and then there."

The Koriak cosmos was populated by a congeries of beings, each of whom interacted with living persons. The universe was porous yet of vital force. Superhuman beings keep vigil over its borders.

Young people today have forgotten how to listen to their dreams. My eldest son who lives at the end of the village had been drinking heavily. I was very worried. In a dream, I saw how two men attempted to tear down my house. The roof was already gone. The two men in my dream were Russians, and they told me not to worry. They said that everything would be good. One man was black and kindled a fire. I felt more at ease because fire means life. Two days later, my son came to me and told me he would go into the hospital. He wanted to stop drinking. You see the dreams show you everything. You need to learn and see.

For many Koriaks I knew, dreams were not a reflection of the past. Dreams did not belong to the realm of the ethereal and vague. Instead they showed the concreteness of the future.

□ □ □

**My mother died, and now she lives in the Other World. Anang also lives there. This god is the god for the entire world. There is no other god. At night, god comes down to the earth and walks from apartment to apartment. He sees every person, and he looks into every apartment. He sees when something is messy, and you will suffer for this in the Other World. If your apartment is neat and tidy, you will have a good life in the Other World. I know this because my grandmother and my father told me.**

This is not a naive statement, echoing churlish ideas. The meaning of this statement is unintelligible from a perspective outside the tundra. When Koriak herders broke camp to move on to another location, they took much care to burn human traces and remains. Food remains, any equipment, for example, indicated the presence of people and a used site. Dangerous animals, such as bears, could then easily trace whole camps. Meticulousness and certain rules of discipline did not mean arguing over the rules of propriety but involved issues of morality and identity making. Keeping a camp ordered and neat was a communal act. Everybody benefited from this order; everybody had to participate.

In northern Kamchatka villages, untidiness is a sign of modern life. As people began to dump garbage in the proximity of the villages, bears began to forage in the neighborhood of people.

**My father and grandmother's faith was strong, but they never talked much with others about it. Humans are the children of god. God sends spirits to protect the people. The spirits are strong and good; they live with us. God created animals and plants. But not clothes—clothes are already thought of and made by humans. God himself dresses simply. He wears fur and fabrics just like us. He lives in the sky and sees everything. There is still somebody else who lives where god is. The Other is dressed in gold. He wears golden necklaces, and golden bracelets hang around his arms. His breast is golden. God and the Other sit there and play cards all the time. When god loses, nothing grows: There won't be any berries in summer, and the reindeer are ill. When god wins, everything grows: the fish, berries, and reindeer.**

This is theology. This is insight in religious creed. The Supreme God is powerful but not almighty. In continual play, a diabolic other challenges god's divine and creative powers. In this image, the Other and god are the world's most potent yet also most unbalanced couple. The cosmos is shaped by the

□ □ □

unpredictability of card playing. There is no teleology, no purpose, only the capriciousness of power games.

In her theology, Ekaterina calls attention to the unpredictability and frailty of nothing less than life itself. The world is an erratic place to be; histories emerge through continual processes of their own unpredictable displacement.

**I was already twenty years old when I married. That was very late. I was not at ease with my first husband. Maksim was my second husband. He and I had known each other for a long time. But then he went away to fight in the war. So I married my first husband.**

As in other places, in northern Kamchatka first loves were thwarted by the onset of World War II.

**I left my first husband a year later. He drank very much. He started to drink and beat me. I threw him out because he slapped me in the face. Nobody should do such things. Koriak men never beat their wives except when they are drunk. They might even kill them, like last year when . . . stabbed his wife.**

The violence of drinking devastates marital relations. Its ultimate terror is death.

**I went to Ossora to attend the regional party's plenary sessions. Until 1959, I traveled very much. Koriak women and men from Anapka traveled to Ossora to a plenary session with the Communist Party for three days. We discussed all the problems in the Karaginskii district. We had to build houses because more and more Koriaks came to live in the village. Our houses were not solid. They brought prefabricated buildings from the area of Vladivostok. Many of the houses collapsed, and we started to build other ones.**

**At that time, the roofs in Ossora were still thatched. Then, in 1959 or 1960, I stopped traveling.**

In the context of Soviet community buildup, women could also be leaders.

**My husband beat me because I traveled to Ossora. He did not like my traveling. Oi, I never wanted to marry. I did not like men. My father wanted me to marry very early, but I rejected all men. I am not a flower you can give as a gift to somebody else. I loved to travel in the tundra and to other places. I liked other people. They were interesting. When a ship came to Anapka, I watched everybody who left. When I married, I was like a dog on a leash. They did not allow me to travel, and I had to stay at home.**

□ □ □

But male preeminence made political engagement hard for women. Ambitions are thwarted.

**In Anapka, I worked as a teacher in the kindergarten. Later I worked in the boarding school. Maksim came and took me with him into the tundra. We lived there for several years. They asked me to keep working in the boarding school, but I said: "Why should I stay here? I need the tundra. Here in the village, the air is bad. Sometimes I cannot breathe. Why should I stay in the village?"**

**In the villages our lives became sad; now many Koriak women and men are timid and afraid. But the village life in Anapka was still better than in Ossora. Here in Ossora, everything is bad. This village stinks. Do you smell the radiators? My head hurts all the time. The air in the tundra is good. I did not know dizziness when I lived there. Living in a tent makes me feel healthy. But since I lived in Ossora, I have felt sick.**

The village is a place of illness and dis–ease. Ironically, life-improving technology that exists to guarantee health aggravates the situation.

**From 1958 onward, I worked for five years in the kindergarten and boarding school; then I went with my husband into the tundra. I worked in the fourteenth brigade; we were close to Palana. It was very different there. Too many hills and mountains. The tundra in Anapka was plain and open. We could drive everywhere by reindeer sled, but where we lived with the herd we could not drive; we had to go by foot. When we were in a valley, we had to climb up immediately.**

In contrast to the popular imagination in which the tundra is an undifferentiated landscape, offering no special place of orientation, from a Koriak vantage point no place is ever the same. Spatial attachments are forged in relation to the country's physical features and the activities they demand.

**When I was seven months pregnant with Olga, I had gone ice fishing and fell on the ice. My arm was broken. I lay there all night long. I could not move. The sun was already rising, and they still had not found me. Somehow I managed to get up and crawl to the compound. Maksim saw me and brought me to the village.**

**When they found out in the village that I was pregnant, they forced me to give birth there. The doctors did not believe that we should give birth to children in the tundra. They didn't know anything. They said that mothers and babies could catch a cold. Nonsense! We never had a cold.**

□ □ □

The doctors' argument illustrates the inescapable dilemma in which the Koriaks were caught. For her endurance and strength in the tundra, Ekaterina was called brave, but in the village they spoke of her carelessness and ignorance. The virus carrier for the common cold is the cow; Koriaks were unfamiliar with such animals before. The logic of science dislodges its own authority; it is an alien in the tundra.

**They brought me into the hospital of Anapka. They put me on a chair, and my legs were up in the air. It was terrible. Koriak women did not give birth like that. We knelt down and rested our elbows on a heap of fur. Other women helped with the birth. Only women helped. No man was present or saw it. But in Anapka, the doctor was a man, and he assisted while I gave birth. I was so embarrassed.**

The gaze of science is professional but not gender neutral. In the light of obstetric techniques and means, it provokes embarrassment and shame, posing its own culture as the center.

**Slowly we have become like white people. In former times, we showed respect to other people. Nobody was a thief. Since we have lived in the village, many of us have started to steal and drink. We have become like the Russians. Never show anything to a Russian. They destroy it immediately. My grandmother said we have to obey and be friendly to them; otherwise they will beat us to death. I am not sure.**

Ethnographic descriptions highlight progress and improvement. Many Koriaks tell stories of destruction and fear. Yet Ekaterina Ivanovna's argument suggests that submissiveness is not the appropriate means to deal with the effects of change. One's own dignity will falter in vulgar imitation of the master. The result is a void of respect.

**In 1974, our village was closed, and many of us were relocated to Ossora. Others had to move to Tymlat or to Il'pyr. My great-grandmother knew how to talk to spirits. She sang night and day. At night, I often lie awake and sing. Just like my great-grandmother. In Anapka, I even sang more because I still had the drum. But when we moved from Anapka to Ossora, the elders told me to leave my drum. They said that there are too many Russians in Ossora and that they do not like singing. They said they would sue me at the court. Our singing disturbed the Russians. They were angry. I left the drum in Anapka. There is a sacred place, not far from the old village, and that's where I laid my drum. I never threw things away.**

□ □ □

This is also fear, but here fear leads to circumspection and self-respect. Elders are careful not to expose themselves to vandalism at the hand of the state. If they lost the power to take care of ritual objects, then they return them to the place they belong.

**I still pray in the morning. When we came to Ossora, I used to do that outside, but the Russians started laughing. So now I go inside. I make a fire in the stove. The elders said that every apartment should have a stove and not hot plates. You can't make a real good fire when all you have is a cooking plate.**

In traveling through the villages and encampments at the northeastern shore, I was constantly reminded of the extraordinary power of fire. A fire's glow and strength of flames told a person much about her life. "The way you kindle and keep a fire burning shows you how you live your life," Koriak women and men said. They fed the fire by tossing pieces of seal fat and dried meat, tea leaves, and small-sized beads into the flames; they spoke stories into the flames; and they never damped the embers. A person's fire—and thus her life—was a matter of her own care and responsibility.

Fire, then, also guards a person's life. I clearly remember Grandmother's efforts to light a fire outside the apartment's door when I visited Tymlat a second time. She would not let me pass into the house before I had walked three times around the fire, following a path that began in the east and proceeded toward the west. The flames bring cleanness to a person's arrival and greet her with the warmth of hospitality; they offer good fortune, health, and care. Yet the flames of Grandmother's fire refused to grow strong. They were meager and small. Relatives, neighbors, and I watched as Grandmother moved the fire from the house farther into the tundra. This was not thwarted expectation. This was insistence on life.

A good fire can surely burn in a stove; but a cooking plate creates only heat, a meek allusion to the power of fire. Cooking plates are an insufficient means of creating a life. In their own way, they symbolize a form of social death.

## Ekulina Ivanovna Chechulina

Ekulina Ivanovna and I spent only one afternoon with each other in the summer of 1992 in her small cabin in the village of Karaga. One of the women I knew in Ossora mentioned that Ekulina Ivanovna Chechulina was

□ □ □

interested in speaking with me. She recommended that I go talk to her for Ekulina Ivanovna had an unusual story to tell. At first, I hesitated to visit her. I had never met her and did not feel comfortable intruding on her. Yet she insisted on my presence. And thus, one summer day, I hiked down the long, dusty road that connects Ossora with Karaga. As I entered her home and introduced myself, Ekulina Chechulina—without much ado—sat me down at the table, asking if had a paper and a pen. I was surprised at her brisk manner, even more so at her assertiveness. This is the story she told:

**I was born the twenty-third of May 1915, in the village of Voiampolka at the western coast of the peninsula, in the gubernatorial district of Tigil'. My father lived in the tundra, but I went to attend the school in the city [Petropavlovsk-Kamchatskii]. Then I traveled on the steamer "Lenin" from the city to Karaga. They sent me to the Karaginskii Island to work in the school and teach them.**

Ekulina Ivanovna was the only person I met at the northeastern shore who had spent time on the island. When I visited the region, the island was a restricted military zone. No villager was allowed to enter the three-kilometer restricted zone. Only state-employed hunters, administrators, and police personnel were allowed there.

In the mid-1920s, the district of Tigil' played a formative role in the creation of regional differentiations and administrations (Antropova 1971, 115). It accommodated important government and administrative institutions; a state-endorsed educational and transport infrastructure was in place there.

**Many kulaks lived at the western shore of Kamchatka where I was born. They had shops and exploited other people. Life was bad then. People were poorly dressed, and nobody could read and write. Japanese fishermen lived in Voiampolka. They fished and lived with us. Some of them were like pirates. They were rich. We lived poorly. There was never enough bread, our clothes were dirty, and there were no rubber boots. We lived badly.**

Ekulina Chechulina's views reflected the ideas of state-endorsed propaganda most closely. She was the only person I knew who deployed the rhetoric of stark economic contrasts, of oppression and exploitation, in an undiscriminating way. The self-assurance of her tone brought the Bolshevik universe of binary distinctions into local relationships.

**There was one Russian kulak in Voaimpolka: Fedorov. Sometimes he came to our tent, and we gave him fish. He left the village and drove away. Then the collective farms were founded. Koriaks**

□ □ □

**started to live a better life. Fedorov did pay us little for our services.
He kept us in poverty.**

As long as social conditions do not change, the rhetoric of the state
remains the same.

**Then I came to the Karaginskii district. I began to work as
a teacher on the Karaginskii Island. Aleksei Kolegov watched the
weather carefully before he sent us over. He died a long time ago.
We drove with long wooden boats from Karaga to the island.**

Weather conditions at the northeastern coast are erratic and rough. In this
windswept piece of land, surrounded by treeless mountains, the directional
change of wind can take on formidable complications. During fierce winds,
few villagers would risk boat trips to travel or hunt. Death by drowning is
frequent. Elders say that the ocean takes drowning individuals as a gift; in
return for the richness, the fish, and the sea, the ocean yields itself.

**At first I did not want to go to the Karaginskii Island, but they
needed teachers. The Koriaks who lived on the Karaginskii Island
were reindeer herders and caught fish and seal. They were poor. They
were badly dressed. All they wore was fur. In the summer months
when it was warm, they scraped the hair off the skin to dress in
lighter fur clothes. I married my first husband on the island. He was
a Koriak teacher, just like me. We worked at the same school. People
were dressed very poorly, and we both tried to change that.**

Ekulina Chechulina turned the ambitions of the state into her own. The
state gave her influence and power in return.

**In 1934, they opened the school on the island, and in 1935 they
opened a boarding school.**

The fight against backwardness and for state primacy moved fast.

**Only a few people lived on the island. A man, his name was
Egor, lived on the island. He had two wives: Maia, she was already
very old, and a young one, Eviki. Egor was the eldest; he had all the
authority. He also had many reindeer, but Ekaterina Lazareva had
more reindeer than anybody else; she kept seventy animals. Tiazhelo
and Innokenti also lived on the island. All the reindeer there were
private; there was no collective farm on the island. When I came to
the island, all of them earned only a little.**

Koriak structures of authority are tied to age, not wealth. Yet a well-kept
herd makes a strong impression. Women can challenge men in accumulating
wealth of their own.

□ □ □

**Americans had been on the island. And Cossacks. When the war was over, the Japanese came to us. The Koriaks wanted to prevent the Japanese from landing on the island. But the Japanese leapt out of their boats into the water to hide behind them. They managed to enter the island.**

The island was a crossroad of different cultural influences and ways of life. Instead of being a place of backward and stagnant culture, it was a much-contested place.

**A church stood on the island, but later, in 1935, the church was transformed into a public bathhouse. The Soviet power did that. The church had been built before the Revolution. Everybody who lived on the island was baptized. We had a big kettle with water, and the entire body was dipped into the water. Then, after the Revolution, they [Soviet soldiery] shot at the icons in the church with bows and guns. They laughed.**

In Ekulina Ivanovna's story, this segment introduces a different tone and change in perspective. Now the representatives of the state are no longer humanistic and enlightened but vicious and without respect. It is one matter to work against illiteracy and for progress. That is Ekulina Ivanovna's job. Yet it is another matter to willfully deconsecrate sacred objects. That is violence and blasphemy.

**There are stones that live. They talk, and they give birth. On the island lived one stone: *Kigniceng*. This stone is like a god. The brother of my husband wanted to be strong. Every day he pulled stones. But he never touched that rock. Even though the stone was very heavy.**

In the Koriaks' universe, everything is imbued with life, even rocks. I heard about several rocks at the northeastern shore that were sensate and would talk. They also changed their locations, moving from place to place.

**In 1959, I came to Karaga. In 1960, everybody had to leave. Here in Karaga lived a shaman: Nikifor Nikiforov. They called him Lauku. He healed people. In the 1960s, he died. He could tell fortunes and heal people. He always carried a piece of white hare fur with him.**

Rituals and shamanic curings continued despite government bans. White hare fur plays a pivotal role in healing rituals and in local magic. Like Lauku, many Koriak women and men I knew carried white hare fur with them or they kept some of it for special occasions in their houses, in bags and chests.

A woman lived in Karaga: Fenia Iadonovna. She was in pain. Many eczemae covered her breasts. She was crying often. We did not know how to help her. A group of medical doctors came to Karaga. They went to see her. Lauku was with her at that time. He hid under the bed when the three doctors entered the room. The children had warned him they were coming. It was forbidden to be a shaman, and the government would have killed or imprisoned him. Fenia wore a long fur dress. The doctors told her to undress. She was very embarrassed. They gave her a bottle with medicine. The eczemae disappeared, and she became healthy again. The doctors had given her the medicine, but Lauku had helped her. He helped many people; he danced and played the drum.

Shamanic curing is more powerful than the medicine of the state. Physicians provide medicine and other remedial means, but it is the shaman who knows how to put their powers to work.

One day I went to see my neighbor, Ivan, who was Chinese. He looked sad. He sat on a chair, holding his head between his hands. He said: "I feel bad. I feel sick." You must know, his wife Mariia was friendly with another man. I said: "Why don't you go to Lauku?" Then he went. Lauku came to his house and wrapped white hare fur into a bundle of *lauteng.*

Besides white hare fur, *lauteng,* reed grass, is one of the spiritually most powerful elements for shamanic performances and rituals.

He stroked Ivan's head and his arms with this bundle, and he said something I did not understand. The next day, Ivan began to laugh again. Mariia returned to him, and they lived together until he died.

Shamans are people with ferocious power. They are able to cure the sick. They are also capable of healing human relationships.

I knew Lauku well. He could become very angry. One day, he sailed in a small boat on the river with his wife. She held a small child in her arms, and that is why she could not hold the paddle. The boat began to float backward. He was very angry. He screamed at her and pulled her hair. She should take the paddle, he said. She should help him. She had to put the child on the wet floor. He was very strict, but he also healed very many people. Like everybody else, he worked in the collective farm.

But then, shamans are ordinary people, just like everybody else.

□ □ □

Of all narratives featured here, Ekulina Chechulina's story most adamantly confirms government authority and the vision of the state. Yet it also offers much insight into local knowledge and tradition. When she told her story, she offered two bounded blocks of histories and themes. In the first part, she appears as the unquestioning, obedient follower of the state. In the second part, she casts herself as an unswerving traditionalist with strong spiritual beliefs. These two aspects of her narrative build a seeming contradiction. One contradicts the other as her story moves along.

In the beginning, I was irritated by her antithetic presentation. The narratives she offered, I thought, were irreconcilable in both attitude and theme. Yet as I contemplated their apparent opposition, I began to see unexpected connections. I did not know Ekulina Chechulina very well, yet I think that she must have been both a traditional and an ambitious woman. She used the power offered to her by the state to gain preeminence and influence. That is why she became a teacher. And she continued her belief in and practice of traditions and cultural styles that were useful and meaningful to her.

5 | □ □ □

# Research Connections

Much of the literature on the political culture of the Russian North stresses the way Soviet and Russian state policies mandated government rule and national standards for identity. This focus has made it possible to think about how the state has argued for its necessity in indigenous communities in the Russian Far East on the grounds of socialist temporal notions of progress and development. In many of these admittedly rich works, however, intersections of gender and political development are peripheral to understanding the relevance of regional hierarchies and identities.[1] Such a focus forces attention on the gendered negotiations of inequality and power, illuminating and challenging the unifying features of gender and ethnic homogeneity.

In contrast, a central concern in recent post-Soviet research on gender is the issue of gender inequality and hierarchy.[2] Scholars describe how in the recent Russian context of great economic and social distress women are far more disadvantaged than men. They are harder hit by poverty, suffer from the sexualization of hiring practices, and undergo violence from men. There has even been a tendency to see women as the true victims in the current transition, given the increase in sexual violence, the unequal burden of child care, and the heightened emphasis on domestic work (Koval 1995; Pilkington 1996; Roudakova and Ballard-Reisch 1999). In the current reconstruction of Russia, the immediate effects of change are certainly experienced differently by women and men, and women may have to struggle harder to assert themselves. Yet the perspective of women as victims overlooks the ways in which women actively respond to and struggle with their situation.

The following chapters pose challenges that criticize both sides of the intellectual tension I have described. They bring the issue of gender power and differentiation into research on contemporary northern Russia while opening up the orientation of recent post-Soviet gender studies to an engaged notion of agency.[3] At the same time, they depart from both northern Russia-focused anthropology and post-Soviet gender research as they call into question the dichotomy of oppression and victimization. I argue for more nuanced and contradictory specifications. An important insight for this project of specification was the recognition that women (as well as women and men) were rarely in full agreement with one another but struggled with the conditions of economic dependence and limited social possibility in fundamentally different ways. In this context of community differentiation, the challenge is to construct accounts of people's responses to, and struggles with, change without trying to erase the differences among them. While bearing the contrasts among women and between women and men in mind, I do not examine questions of gender and agency from the perspective of community-oriented analysis but use stories to ask how individual Koriak women experience and live out the historic changes that ravage Russia today.

## Conditions of Telling

Attention to individuals' stories requires attention to the ways in which the stories were "gathered" and the ways in which they were told. If the links between the specific formation of stories and the circumstances of their telling are to be appreciated, I must provide some background into the conditions of their accumulation. First, I return to the issue of my own research; then I attend to ethical problems about the telling of individuals' stories.

I have already mentioned that in the process of my research my uneasy relation to "foreign-ness" surfaced in different ways. Because I was a foreigner and a single woman traveler in the region, Koriak women and men were at first shy about talking to me. During this time, when I felt distraught and confused, an unexpected event helped turn around the issue of shyness.

*During much of the time I spent in Tymlat, I lived in Galina's household and shared the two rooms with her, Grandmother, and Galina's three children. After I had lived in Galina's household for several weeks, her youngest son became seriously ill. Galina was forced to travel with him to the hospital in Petropavlovsk, a two-hour flight away. When she asked me to take care of Grandmother and her six-year-old son Valerii and her three-year old daughter Nina, I must admit that I agreed only hesitantly. I would*

□ □ □

*not know how to take care of the children and Grandmother (who was half-blind), I said. I was to run the household, Galina said. Truly I was a young woman, and healthy, she replied. Certainly I could take care of them all. There was nothing to it—she did it all the time. All I had to do, she said, was to cook and make sure that the children were washed and wore clean clothes to kindergarten or school and that Grandmother always had tea.*

*Galina and her son left for Petropavlovsk in mid-February, when it was cold. I tried as best I could to keep things afloat. I cannot say that there were no problems or that things always worked out for the best. Yet somehow we managed. In this situation, Valerii became one of my most valuable teachers. He knew exactly how Nina should be dressed, how much she should eat, when she should be in bed; he told me how Grandmother liked her tea and what she asked for or said when she spoke to me in the Anapka dialect. Together we went ice fishing, with me holding the drill (to drill holes in the thick layer of ice) and the rod, while he explained to me how to use them. One of Galina's uncles dropped by from time to time to check that "everything was all right" and then left. Female neighbors visited to see if things went well. In this context of my own insecurities and not-knowing, Misha's help made my help possible.*

This time at the beginning of my research has various meanings for me. The one I emphasize here is that with Valerii's help my own involvement opened a passage into discussions and relationships with Koriak women and men at the northeastern shore. Women especially gave much of their time and offered support; they created an environment in which I could feel welcome and safe. Our discussions called my attention to the daily struggles these women faced and how they fought for social possibility amid conditions of violence and penury. Through these friendships, I learned something about the problems women experience in bringing up children, about their choices in sharing romantic relationships with men and creating lives of their own. They also taught me about the (im)possibility of ethnographic detachment and writing.

*At the beginning of my research, I decided to learn the techniques of tanning and sewing reindeer skin. A friend took me to the* masterskaia, *the workroom where Koriak women labor to transform untanned reindeer hides into supple skin. As I began to learn, women first assigned easy tasks to me: I was given four pieces of reindeer lower legs, and Mariia showed me how to move the long wooden bar with an inserted round stone along the skin. As I tried hard to move the bar in a smooth way to avoid digging holes into the skin, the children of some of the women who worked in the* masterskaia *were playing*

□ □ □

FIG. 9 | Valerii (photo: author 1992).

*with some fur segments. In the course of their play, some pieces vanished; so too one piece I had been given by a friend.*

*In the following days, I began to ask whether one of the women I knew could save a small piece of her material. I knew that this would be difficult; I also knew that in the village pieces of fur were hard to obtain and thus particularly esteemed. When I inquired among the women who worked in the* masterskaia, *Lidiia, the brigade leader at that time, looked at me in disdain. With a bare shake of her head, she rejected my request. From the beginning of my arrival in Tymlat, she had been very antagonistic and cool; not knowing what was going on, I had no explanation for her behavior. Fortunately I heard Mariia's voice coming from the dark corner of her place in the workshop. She told me that she could give me the missing piece. She also told me to come and visit her in the evening: There we could drink tea, and she would show me how to better my technique. This offer marked the beginning of a friendship that persists until today. As Mariia began to introduce me to the artistic finesse of working with fur, our friendship grew. Other women in the* masterskaia *began to taunt me with ease, yet my relationship with*

□ □ □

*Lidiia became very aggravated. Sometimes she was flaming with scorn, not knowing whether to ignore me or pour sarcasm on me. According to my first impression, Mariia and Lidiia did not get along well. Mariia frequently ignored Lidiia's orders as a brigade leader, and in return Lidiia raged against her with anger. The working situation in the* masterskaia *grew quite unbearable: Several women began to stay away, and sometimes only Lidiia was left, along with her supporters. Around that time, however, I was poised to leave for the tundra, and I gladly escaped the tense situation.*

*After two months, when I returned from the tundra, I went to see Mariia. I was surprised to find Lidiia at her house. When I greeted her, she replied with a short nod of her head. Pondering her hauteur and contempt, I began to ask others for explanations. Lidiia, so I was told, had always very been jealous if somebody had tried to befriend Mariia. Many other women did not even try to be friends with Mariia anymore. However, they said, with me the situation was different. I had come as a foreigner, and I should be well greeted and helped. Lidiia, as far as the general opinion went, was resentful because Mariia spent much time with me. She felt left out. In the end, the tensions between Lidiia and me eased, yet reservations persisted.*

Friendship is never a neutral issue. Drawing on friendship and individuals' commentary as sources of insight, as I do in this book, requires attention to ethics. Indigenous scholars have argued against the use of biographic and personal information in ethnographies and other forms of documentation that may lead to the exposure of private lives (for example, Bentz 1997; Allen 1998). They have called into question anthropologists' conventions and practices that often use individuals' lives and stories to demonstrate the idiosyncrasies and limits of dominant cultural categories of structural formations of power. They have rightfully argued that anthropologists feature private lives in great detail without paying attention to the negative repercussions such descriptions might have for the person or persons described. From this perspective, detailed descriptions of individuals are a form of cultural analysis that offends and hurts.

Other indigenous scholars, however, have suggested that life histories and individuals' stories are a good place for cultural analysis. For example, the indigenous writer Elizabeth Cook-Lynn (1998) takes issue with the idea that stories of individuals' lives are stories that hurt. She emphasizes that stories of people's lives may actually further communication and understanding because they touch on a more personal level than do disembodied academic descriptions of cultural existence. To emphasize the possibility for dialogue and communication across cultural and political borders, the cultural critic Cornel

West (1990, 34) similarly writes of "the importance of creating a culture of critical sensibility and personal accountability." To take his argument seriously requires the willingness of a self-critical engagement with the conditions of one's own thinking and writing. I do not exclude my own responsibilities and practices.

Some stories I tell may not be the kinds of stories Koriak subjects might want to be told about them.[4] In my own disciplinary tradition, the critique of anthropology as a form of Western colonial discourse is by now well known and has initiated a discussion about the political assumptions and cultural representations in which such colonialism is bred. Anthropologists and everyone interested in cultural dialogue and interaction can no longer afford to overlook this debate. At the same time, anthropologists (for example, Aretxaga 1997, 17) fear that if they shy away from engaging potentially contentious issues they give up their voice in matters of public debate. I cannot avoid such issues; I can only maneuver within them. A central challenge for this work is to position the statements of cultural subjects politically. The following chapters try to make room for the way in which Koriak women experience and engage broad regional and local configurations of power while showing how these configurations give shape to strategies and experiences in the first place. In this way I hope to convey something of the struggle of life at the northeastern shore without abandoning the project of ethnography altogether.

□ □ □

# 6 | □ □ □

## Agency in Dire Straits

The social context of poverty and power disadvantage defines the kinds of social possibilities that Koriak women can enact to craft better futures for their children, their communities, and themselves. Yet as Koriak women, they are frequently in disadvantaged positions vis-à-vis regionally defined forms of gendered and ethnic inequality. Both Koriak women and men spoke about the conditions of economic and social hardship at the northeastern shore, yet Koriak women also argued that they were more encumbered than men. As women, they complained about the irresponsibility of men by whom they mothered two or three children, the problems of raising children on their own, and issues of male drinking. The Koriak women I knew loved their children and were aware of the men's problems relating to the lack of work and unemployment, but they also expressed themselves about their own anxieties and fears in the context of social hardship and distress.

The subject of this chapter is the possibility of agency amid the desolate circumstances of post-Soviet life. Specifically, it is concerned with the gendered formations of social possibility for Koriak women in Ossora at Kamchatka's northeastern shore. I ask about the conditions and social opportunities Koriak women can and do find to create and enact social projects to forge a future of their own. But instead of showing the formations of agency from the perspective of either political movements or community-oriented analysis, I try to show them from the perspective of two Koriak women, individuals who called my attention to the ambivalence and fragility of the conditions of social instrumentality and action. In trying to understand the formations of Koriak women's agency in Ossora, I suggest that the analysis requires attention to the individual conditions of this agency, in tandem with the social circumstances in which the agency is set. I thus ask about both the possibilities and limitations of Koriak women's agency, for these horizons constitute the very precondition of this agency. The point is related to that made by the theorist Judith Butler (1995) in her criticism that agency is neither the ground for, nor the product of, particular actions. Rather, agency is a permanent yet constantly changing social possibility.

In this chapter, I tell the story of two Koriak women, Lidiia and Zoia. In my analysis of their stories I draw, first, on insights of how regional structures of inequality create sites of gendered vulnerability and exclusion; second, how national frameworks of gender play out in locally specific ways; and third, how women work to challenge conventions of sexual and gender propriety. To appreciate the efforts of Koriak women in attempting to enhance the conditions of living for their children and themselves, readers must follow me through the terrain of local poverty and women's experience of contemporary social change, nationally ramifying gender formations, and transnational links of male-oriented, authoritative discourse. Then it becomes possible to see the social betterment women are trying to achieve. In many places I visited at the northeastern shore, stories like Lidiia's and Zoia's surfaced in various yet equally troubling ways.

## Lidiia

In describing Lidiia's story, I begin with a narrative that called my attention to the way in which Koriak women are frequently described as scruffy and vulgar if they fail to keep their houses clean, neglect their children, and embark on sexual relations with Russian men. Indeed the following story framed my possibility of asking about the structure of Russian-Koriak relations, issues of regional and gender domination, and the dynamics in which claims of cultural and male authority are set.

In the summer of 1994, I met a Russian writer who was traveling across the northern Kamchatka peninsula to collect material for a book on the contemporary lives of Koriak women and men. When he arrived in the village of Ossora on the northeastern shore, he stopped at the home of a woman whom he had known for several years, and whom I by comparison had then known for approximately one year. Their encounter was neither casual nor accidental; in fact, he stopped by to ask her how she, an impoverished,

□ □ □

middle-aged widow with three children, managed to get by. While he sat on the only chair in the only room of her apartment and she was in the midst of preparing a meal, he began to comment on the domestic disarray he discerned. The cooking pots were not cleaned, the window shutters were askew, and the floor was soiled with pebbles and small chunks of mud. Silence ensued. While the conversation among us dragged, her lover, a young Russian man, unexpectedly appeared. Not yet ready with the meal, she sent her youngest daughter Lena—who was eleven years old at that time—to buy several bottles of *samogon* (self-distilled schnapps). Slipping her daughter some ruble notes, she reminded her not to forget to pick up some videos, which had begun to flood Russia's market in the beginning of the 1990s.[1] Once Lena was on her way, the rest of us continued our awkward conversation. When Lena reappeared with the alcohol and some tapes, the writer and I decided to leave. We had barely stepped out of the house when he turned to me and said: "She is a hopeless (*beznadezhnaia*) case. She is already far gone."

Lidiia had a brother, not much younger than she, who had also known the writer for a long time. Indeed, he liked the man so much that he had arranged several meetings to help facilitate the writer's project. By nature accommodating and helpful, he also took us along to meet his male Russian and Koriak colleagues at the power station where he worked. It was on our way to this station that the Russian writer shared his thoughts about Lidiia with her brother. Initially I was surprised to hear that her brother did not raise his voice in protest but de facto agreed. Yes, he also thought that his sister was really going to the dogs and, worse, was not decent. Why, he wondered, did she not take better care of herself and the children? It was a mystery to him. She might end up with nothing, on the street. But, shrugging his shoulders, he asked: What could someone like him do?

## Delusions

When I knew Lidiia, she lived in one of the decrepit houses that skirt the edges of the village. Here she inhabited, with her two teenage daughters and a six-year-old son, a rickety one-room apartment. While she slept on the creaky bed that with thin, musty-smelling pillows was set against one wall, her youngest daughter and son were bedded down in a cubbyhole built into the narrow hallway. Her oldest daughter continually complained that during the night she could feel drafts of cold air spinning around the air mattress on which she slept; the apartment offered no insulation against the cold. Crumbling cement flakes chipped off the wall and divulged an ugly skeleton of prefabricated architecture. Shamefully hidden in an entrance corner was a stained bucket that served as toilet. A water pump across the muddy road provided water for drinking and cooking and in a limited way allowed them to wash away the "daily grime."

## Decisions

Lidiia felt caught in poverty and generally dejected. But Lidiia had once had, as she said, "the opportunity to live a different life." When she was a young girl, one of her teachers in the boarding school recognized Lidiia's fine talents as a student and suggested that she attend a special school in the city of Novosibirsk (a major urban center in Central Siberia with approximately 1,400,000 residents) to become a forest warden. The teacher was so convinced that Lidiia would do well that she went to discuss the matter with Lidiia's parents. They did not want to let Lidiia go, but they also knew that they did not have enough authority over the process. Lidiia left.

Lidiia was approximately seventeen when she moved to Novosibirsk. It was not the first time that she had been separated from her siblings, parents, and friends. When she was a student in the boarding school, her brother and two sisters had, for reasons unknown to her, attended a different school. Lidiia remembers the long nights she lay awake, thinking especially about her younger brother with whom she was very close and about the two short months she was allowed to spend with her family in the summer. She also remembers the isolation she felt and her deep wish to be with her parents and siblings.

In the institute in Novosibirsk, she had not felt so alone; she liked to learn and found friends quickly. She also liked the city and the excitement, but in the end she decided to discontinue her education. Four years of training meant a long time away from her family. Even more important, in the long run she could not imagine living as a forest warden, for this would have meant a life away from her home. There is no forest in northern Kamchatka; above all, there is tundra, muskeg, bog, and sheets of water that layer the soil. In northern Kamchatka, there would have been no work for her. Thus she opted to give up a career as a forest warden and return to her home.

Today, Lidiia often regrets her decision. She believes that she and her family would be much better off if she had finished her education. She would have more chances of well-paid work if she had stayed in Novosibirsk, she explained. Why would this be? An important factor was that all students were forced to take English lessons in the institute. Today in Russia—where a consumer-oriented market economy, entrepreneurship, and privatization of collective property regimes call attention to the unstable conditions of transition—speaking English is a much-sought skill. But as Lidiia said: "At that time [in the mid-1970s], I did not know why I should waste my time with it, anyway. Then it was of no use. Now I wish I had spent more time learning English and taken my studies more seriously. But what did it matter at that time? Who could then foresee the future? Who could know what would happen to Russia and to us?"

How did state-endorsed constructions of gender make it possible for Lidiia to move to Novosibirsk in the first place? This is not only a question of ethnographic importance; it also involves attention to the irrevocable power of decisions made. Every decision entails the future.

To some extent, the possibility Lidiia was offered must be seen in the light of Soviet state models of gender and government programs. In the mid-1970s when Lidiia lived in Novosibirsk, Soviet government programs encouraged the active participation of women in industry and labor. Indeed, the state-endorsed ideal of the "Soviet Woman"—the idea that women were not separate from men and should be men's equals in economic and social relationships—was deeply integrated into the gendered fabric of Soviet every-day life. Born in the Revolution and the civil war, the Soviet Woman became the leading, pan-national ideal for all women workers (Clements, 1985, 220). Spending her days toiling in factories, plowing fields of gigantic proportions, or fighting bravely in wars, the Soviet Woman was deeply implicated in, and shaped, the gendered fabric of Soviet life. Indeed, her history has been written as one of conspicuous achievement, in which prestige was won through the heroic performance of work ("Heroines of the Soviet Union," "Heroines of Socialist Labor," and all the other heroines of the five-year plans),[2] together with the display of modesty, courage, boldness, and dedication (see Clements, 1985, 220; Bridger, Kay, and Pinnick 1996). Thus linked in its political origins to a revolutionary ethos and ideal of economic emancipation and work, labor was the key category of femininity. Ethnographic records, too, imply that Koriak women had professional expertise and were engaged in wage labor, just like men (Antropova, 1971, 192). It was in this context of state encouragement and programs that Lidiia was offered the opportunity to prosper and learn. But then she decided that this was not the kind of education she wanted.

## Marriage

Back in Ossora, she again met one of her former schoolmates, Oleg. It was not long before they decided to marry. Their families agreed. The marriage,

Lidiia explained, was a joyous occasion. Out of white reindeer furs, one aunt sewed her a dress, and after the wedding registration her mother drew a Greek cross with reindeer blood on the couple's foreheads. Many of their relatives attended the wedding. There were crisp cakes, cold dishes of chopped fruit, vegetables, and fish, seal fat, fish soup, and even some frozen reindeer brain and marrow. Lidiia said that she thought that she and Oleg were off to a good start.

And so it seemed. They had no difficulty in finding an apartment in Ossora. One of Lidiia's maternal uncles who had worked all his life as a herder in one of Ossora's state-run reindeer brigades had obtained occupancy of an apartment near the house in which Lidiia's mother lived. Preferring a life in the tundra to the, as he said, "dull" life in the village, he did not find it hard to offer the newlywed couple his one-room suite. In light of the notorious housing shortages in the Soviet Union, and the local conditions that privileged Russian and Ukrainian families in obtaining adequate housing, the couple felt lucky. Unlike other young Koriak (and sometimes Russian) couples who were forced to spend the first years of marriage in their parents' homes, they had a place of their own in no time.

In the beginning, their marriage went well. Lidiia worked as a clerk behind the counter in one of Ossora's collectively owned food stores, while Oleg earned his living as a machinist. In Ossora, these were standard work activities for many Koriak women and men I knew. Because Koriaks are considered to be bumbling know-nothings who are inept at technical skills, they are frequently denied work or get poorly paid jobs. Many Koriak women and men I knew find it hard to challenge the insidious indications of this argument and retreat either into quiet despair or silence. But Lidiia and Oleg were content in making their living with what they knew best. They earned the money they needed, and they could even afford to buy a refrigerator. Two years into their marriage, Lidiia gave birth to a daughter, and three years later their second daughter was born. Lidiia felt that her life was going well.

Oleg was, she thought, also satisfied. Since the beginning of their lives together, Oleg had doted on his daughters; he played with them and took them out to fish and camp. They also adored him. But slowly, fissures appeared. He appeared discontented, tense, agitated. His answers grew short, and he ceased spending much time with his family. Lidiia remembered how he began to talk about wanting a son. He loved his daughters, he said, but only with a son could he go hunting and explain machinery and other technical devices. He also complained about the narrow space in the apartment. There was not

□ □ □

enough room for everybody in the family, he said. He began to stay away from home; he also began to drink.

To allay her husband's yearning for a son, Lidiia decided to give in to her husband's desire and complaints. The couple adopted a six-month-old boy.[3] Lidiia also hoped that she could persuade Oleg to take care of his daughters again and to spend more time at home. Although she had never been entirely sure that adopting one more child was truly a good idea, she remained hopeful that in the end everything would work out. She expressed some of her doubts about the rightness of their decision in explaining: "I gave in to Oleg because I wanted to do him a favor. I hoped he would come back to the family."

## Hanging On

But although Oleg very much cared for his infant son, he continued to drink. He also continued to stay out all night long. Sometimes, bingeing with his friends from the village, he would not come home for days. Lidiia grew weary and quickly flew into a rage. The children either withdrew into silence or threw fits like the ones they had seen. In the end, after several years of alcohol and hard drinking, Oleg collapsed dead on the wooden staircase of the house. Although Lidiia, Oleg's neighbors, and close kin explained that his death had been imminent ("the way he was drinking he was bound to die"), it still came as a shock. Not allowing anyone to lay blame on her husband or his friends, Lidiia explained: "He was tired. He was fed up." And she continued to explain that he simply had not wanted to live in this world anymore: "Look at us! Look at how we live! Do you call that a life? Even the dogs here live better than we do." And the worst thing, she added, is that only a few people believed in the possibility of betterment or could muster even a bit of hope.

Among Lidiia's family and friends, Oleg's death sparked different and contradictory responses. Members of Lidiia's family helped in their own ways. Her mother and oldest sister, who lived together in a neighboring house, cooked for Lidiia's children. Lidiia's brother, who spent much time— often weeks on end—at their mother's place, helped the children with their homework and school assignments; he also took them fishing and took Lidiia's son on hikes in the tundra. Lidiia's youngest sister showed her nieces how to use makeup and how to alter skirts so that they looked like new and talked with them about contraception and various means of birth control.[4] Lidiia appreciated the loyalty and efforts of her kin, but she began to express some anger and dissatisfaction about the pressures she experienced from them. For all the help they were able to give and were willing to provide, they also began to express opinions that Lidiia was losing her footing in life, that she was becoming irresponsible with her children and unresponsive to criticism, that her behavior was erratic and her changes in mood hard to bear. Lidiia's neighbors agreed. In the house, they could hear her scream and yell, they complained. And often they would hear strange sounds, as if something was falling with a thud. Maybe Lidiia was drunk? To this question, Lidiia sharply replied that her neighbors were drinking as well; she had known that for a long time, and they should keep their noses in their own affairs. And other friends could go to hell if they really thought that she had turned into a slovenly and bedraggled woman.

This was not the kind of answer her family and neighbors expected, and they grew increasingly impatient with her. But Lidiia's snappishness and fits of anger were not exclusively fueled by her husband's death and her feelings of dependence on her kin. They must also be seen in the larger context of economic and social change that exacerbated life in Koriak communities to such an extent that I heard Koriak women and men frequently express themselves about poverty making them feel worthless.

*Frustration*

Together with other Koriak women and men, Lidiia also experienced the sharpening of poverty and financial worries in the mid-1990s when many workers in Ossora did not receive salaries for three or four months at a time and others, including Lidiia, went unpaid for as much as eight or nine months. But she also felt fortunate that she had been able to keep her job. In Russia, a serious consequence of market reforms, renewed emphasis on economic initiative, and private entrepreneurship has been chronic unemployment, the consequences of which, in Ossora, are directly experienced by those who worked in former state-run economic structures and institutions. At the same time, runaway inflation and the failure of government to agree on charges for even such essential products as bread and tea caused prices to spiral to previously unimaginable heights and left many in dire poverty and without any economic possibility. In this context, women were generally acknowledged as a group that is seriously disadvantaged by the process of economic restructuring. In Russia, women have been hit much harder than men by unemployment and were expected to suffer severely as mass layoffs in the industrial sector became an inevitable step in the privatization of state enterprises. For Lidiia, this fear was doubled by structures of regional inequality that disadvantage Koriak women and men. Her daily work—

heaving countless heavy sacks of sugar, flour, barley, rice, and other grains into the storeroom behind the counter, lifting parcels of sugar, coffee, tea, and cans of fruit and greens onto high racks and shelves, and arranging glasses of conserves such as tomatoes and hot peppers into artful pyramids—still gave her an income, albeit one that was rarely paid. But the work also exhausted her. She was frustrated. In the evening hours, she began to stay behind with her colleagues, spending increasing portions of her salary on drink.

Thus Lidiia's drinking increased. She also worried that she lacked the strength to keep her family together. This concern was particularly stirred by the fact that her oldest daughter, Zina, had turned into a difficult and self-willed teen. When Zina was approximately fifteen years old, she decided to leave home and move in with her boyfriend, a young Koriak man from a neighboring village. She moved to his settlement; the couple had no money and lived in a small tin-roofed, debilitated shack close to the shore. Rumors flew to Ossora that Zina's husband did not allow his wife to leave the hut; that she had to stay all day long with his grandmother who did not speak Russian (and Zina spoke no Koriak); that Zina looked disheveled and starved; and that she was pregnant. Lidiia became enraged; communication between mother and daughter ceased. In public, Lidiia voiced her vexation in strong words: "He is handsome, but he is also fucking nuts. I cannot see how she throws her life away. She doesn't go anywhere. All day she sits at home. Waiting for him. She lives in dirt. He ruins her life."

But in spite of her public display of rage and lack of forbearance, Lidiia was not the tough-minded parent she seemed. She began to blame herself for allowing the situation to erode the way it had. She troubled herself with questions of why she could not take care of her children well enough and why their father had to die. She also thought about the ways in which she could improve her situation. Should she leave Ossora and move to another place? Or become a street trader, open her own kiosk where she would sell clothing, cosmetics, and other articles?[5] In the end, however, she dismissed these options as foolish and absurd. They were unrealistic because she did not have the money to carry them out. And this fact was part of the problem, she said. Indeed, it had created the problems between her and Zina in the first place. How would she have been able to provide some space for the couple? She did not have the money to buy a new place. And, of course, she could understand that Zina wanted to leave home because she had no room of her own, that she was fed up with taking care of her younger brother all the time only because her mother could not afford to keep her son in day

□ □ □

care, that she wanted to go out with boys. What teen in Ossora did not? But she also thought about the fact that Zina was young. She wanted Zina to make her decisions carefully and without haste. She did not want her to miss any opportunities, to live in poverty, to end up without money or an education. It was enough that it had happened to her; why should Zina be affected by it? But now, what did she do? Fifteen years old, a dropout from school, pregnant, and without any visibly worthwhile future. Lidiia was both worried and enraged. But in the end, Lidiia's concerns could not affect Zina's decision. Zina had moved out.

For what it is worth, Lidiia's open condemnations of Zina's actions did not mean that she refused to assist her daughter when she asked for help. When Zina was seven months pregnant, she left her husband and decided to return home. Lidiia offered to clear out one corner of the apartment so that Zina and the newborn could stay. And that is what she did.

## Romance

As Lidiia found it increasingly difficult to hold her life together, she also incurred the anger of her kin. In 1994, a Russian racketeer, Dimitrii, was Lidiia's lover. Dimitrii was handsome and young; he was also aggressive and bold. Unwilling to put up with his illegal business practices and the bragging of his friends, his mother had thrown him out of her house, not caring about his whereabouts. Dimitrii had walked straight to Lidiia's place. This situation was disturbing to her family, who expected her to be more temperate and reliable. Her children complained that they were often not allowed into the apartment's only room but were forced to stay in the kitchen or hallway. They sought solace in slighting remarks and sneered in rage and scorn at both adults. Lidiia's sisters expressed their contempt for her lover and said that if she continued to act like a promiscuous woman she would soon be on her own. Her brother slowly turned his back on her and explained that he could not understand what had got into her. Lidiia's mother remained silent.

Lidiia's romance with Dimitrii was a romance of ambiguity. Initially, Lidiia said, she took him as a lover because, truly, she was fed up with the depressing conditions of her life; what she needed was a change, and a lover was good for that. But then, Dimitrii continued to stay at Lidiia's place for weeks on end. She prepared him meals and bought vodka, cigarettes, and hard-to-come-by luxury foods such as butter and cheese. But although she lived with him, she refused to take care of his laundry, invite his friends, or keep her house clean for him in a special way. She was no maid, she said. She had no master.

□ □ □

But her argument did not bode well with some of the Koriak women who lived in Lidiia's immediate neighborhood. Many of them, like Lidiia, were forced to raise their children without the help of husbands or former lovers; yet in contrast to her they lived in even more distressing conditions. There is a dark, damp bunker-like place at the edges of the village; women without any form of support from kin or friends move here with their children. Because I knew some of these women well, I often visited them. They doubted Lidiia's concern for her children, saying that as a mother she should take better care of them. What, they challenged, had her lover to offer? The bit of fun he could provide was surely not enough to take him in. And on top of that, Lidiia even fed him. Why would she do that? To these questions, Lidiia only piercingly replied that she had heard this all before, thank you very much; she was the one to make decisions in her own life, and anyway, her children were not worse off than theirs. Sure Dimitrii stayed at her place, and although he was commanding and arrogant, she did not give in to all of his demands.

The different opinions swirling around Lidiia's affair draw attention to a regional pattern of power and meaning: As the sweethearts of non-Koriak men, Koriak women are often viewed as women of sexy docility and lewd passion. This is a meaning that, in the Russian context, organizes much of its alleged insight around conventional ideas of economically marginalized women and, more internationally, helps to create a world in which Westerners (or other privileged groups and individuals) are not surprised, or even expect, that socially disenfranchised women, including Koriak women in northern Russia, may become personal sexual slaves. It is in this context of such widely accepted truisms about "these kinds of women" that the writer's comment mentioned at the beginning of this chapter was set. Yet to discuss the culturally specific and power-differentiated contours by which conventional knowledge about Koriak women is shaped, I turn to the interrelated discourses of "primitivity" and femininity on Kamchatka's northeastern shore. In the following section, the tone of my analysis must shift as I describe the political and ethnic contours of regional dominance and gender differentiation.

### Social Hierarchy and the Wilderness

On Kamchatka's northeastern shore, common formulations about cultural difference and social hierarchy are framed in Koriak-Russian dialogue by drawing distinctions between the civilized and the wild (*dikii*). Although most Koriak women and men who live in Ossora rarely spend time in the tundra (except in summer and in fall when everybody—Russians and

Koriaks alike—harvests berries or mushrooms), in the Russian imagination ideas about the tundra are nevertheless linked to the ignorant and untamed. The Russian women and men I knew often warned me not to travel through the tundra, saying that wild animals would attack me. My reply that there were no particularly aggressive animals in the area[6] was frequently greeted with disbelief or mild smiles at my innocence. The advice I received was usually accompanied by explanations that Koriak women and men "still sleep on fur" (that is, reindeer hides) and "eat raw flesh" and "rotten fish heads" (*kislye golovki*). It was at this point that I began to think about the comments and explanations that should prevent me from traveling through the tundra in the context of cultural differentiation and boundary making. Fur, flesh, and rottenness—from a vantage point outside the tundra, the imagery of raw nature truly infests white-Koriak relationships at the northeastern shore.

Although Koriak women and men do not easily shrug off the negative characterizations of their Russian and Ukrainian neighbors, the terms of these interpretations do not go unchallenged. In being associated with the wild, Koriak women and men are not at a loss for words. They often choose to turn these accusations around; their strategy is one that involves transforming the rhetoric of primitiveness into the rhetoric of knowledge. The Koriak women and men I knew made fun of Russian women and men who "do not know how to dress in the tundra" and thus constantly complain about the cold; about Russian women "who walk with high heels in the tundra," who cannot walk but instead dangerously stumble along, and who shriek when they hear stories about "wild animals" such as bears. They emphasize, too, that tundra places as a space of living involve forms of knowledge that can be claimed as expert knowledge in the context of white-Koriak social relationships.

The cultural bias expressed in white regional conversations about Koriak women and men as simple, primitive, and wild is only one component in the discourse of cultural relationships at Kamchatka's northeastern shore. A second dimension emerges when the alleged lack of propriety and cultivation of Koriaks and the devaluation of women come together in images of Koriak women as racially deformed or as submissive creatures who need not be convinced to spend amorous and sexually defined time with men. This recognition was powerfully impressed on me when I met a Russian biologist who had hiked up and down the peninsula to produce a book on its bird life. Literally within the first minutes of our acquaintance, and without further ado, he asked me whether I also took the view that Koriak women are "physically bad looking." "Their necks sink in their shoulders," he explained, and "their protruding lips are clearly markers of another race." But the most memorable incident that pointed to the entrapment of Koriak women as willing sexual servants in the double-crossed discourses of cultural difference and gender occurred when another ethnographer and I were invited by two local newspaper reporters to give an interview on our work in northern Kamchatka. While we were finishing up the interview, one reporter decided to feature a picture of us ("as a joint venture, so to speak") on the front-page. For the picture, however, he asked me to sit on my colleague's lap; I refused. The ethnographer began to press me to sit on his lap. I refused again. After some quarreling back and forth, the reporter ended the argument by saying: "You are just not like a Koriak woman." I tensed at this, but no one seemed to think much of it. After all, this comment only reflected what nearly everybody thought.

Here, however, let me clarify an important issue before I explore how Russian-centered notions of femininity are extended in Koriak women's lives. Here I do not argue that Koriak women and men consider all white women and men in Ossora with the same insolence and disdain, as if the latter were a homogenous group. Some of the Koriak women and men I knew were good friends with their Russian neighbors, and they helped one another by sharing food and, if they were younger women, cosmetics and clothes. They also (albeit not very often) visited one another to party, dance, or play cards. But in the broader picture of Koriak-Russian relationships, Koriaks and Russians each stuck to themselves and associated rarely with each other. In this sense, I have shown how categories of cultural difference are a site of critical engagement with social hierarchy.

The intertwining of cultural difference and natural hierarchy is only one set of meanings in which to explain Lidiia's story. Recalling her words that she does not consider her white lover as her master makes it a little less possible to assume that she fully accepts the terms in which white power is set. Lidiia does not see herself as the docile lover and sexual servant of a Russian racketeer. Although she cooks meals for the man she lives with, allows him to sleep in the only bed, and takes care of his comfort, she is not overwhelmed by his power. Yet while her insistence on her own (albeit limited) autonomy offers a context that allows us to see why Lidiia does not (entirely) accept the sexually docile role in which white men place Koriak women, it does not entirely explain the domestic dimensions of the writer's comment. To explore these dimensions, I must return to the politicized context of gender in Soviet Russia and its concomitants in Russia today.

□ □ □

## *Gender Difference*

One much commented-on feature of gender in contemporary Russian life is the bias that women are expected to carry the burden of domestic labor.[7] Indeed, in contemporary analyses, one key concern is to examine how and why women are expected to perform the myriad chores of housekeeping: cooking, cleaning, mending, and caring for children. These studies are not satisfied with exposing the "terrible weight of the double burden," of the combination of domestic and familial obligations that have been ascribed (with the support of the state) to women; they are also interested in how these assignments are involved in the creation of feminine subject formations. To some extent, feminist scholars suggest (Kay 1997), the return of the feminine can be read as a reaction against the idea of the Soviet Woman: that is, the public endorsement and appreciation of feminine values.

As a response to the notion of the Soviet Woman, then, hackneyed stereotypes of women as fragile, family minded home keepers make headway in newspaper columns and public behavior and talk. Along with a renewed emphasis on the "essentially feminine" (Kay 1997, 81) has come a public endorsement and affirmation of traditionally restrained notions of femininity. But although housework and the conspicuous display of beauty and freshness and the prestige granted through fashion are imperative in the ceremonial display of femininity, they are also an important element in gender boundary maintenance: that is, in setting female and male worlds apart. Yet why does Lidiia's brother agree with the Russian writer's evaluation of Lidiia?

In contemporary life, young and middle-aged Koriak men—like many white men—use claims of a bold and aggressive sexuality to establish male power and reputation. Yet at the same time, marked as nonwhite and as part of the "wild," they also enter into racialized discourses and are often humiliated in front of Russian men. These experiences are painful and can be destructive, yet they also encourage the idea that male strength is linked to expressions of sexual assertion. This common understanding makes it possible for many younger Koriak men to transform their "discursive" impotence in interethnic relations into sexual prowess at home. Because such notions are supported by white men, they also accrue additional political meaning.

But this strategy of transforming humiliation into strength is not one of Koriak men's own making; it is one that has been, perhaps unwittingly, endorsed by the state. Let us return, for a moment, to the experience of boarding school education on the northeastern shore. Because in the 1930s

□ □ □

and 1940s this education was imposed on all Koriak children, the majority of women and men around and below fifty years of age lived in boarding schools for ten months a year. Although these government programs and interventions were not intended to create distinctions defined by gender, they created gendered distinctions to the extent that Koriak men were encouraged to assume authoritative roles in their families and vis-à-vis female kin. This is not the kind of gender segregation Koriak women and men elders describe. Although they explain that they knew divisions of gender in connection with household tasks and raising children, they also point to the fact that both women and men were quite capable of performing each other's tasks. In particular, Koriak women elders reprimand young Koriak men for behaving in boisterous and assuming ways. Theirs, they say, should be a behavior of respect and consideration, not of female humiliation and male self-admiration.

## And Dignity

Many Koriak women like Lidiia have no choice but to deal with the issues of difference and the conventions of gender in relation to both regional inequalities and local male authority. They are not demure; even the most shy offered criticisms and ironic remarks. Their comments make it difficult to assume that such assumptions are stable.

In the summer of 1994, what had only been rumored in Ossora for several months came true: A bar was soon to open its doors. Much anticipated, this was a noteworthy event in Ossora. Although cheap stand-up *pivnojs* (beer halls) had spouted across Russia, Ossora had never housed such a place. Neither had its *dom kul'tury* ("house of culture"),[8] which accommodated a gussied-up counter at which alcoholic drinks were served. But for the young Russian man who opened the bar and the customers who frequented it, the bar was not a marker of decadence but of new middle-class aspirations, a sign to map the new Russia of money and enjoyment onto Ossorian space. It was part of the desire to participate in the "new Russia" and to capitalize on a particular moment in its history.

Asked to work as daily helper in the bar, Lidiia was hesitant to take the job. To be sure, it would have meant more money. Maybe she would be able to buy a larger apartment. May be she could afford to buy some clothes for her children and something for Zina's baby. But maybe she would fall even deeper into drink and despair. Would people begin to think that she was low-minded and risqué? Would she, in the end, prove them right by becoming unkempt and lowdown? On the one hand, the offer was seductive enough for her to

□ □ □

give it some serious thought. On the other hand, it would associate her, even more so than before, with uncouth behavior and the stigma of drinking.

Her fears were plausible and judicious. Apart from being a marker of middle-class aspirations in Ossora, the bar is also a threshold space, lying seductively, yet within easy reach, in the zone between pleasure and degeneration. Lidiia was aware of these meanings. I remember one evening in which she struggled hard to find some answers to her questions. Wavering back and forth in her decision about the job, she asked everybody she met what she should do. Yet she felt unable to make the decision.

In the end, Lidiia decided not to take the job. She explained that it would not be good for her reputation, and her family would probably take it badly, too. More important, in the long run it might harm her children. Although her life might be filled with pain, negligence, and levity, she also worked to craft a personal agency involving dignity and pride. For that was what it meant to be a person.

## Zoia

Lidiia's story influences the kind of story I can tell about Zoia. Like Lidiia, Zoia lives as a single mother—with a nine-year-old son—in a run-down apartment in Ossora. She also wants to escape the conditions of poverty and embarks on romantic affairs with non-Koriak men. Like Lidiia, she is caught between her own self-improving efforts and social disrespect, but at the same time she is more daring. I begin her story with the beginning of her marriage.

### Love

In the early 1980s, Zoia and her childhood friend Oleg decided to marry. They had known each other for a long time. Born at the beginning of the 1960s in a northern coastal village, they had spent their early childhood playing in the shallow waters of a nearby bay. When they were six years old, they were sent to boarding school in another village, about a four-day hike away from their homes. In the summer, they would return to spend the short summer months with their families. They were barely eighteen years old when Zoia told her mother that she and Oleg wanted to marry. Zoia's mother pleaded with her daughter to avoid a hasty marriage, but Zoia tossed all motherly warnings to the wind. She insisted that she knew what she wanted. Oleg, she explained, had been a much sought-after man: "He was handsome, tall, and strong. So

□ □ □

many young women were in love with him." She also explained that Oleg had been an affectionate man. He loved her so much, she said, that he would even help her cook and scrub the floor. All she wanted was to live with him.

The first years of their marriage went well. Although they lived in Zoia's mother's apartment, they rarely fought. Zoia worked as a salesperson in one of the local collective farm–run food stores, selling comestibles such as bread, milk, butter, sugar, tea, pulses, and wheat. In the collective farm office, she was known as a hard and reliable worker and was soon promoted to the position of manager. Zoia took much pride in her success and the financial independence she had gained because of her own labor: "I was even able to buy Oleg a motorcycle for his birthday with the money I made. He was so surprised. He liked driving around." Together they also bought an electric stove and a refrigerator, two epitomes of success and prestige at that time.

Three years into their marriage, their son Misha was born. Zoia was so proud that she wanted Misha to have only the best. Only the nicest toys and prettiest clothes, she explained, were good enough for him. In the evenings, after she had returned home from work, she frequently sat down to sew a coat or some shirts for her son. At that time [in the mid-1980s], Zoia stressed, Ossorians were still able to buy good-quality fabrics. But it was also around that time, Zoia explained, that she began to experience frequent migraines and severe abdominal pain. She grew so desperate that she went to the hospital where she stayed for several weeks. She took medications, but the pain persisted. At times, she was forced to stay at home.

Yet in spite of Oleg's urgings to give up her job, Zoia insisted on working. She was not willing to barter her financial independence for an existence at home. She was open about the fact that she enjoyed the contact with clients and a chaste flirtation with male customers across the counter. She was also loath to miss the friendships with her colleagues. At special occasions, after closing hours, Zoia and her colleagues would stay behind in the shop to celebrate. "We celebrated one another's birthdays and all the other holidays. Our husbands were often upset because we also drank." Sometimes, Zoia admitted, she had come home inebriated. Oleg, she said, was raging. He prohibited her going to work or leaving the house without his permission, and he forbade her to talk to other men. "He was so jealous, so very jealous, because I was beautiful and vivacious," she said. "In the beginning of our marriage, I liked it. He seemed so caring. I took it as a sign of love and devotion." But, she continued, what she had taken as a sign of love and devotion quickly turned into possessiveness and control. Their continuous

□ □ □

altercations grew into acrimonious fights. Seven years into their marriage, Zoia told Oleg that she wanted to split up. She asked him to move back to his mother's place and to leave her alone. After the divorce had been settled, Oleg began to pay child-care support. Together with Misha, Zoia moved back to her mother's place.

## Image Making

One source of contention between Zoia and Oleg was Zoia's unseemly behavior with her colleagues; another more important arena of conflict was the way she flirted and dressed. Although her husband reproved and scolded her, Zoia was not willing to submit to the decorum expected of her as a wife. In contrast to the coarse, heavily woven cotton jackets and plain sport shoes that were the usual summer wear of Ossorians, she confounded her family and neighbors with open sandals, bright red lipstick, and frivolous skirts. In winter, Zoia would stroll down Ossora's main road in high-heeled boots, her red-colored hair tucked under an outrageously showy fur hat, her dark eyes thickly encircled with black kohl. Frequently, people she met in the street whispered behind her back, and some Koriak women I knew slighted her for wearing dainty and frivolous skirts. Usually Zoia ignored contemptuous and sneering remarks, yet her feigned indifference did not mean that she did not feel the hurt. Zoia did not easily shrug off the disdain of family members and neighbors, but she refused to give in.

In her own conspicuous style of image making, Zoia drew a great deal of inspiration from the Russian rock star Alla Pugacheva.[9] Zoia admired Alla Pugacheva's individualistic style and success. She also admired her passionate temper and luxuriant red hair. "Alla Pugacheva was never afraid to say what she thought," Zoia explained. "She would play her music even if the party bosses didn't like her. And she always looked sexy and bold." Pictures of the star decorated the walls of her room, and to the annoyance of her mother she would play the star's songs—on a cheap recorder run by batteries—loudly over and over again. Zoia also spent much time emulating the star's hairdo. Her efforts involved the seriousness of a fan who through imitation hopes to obtain part of the qualities of the person adored. In particular, Zoia stressed, she wanted to have the star's self-reliance and nerve.

Yet Zoia's insistence on wearing frivolous skirts and her refusal to countenance the plainness of Soviet-style femininity not only annoyed Oleg but caused offense to her family. Zoia's conduct and style of living, indeed, generated so much conflict between family members and herself that in the

□ □ □

end she decided to leave her mother's place to move into an apartment of her own. How were these conflicts structured? Why did they emerge in the first place? Apart from the narrowness of the apartment, which aggravated existing tensions, I believe that these family conflicts emerged from deeper roots because Zoia's style crisscrossed some of the deepest fault lines of Koriak and Soviet models of gender and work. With regard to their own political and gendered positions, there exists no homogeneity among Zoia's family members. Rather, in relation to her or his own circumstances and ideals, each person was situated differently in the context of gender conflict. Such different positions allow me to explore issues of gender and femininity, involving the web of relationships between women and men but also among women and generations.

*Conflict*

In the context of Zoia's family, her mother was the person least openly expressing her concerns and dismay about her daughter's behavior. But her silence nevertheless carried a mute reproach. A respected Koriak woman elder, Mariia Nikolaevna had grown up and spent most of her life in the tundra. As a young woman, she said, she had helped her husband to herd reindeer, had spent days without end tanning and sewing, took her children in the summer to collect berries, herbs, and wood. She said that her children had rarely bothered her when she cleaned the tent or cooked. Along with other Koriak women elders, Mariia Nikolaevna implied through her stories that women and men had been differently positioned with regard to labor tasks and raising children, but she also stressed that women and men had been capable and always willing to perform each other's chores. The Koriak world that Koriak women elders described saw women and men not as different beings but as equally important to the social community. In fact, Mariia Nikolaevna emphasized, women had frequently worked harder than men to keep families and other social networks together. For example, decades ago, when her by-now deceased husband had started to drink, he had repeatedly invited her to join him. But she had always declined. Who would have taken care of her children, she asked? What kind of life would they have lived?

Out of these feelings of responsibility for her own children also grew Mariia Nikolaevna's distress about Zoia's relationship with Misha, her son. Part of Mariia Nikolaevna's concern was that after her divorce Zoia began to see different men. The attention Zoia received began to make her feel both irritated and overwhelmed. Some of her suitors were so persistent that they

□ □ □

would ring her up in the middle of the night, throw pellets at her window, bang at the wooden framing of the house, or yell to make her open the door and talk. Her mother sighed and complained; her sisters cursed, and her brother, bursting with rage, went out to tell off her lovers. But while Mariia Nikolaevna and Zoia's family grew increasingly aggravated at these nightly disturbances, Misha became fearful and withdrawn. He ceased to respond to his mother's questions, stayed home alone, or disappeared for hours on end. In response, Zoia grew increasingly impatient with her son, paid little attention to his behavior and appearance, and left him alone at night to spend time with her friends. Mariia Nikolaevna watched all this with a troubled expression on her face, cooking for Misha, mending his clothes, and sitting with him when he appeared quiet and alone. From time to time, Mariia Nikolaevna would forcefully, but never loudly, reproach her daughter for her apparent irresponsibility toward her son. Yet at the same time she also acknowledged that her daughter's behavior was not entirely her own fault.

Mariia Nikolaevna blamed her daughter's upbringing in the boarding school as a key factor that explained Zoia's lack of responsibility and drifting. Together with her siblings and other children, six-year-old Zoia was sent to a school away from her home. In the two summer months, she would return to spend this time with her parents in the tundra. She relished the free time away from school, but she resented much of the work her mother assigned to be done. Most of all, Zoia said, she hated the assiduous labor and tremendous efforts that went into the collection and preparation of foods. She said that she had always made herself scarce when it came to these tasks. Collecting berries and wood; catching, gutting, salting, drying, and smoking fish; cooking haddock, pollock, hake, herring, and crab until the entire hut was filled with the smell of kerosene and fat; and feeding the family's dogs with sprats and crushed flounder—these were dirty and greasy jobs, she said. She would have nothing to do with them.

Over the years, Mariia Nikolaevna had tried to reconcile herself to the fact that Zoia rejected such labors as unpleasant and offensive. Still, she tried to communicate to her daughter some of the pleasures and responsibilities that grew out of them, but Zoia did not share the cultural perspective that was at the heart of her mother's narrations. After all, she replied, she lived in a settlement that had been built to relegate customary work and traditions to folklore and superstition. To her, the passionate details of her mother's stories concealed how onerous and unremittingly harsh her life had been; how she had hauled and tugged all day long; how infections and diseases had taken

□ □ □

their toll; and how famine had sometimes menaced elders' lives. Zoia found it difficult to imagine a tradition-based life as useful and worthwhile; this life she identified as boring and benighted. She expressed herself clearly about her desire to live what she considered a modern life.

Zoia's relation to work was also the key site of conflict between her and her older sister Tatiana, albeit in a different way. Tatiana's key objection to her sister's frequent flirtations, staying out late, and, in her view, scandalizing apparel was rooted not so much in the neglect of her son as in Zoia's refusal to search for work. This was not harshness; Tatiana did not imply that her sister was lazy or idle. Her criticism rather involved a concern over her ability to support herself. Certainly, Tatiana knew that finding steady work would be very hard and maybe impossible, but she was greatly upset about the fact that Zoia did not even try. She was also aware of the fact that her sister felt frequently ill, although no doctor had been able to find the source of her weakness and heaving stomach. Tatiana was protective of her sister and took care of her when Zoia was confined to bed, but she also criticized Zoia for living off her former husband and her mother and not trying harder.

But why was Tatiana so adamant in her insistence on wage labor? How did this insistence emerge in the first place? To understand Tatiana's reaction and vehemence, I must turn to her political commitments and social ideas that she continued to support even after the break-up of the Soviet Union and economic demise of the country.

In the beginning of the 1960s, when she was approximately eighteen years old, Tatiana had joined the Communist Party with enthusiasm. At that time, government programs encouraged the active participation of women in government. Tatiana was offered the opportunity to politically prosper and become engaged in the Party.

Tatiana speedily advanced to the position of leading local administrator. As an influential official, she frequently traveled to Moscow and Khabarovsk; in the 1970s and 1980s, she even embarked on several trips abroad, most notably to London, Paris, and Madrid. She had liked these cities, she said, but she had also seen some of the poverty in them. Now she wondered why so many former Party officials said that a market-based economy was better than what they once had had, implicitly criticizing them for changing with the wind. The new government might be wrong, she said. She knew that in the West not everybody could find work. Was that a good thing, she asked? Why would a market-based economy necessarily be better for Russia than the Communist system in which she so firmly believed? Certainly, she would

□ □ □

not go so far as to say that everything had been good under Communism. She had always disapproved of the state's resettlement programs and policy of collectivization. But it was also a well-known fact, she explained, that during the time of Communism the overwhelming majority in Ossora had worked, that nobody had starved, and that there was a sense of order and, in particular, for many Koriaks, self-respect. Now the situation had deteriorated so much that people went hungry and their sense of dignity was gone. Would I call that a better life, she asked?

In the village, Tatiana was known as a somewhat rigid and demanding person, but she was also known for her helpfulness and fair-mindedness. Young Koriak women sometimes found it hard to deal with her domineering ways, yet they also appreciated her efforts to find work for them. And often Tatiana succeeded, putting past Party connections to use. She never ceased to believe in a just future, Tatiana said, arguing that this future came with the possibility and equality of work. This was precisely what was lacking after the breakup of the state, she said. That was why so many young women, like her sister, had all this nonsense in their heads. If they could find work, Tatiana said, things would indeed get better for them.

Zoia appreciated the experience her sister had gathered abroad, but she did not care much for her ideals. Zoia respected her sister as a thoughtful person and somebody she would occasionally ask for advice, but she did not feel that Tatiana really understood her motives and desires. Tatiana, she said, was still so closely attached to the ideals of the Party that she could not recognize what a young woman like her could possibly want. "Look around," she invited me. "Look at all the new kiosks that have opened, all the things we can now buy." Would these have been possible with Communism, she asked? No, she replied. Tatiana still believed that a person's worth was won through the performance of hard labor. But what her sister failed to realize, she said, was that now beauty and charm could substitute for work. Hard work did not really get a woman anywhere. History had bypassed her sister's ideals. Her dilemma was that she refused to recognize the changing conditions of work.

Yet despite her mother's and sister's criticizing, the person who most objected to Zoia's lack of responsibility and modesty was her brother Sergei. Only two years older than her, he blatantly expressed his anger that she did not work hard enough to keep the apartment clean, did not prepare the daily meals readily enough, refused to do his laundry twice a week, and in general did not behave demurely enough. Sergei's charges and complaints resembled Oleg's grievances in a surprising way. Like Zoia's former husband, Sergei resented

□ □ □

what he perceived as his sister's slovenliness. One morning in the summer of 1994, Sergei arrived home unusually early from work, obviously expecting to find a meal ready. Noticing that no food had been prepared and that his sister had failed to anticipate his coming, he thundered out that she behaved like a slut, out on the street, trawling for men. Zoia, who appeared unimpressed by her brother's insolent behavior and authoritative style, retaliated by criticizing him for "being such an ass." She was definitely unwilling to accept and submit to her brother's standards of female propriety.

## Commodities and Change

Tired of the apartment's narrow space and incessant confrontations with her family, Zoia eventually moved into her own apartment. Although she had anticipated many complications, the move was surprisingly smooth, helped by the fact that apartments in Ossora became available in increasing numbers because many whites had decided to leave. A consequence of the political turmoil that followed the breakup of the Soviet Union was that Russian and Ukrainian administrators, teachers, and workers in Ossora wanted to return to their respective hometowns. In the context of economic instability and political uncertainty that followed Russia's privatization programs, a great number of Ossora's white residents began to put their apartments, refrigerators, television sets, and furniture up for sale. It was far too expensive, they explained, to ship appliances and other furnishings from northern Kamchatka to their homes. And because they imagined a difficult start once they returned, they put high prices on their apartments, frequently the equivalent of six or seven years of wage labor. Together with other Koriak women and men, Zoia was concerned about such prices, knowing full well that she could not afford a home. Thus, she said, she was lucky that she had managed to receive an apartment under the old rule, via registration on a waiting list.

In response to these developments, many Koriak women and men I knew began to express sharp feelings of abandonment and discontent about the fact that they were unable to participate in the commerce of apartment properties. They also pointed to the fact that the peninsula was assuming a new face. Indeed, the Koriaks that I knew emphasized that only one group of people could afford the asking prices: people with money, people who knew how to make money. Many of these people came from urban centers such as Moscow, Vladivostok, or Novosibirsk; some of them were racketeers and dangerous, Koriak women and men explained, but all of them were making money fast and well. In the village, opinions strongly differed about these

□ □ □

newcomers, oscillating between affirmation and depreciation. For example, Koriak elders that I knew stressed that many whites who were now leaving the peninsula had been well-meaning and good. Certainly, they said, the majority of them had arrived to make money, just like the newcomers today. But nevertheless, many of them had tried to behave respectfully, if not always adequately. Now they were abandoning the region, leaving behind economic despondence and humiliation. And what came in their place, elders asked? Different whites who did not express regard, who did not care about schooling and work but who wanted to line their pockets through dubious business and racketeering, who established tourist businesses on Koriak lands without consulting them and used business connections they enjoyed with U.S. and Japanese entrepreneurs to further only their own causes. Elders in particular found it hard to understand why these whites were so appealing to their grandchildren, daughters, and sons. Mariia Nikolaevna, for example, was openly indignant about the fact that Zoia called many of these newcomers her friends. She said that she would never allow any of these men into her house. And she never did.

Zoia did not take her mother's indignation lightheartedly, but neither did she allow herself to be disquieted by it. In general, she explained, elders did not understand the way things were now. People like her mother, elders, she continued, had spent a great deal of their life trying to avoid the whites' attention. They had also tried to mitigate the effects of state policies such as resettlement and collectivization by eschewing contact with local authorities and administrators. But the conditions of living at the northeastern shore had changed, Zoia said. Now kiosks and privately owned retail shops were blossoming. Along with cosmetics, clothes, and perfumes; wool cardigans, cashmere scarves, and silk blouses; video cameras and recorders; alcohol, pralines, and exotic foods had come a world of allure and promise: the promise of social betterment. Like Lidiia, Zoia was intrigued by the opening of the bar; but in contrast to her, she saw it as a place for entertainment and social possibility. Zoia began to "hang out."

Like many other Koriak women and men I knew in Ossora, Zoia, too, took these new economic developments as signs of hope. In the impoverished world of Ossora, western commodities are particularly appealing because of their glamour and prestige. More important in the context of economic insufficiency and limited social possibility, they mirrored a carefree world of ease, encouraging fantasies of economic and social betterment. Igor Kopytoff (1985) suggests that commodities are created in what he calls a process of

□ □ □

becoming. In contrast to the orthodox view that commodities begin to exist once their use-value has been matched by a certain exchange-value, he professes the notion that commoditization (that is, the active process of making commodities, or economic goods) evolves through the interconnections and entanglements of historical phases and change. Trafficking through various configurations of history and power, commodities take meaning in particular historic, social, political, and economic circumstances that engender their significance and making. Following Kopytoff's insight, then, it is important to note that in the impoverished Koriak world of Ossora, Western commodities are imprinted with an impressive history of economic success. If in the state-dictated economy of the Soviet Union the commonsense definition of the commodity imputed use-value and its moral companion of constraint, then, by contrast, Western consumer goods can be called enchanted commodities or, as Ann McClintock (1995, 84) suggests, "impassionate objects." Traveling across borders now open but formerly closed, commodities unleash a welter of promises that encourage fantasies of social betterment and hope. The unrestrained range and lavish wastefulness of enthralling goods exhibit the surplus value of exchange as *surplus fantasy* and illusion, therefore placing the commodity at the ambiguous threshold of social possibility and hope.

In the way she talked about western commodities, Zoia implied that for her they held—as for so many others—a specific promise: the promise of social betterment. Maybe now, she would be able to buy better medication for herself, prepare better meals, be able to mend the leaking drain in the kitchen, and finally buy fine clothes. In these plans, she felt encouraged by the life of soap opera characters and movie stars whose film stories she watched on television. In the beginning of the 1990s in Russia, serial dramas and Hollywood films had begun to populate television screens in previously unimaginable ways; their effect was thrilling and exciting. In the summer of 1994, nearly every Koriak and Russian family I knew was eager to catch every installment of the Mexican melodrama "The Rich Cry Too." Every evening, with only a few exceptions, families who did not own a television set visited neighbors or friends to watch, leaving as soon as the credits began to roll. In the same summer, the movie "Pretty Woman," starring Julia Roberts and Richard Gere, flickered on Russian television screens. Zoia loved the serial "The Rich Cry Too"; she loved "Pretty Woman" even more. In both movie and sitcom saga, a penurious woman of the streets gains the riches and love of a powerful man. This story, Zoia implied, resonated with her. Why was it so powerful in her life? In a context in which women feel "peripheral and disadvantaged compared to the urban and the white," anthropologist Lila Abu-Lughod (1995, 64) suggests, "the possibilities expressed in these shows enable them to invent projects for themselves and confirm them." If this suggestion is plausible, how was such a project shaped in Zoia's life? What of Zoia's agency in these projects?

## Relationships

Shortly after her divorce, Zoia embarked on an intense but clandestine affair with a married Ukrainian man. She said that Andrei was attentive and sweet. She also liked his brazenness, his laugh, and his quick wit. While she was still working in the collective farm shop, she had noticed that Andrei had cast an eye on her. It did not matter much, she explained, that he was married. He showed the interest of a curious suitor; he was obviously looking for distraction. Why not her? He could offer her the laughter and good times that she longed for so much after her years in monotonous wedlock. He could also offer her some of the material things she longed for.

The couple met at Zoia's place; they wanted no trouble. Every now and then, Andrei presented Zoia with gifts: a pair of stockings, chocolate, vodka, and small amounts of cash. Zoia was satisfied. She was content with what he could give without his wife noticing. She described the time they shared as a time of carefreeness and ease. During their affair, she was sometimes afraid that he would leave her to return to his home in the Ukraine. Because of the political turmoil in the Ukraine, his wife had grown frightened, he told her, and was determined to leave the peninsula. One year into their romance, Andrei and his family left. Zoia was sad, but sadness, she observed, would not help her to make a living. A few months after Andrei was gone, she embarked on another affair. Just like Andrei, Sasha had been insistent in his approaches to her.

Zoia explained that it was much easier for her to embark on an affair with Sasha than with Andrei. She had no scruples about being unfaithful with him; he was far more calculating and shrewd than Andrei. He was also more bossy and domineering. In Ossora, Sasha was known for his deceptiveness and tricks: a cunning fox. He hobnobbed with regional administrators, business executives, political leaders; he explained to me that in the current political climate only the strong and unscrupulous could profit from the general economic chaos—could accumulate considerable private property and make a profit. Sasha traveled a great deal; he managed to get hold of rare goods and to negotiate advantageous deals. Zoia said that he gave many of these luxury

□ □ □

items to her.

What did it matter, Zoia asked, that his business practices were crooked, with a hint of contraband, bordering on the illegal? In these days, she wondered, who had time for such trivialities? In her view, his economic success and the commodities he procured more than made up for his racketeering. Sasha offered her expensive clothes, sums of money, and occasionally trips away from Ossora to urban centers. He gave her so much, she said, that she could live well and free of financial concern. I remember one family celebration at which Zoia appeared in a shiny black leather costume, silk stockings, and high heels. Her mother and sister frowned; her brother chose to remain silent and refused to talk; only one of her younger nephews dared to ask what everybody wanted to know. Where was the costume from? Who had given it to her? And how much had she paid?

In this context of concealment and covert gift giving, how were Zoia's relationships with her lovers structured? What did she have to do to secure some of these gifts? What were her lovers' expectations? How did she experience the negotiation of power in the context of romance and illicit affairs?

Zoia said that there were several similarities between Sasha and Andrei that she found reassuring and attractive. Both men felt bored by the dull routine of their marriages; they were looking for enjoyment and excitement. Their wish was to have fun; neither Sasha or Andrei was interested in marriage, nor did they insist on commitment from her. Both of them offered monetary gifts, comestibles, and clothes for what they received. But there were also differences that made an affair with Sasha more worthwhile and appealing.

Simply, the main difference between Sasha and Andrei, Zoia explained, was that Sasha could offer her more money, more assets, more luxury. Yet his ability to bestow more riches and wealth also involved an adverse effect: because Sasha could offer more, he also demanded more. In many ways, Zoia's relationship with him was one of deference and subjugation. Sasha, for example, would not let her know when he would come to visit her. Thus, during any day, she expended much time shopping: home-brewed schnapps, cigarettes, and meat; expensive treats such as chocolates and even cheese. Sometimes she was able to get hold of some pirated videotapes that circulated in Ossora at that time. In the evenings, she often felt exhausted.[10]

Sometimes, Zoia said, she found it difficult to put up with Sasha's male authority and domineering. Sometimes she even showed some impatience with his displays of pride. For example, one evening Andrei unexpectedly decided to come by with some friends. Not knowing about his plans, Zoia had prepared a meal only for him. He scolded and yelled at her, calling her inept and useless. He also told her that he wanted her to look more dressed up. Why did she not fix her hair, he asked? Why did she not wear lipstick, high heels? What were his friends supposed to think? What was he paying for? Finding it difficult to keep her anger under control, Zoia screamed back at him, but she also felt humbled and let down. "You must understand," she said. "They [men] like it when I serve them. In the end, it doesn't matter, though. I still get what I want."

But being humbled is hard to take. To compound Zoia's agony, she received little recognition from her family or peers. In her conversations with me, Zoia rarely expressed a concern about what others might think about her. She frequently pointed out how double-tongued and sly they could be. "Don't you listen to what they say about me," she advised me. "Many people here do exactly the same thing. You meet them in the street. The act polite and cool. But behind their back they lie and cheat. Just like everybody else." But this did not mean that recognition did not matter to her. Maybe Zoia spoke too harshly; maybe she stated her opinion too bluntly. But she also left no doubt about the fact that she thought most of her neighbors and friends insincere and narrow-minded. But expressing indifference in the face of her peers' disregard also created an isolation in which Zoia found it hard to exist. Then she left her house to see her sister and mother. For all their criticizing, they were among the only ones who still gave her feelings of affection and belonging.

## Agency in Dire Straits

The stories of Lidiia and Zoia I have told are not easy to analyze. They exist beyond the borders of what are clearly acceptable standards of femininity in Ossora and Koriak communities. The stories point to both the courage and the desperation of Koriak women in searching for social possibilities, even if this means to infringe on local standards of respectability and propriety. As regional and national configurations of gender and cultural inequality support the position of men as authoritative judges of morally acknowledged sexual and domestic standards, women find it hard to challenge the conventions in which such standards are set. As long as Koriak men agree with commentary such as the one offered by the writer, "impotence" in interethnic relationships is transformed into sexual prowess at home. Because Koriak men frequently

□ □ □

support such norms, such assertions gain additional political meaning. Thus, instead of condemning Lidiia as "hopeless" or morally inept, it is useful to show her own positionings and stakes in this matter. Similarly, Zoia's going out with white men who "pay" her for her company and appearance should not be seen in the light of slovenliness and indecorum but as a strategy to achieve personal betterment and survival. From the vantage point of social well-being and security, Lidiia's and Zoia's efforts may seem unproductive, lacking in concern for their children and families, and even harmful to themselves. But they are also committed as, at the same time, they draw attention to their own limitations.

In telling Lidiia's and Zoia's stories, I have invoked a common world, full of cultural stereotypes, social hierarchies, and political disadvantage. What possibilities do Koriak women see in such a world to craft better futures? I do not suggest that Lidiia's and Zoia's strategies are the only ones imaginable, but neither do I suggest that they are immoral or wrong. A world of manifest social and economic deprivations is a world that inspires a variety of personal and political agendas. The women I knew acted from the borderlands of social possibility. Perhaps there is not much evidence in their stories that they were successful, but I hope I have given readers a sense that Lidiia and Zoia worked to carve out a sense of dignity and self-respect for themselves. Any analysis of their efforts must sit respectfully against theirs. Here I can only begin to break up the gender-neutral discourse of northern studies of suffering and post-Soviet gender studies with their emphasis on victimization. In this chapter, readers have perhaps not found much descriptive corroboration to support an analysis of Lidiia and Zoia as challenging or even resisting. But neither are their stories rooted in passive acceptance.

How then can I speak of agency if the stories I have offered here provide only fragile ground on which to argue for social possibility and the individual's sense of power? I think specifically about Lidiia's domestic work for a lover who does not really care; I also think about Zoia's docility with regard to her lovers' demands. I think about the hostility and anger of Lidiia's children when she invited Dimitrii to stay, and I think about the open dismay of Zoia's family regarding her refusal to find salaried work. Most important, I think about the affronts and open disdain by other Koriak women and neighbors that both Lidiia and Zoia evoked. How can I speak of women's agency if the very agency I have attempted to describe is torn between the dilemmas of economic disempowerment and the refusal of social recognition? Can I speak here of agency at all?

□ □ □

The dilemma in analyzing the question of Lidiia's and Zoia's agency is rooted in the fact that the things and persons that empower them are simultaneously the source of their disempowerment. The sense of empowerment Lidiia and Zoia achieve comes at the price of submission. For example, in Zoia's relationships with Sasha and Andrei, in giving her what she longs for—money, food, clothes, and occasionally short trips—both men fulfill some of Zoia's strongest desires, thus creating a space of social possibility. But this is an ambiguous possibility that breeds a corresponding dependence on the one endowed with the social privilege of approval. For Zoia to obtain the social betterment she longs for, she must comply with Sasha's and Andrei's desires and dreams. The tragedy embedded in this paradox, of course, is that it forestalls recognition of personal efforts and social agency.

The tension created by this paradox was a tension my explorations could not avoid. Perhaps there are no clear-cut solutions to the analytical unease created in the gap between social possibilities and limitations except for the constant recognition that such tensions exist and social subjects like Lidiia and Zoia, as well as their analysts, can only maneuver within them.

Lidiia's and Zoia's stories, as I have discussed them here, assume an almost allegorical character in illustrating the dilemmas of women's agency in post-Soviet Russia. When I presented parts of this chapter as a talk, a Russian scholar commented that she could tell similar stories about women in urban contexts, in Moscow, for example. I was thankful for her comment and thought it illuminating because it pointed to the fact that Lidiia's and Zoia's efforts were neither unusual nor bizarre and that Koriak women's problems do not exist in isolation. The comment entailed a recognition that can benefit both post-Soviet gender scholarship and northern anthropology studies.

Part of the problem for Koriak women on Kamchatka's northeastern shore is that until now they have had few social possibilities to deal with issues of poverty in a way that they consider promising and fair. As long as Russia's contemporary struggle for democracy, economic growth, and international identity uses familiar colonial logics to refuse political recognition to indigenous minorities; as long as cultural communities find that Russia has laws for legal and cultural equality but equality is restrained by the continuation of regional power structures; and as long as political standards privilege national assumptions of gender and cultural difference, women may find it hard to offer challenges to the formations of political and gender inequality. In this context, women's own agendas may find no clearly articulated political voice. Their opposing strategies exist, instead, in unspoken protest and fleeting refusals

□ □ □

of men's desires. As women are differentially positioned in relation to both regional and gendered authority, throwing out irreverent remarks can become a form of back talk against these various forms of authority. Thus Lidiia did not dare to publicly challenge the writer. But later, when I asked her what she thought about him, she unambiguously answered that she thought he was "stupid" and "arrogant."

□ □ □

# 7 | □□□

## Skins of Desire

If love affairs between Koriak women and white men in the settlements can be ambivalent and shaped by scorn, how are romantic relationships outside the settlement structured? In this chapter, I move the context of the stories about Koriak women I can tell along the twisting tundra paths and across the steep cliffs that separate the locales of Tymlat and Ossora. Traveling along these paths moved my thinking toward the importance of cultural idiosyncrasies and community characteristics, as well as to more encouraging projects of agency and autonomy, along with the conditions in which their promise is set.

Here I take up questions of romance and ask about agency and passion in the tundra. More specifically, I explore how Rekinniki women in Tymlat produce and exchange gifts of fur to entice sweethearts into romantic relationships that offer permanence and reliability. I have chosen to tell the stories of two Koriak women from Rekinniki, each of whom uses her skills of tanning and sewing to draw a man into a permanent relationship. My interest in exploring the aesthetic and identity-creating aspects of animal skin emerged when during my living at the northeastern shore I became increasingly aware that women's tanning and sewing involved more than just the functional aspects of creating clothes. The effort, thought, and care women invested in producing garments for particular men suggested to me that fur products symbolize sign-bearing surfaces that engender beauty and pleasure as sensual qualities of women's selves.

The significance of the love stories I describe is threefold. First, through the transfer of superbly tanned, sewn, and embroidered fur hats, mittens, boots, and coats, Rekinniki women perform and express poetic and alluring aspects of themselves on the surfaces of animal skin. Second, tanning and sewing enable Rekinniki women to express and maintain forms of cultural identity in the culturally heterogeneous world of Tymlat and against political onslaughts. In Tymlat, resettlement has given rise to an interethnic discourse in which tensions and rifts seep through the village to form an invisible border. In particular, women and men from Rekinniki feel unwelcome and frequently slighted. More than any other subgroup, they must defend themselves against humiliating remarks. Koriak women and men from villages other than Rekinniki frequently say that since the arrival of the people from Rekinniki the village has become dirty and strewn with rubbish. They explain that the *Rekinnikskie* still prefer a livelihood in the tundra, drum and dance throughout the night, do not tend their gardens, and have trouble keeping their houses clean. These views frame issues of cultural difference by drawing careful boundaries between an untamed livelihood in the tundra and a protected settlement life. In this context of hostility and tension, Rekinniki Koriak women and men craft distinctive collective identities by highlighting culturally idiosyncratic characteristics. Third, through the process of tanning and sewing, Rekinniki women affirm and maintain symbolic relationships between humans and animals. Each of these aspects is an important element in the transfer of fur gifts from Rekinniki women to men.

In this context of Rekinniki identity formations, I am particularly interested in exploring the meaning of the gift as an embodied metaphor that arouses attraction and desire and creates seductive subjectivities. Gifts have circulated through anthropological theory for a long time, and the analysis of their exchange is often tied to intricate models of social balance, debt, and obligation (Mauss 1967; Thomas 1991; Bercovitch 1994). Gifts, and the people who give and receive them, are understood as being entangled in delicate webs of power and reciprocity, which are constantly subjected to protest and negotiation. Recently, however, Marilyn Strathern (1992) has argued that the examination of social forces to reciprocate what has been given has been allowed to overshadow more performative and emotive aspects of gift exchange. She calls for a more affective reading of the gift by stressing its expressive and artistic dimensions. Taking my cue from her, I explore the affective aspects of gift exchange in light of notions of poetry and performance (Herzfeld 1985; Fernandez 1986; Seremetakis 1994) and the aesthetic aspects of gift exchange (Strathern 1992; Battaglia 1992). Examining the exchange of reindeer fur and skin involves careful attention to the poetic and sensual forces of gift production and exchange.

□ □ □

At the same time, this exchange draws attention to the gender-specific and affective features of particular gifts. As Annette Weiner (1992) points out, objects are instrumental in creating and consolidating relationships, yet the general view of the gift as gender neutral easily conceals the sexual stakes of those involved in its making and exchange. Following her insight, I explore how the gift operates as a gendered metaphor, how agency is embodied in the gift, and to what effect. What difference does it make that gifts of fur are the work of women and not men?

In describing the agency of Koriak women in Ossora, I focused on issues of regional inequality and women's conditions of social possibility. The story I tell here requires a shift in perspective as it locates itself in tradition-based knowledge and in the tundra.

## Reindeer and Cultural Identity

For many Koriak women and men elders I knew, reindeer herding is a culturally specific way of making a living. Many Koriaks understand that they not only live from but also with the reindeer. With the reindeer, Koriak elders said, women and men traveled through the open and vast northern Kamchatka landscape of tussock and bogs, contorted rivers and unlocked plateaus. As reindeer herders, they cared for the animals that in turn took care of them. In their narrations, Koriak elders emphasized that they owe their existence to the reindeer whose meat, blood, guts, and marrow sustained them and whose supple and protective furs provided much of the shelter the humans needed. In response to the animals' munificence, elders said, the humans attended to the animals with great care.

In a world in which physical proximity between humans and animals is of fundamental significance, truly part of the human condition, caretaking includes forms of knowledge that involve familiarity and experience with the animals. Consider, for example, the knowledge and techniques of reindeer herding. Reindeer herders stay with the animals night and day. They know where single reindeer graze, how many reindeer are ill, which animals appear weak, and what are the odds for calves to survive. A reindeer herder will look for a lost animal for hours. Herders know which reindeer are suited to work as draft animals to carry baggage and pull sleds. They debate the number and strength of animals before they decide on a kill. These forms of livelihood

□ □ □

knowledge involve spiritual ties linking humans and animals in an intimate set of interdependent relations.

Humans and animals were joined in a circle of give and take, a spiritual order of reciprocity that Koriak women and men were careful to preserve. In many stories, Koriak elders emphasized that their rituals and celebrations express a deep concern for the well-being of the reindeer. Dances and songs were performed to praise the munificence of the animals. Races and games were arranged to entertain them. Koriak women expressed respect for the animals in their work and art by carefully observing special cultural rules (Chaussonnet 1988). For example, women did not tan or sew while their husbands, brothers, or fathers were hunting or fishing. These activities could offend the animals and could bring harm to the seamstress and her kin. Even today, many Koriak women I know interrupt their work for several days while their brothers or husbands are engaged in tasks that take them away from their families. In obeying cultural rules concerned with the proper treatment of reindeer, Koriak women who tan and sew deepen and reinforce the intimate bonds between humans and animals.

## Settlement Life

In contemporary everyday settlement life, the cultural knowledge tied to reindeer herding has lost some of its significance as a key marker of Koriak identity. Rather than affirming links with the animals while I lived at the northeastern shore, many people were primarily concerned with the direct effects of economic and political transformation on their lives. But while I lived in Tymlat, Rekinniki women and men affirmed greater proximity to the animals and the land than did anybody else. Koriak elders argue that this situation emerged as a historic consequence of the resettlement programs implemented at Kamchatka's northeastern shore. As I mentioned in Chapter 2, in the mid-1950s until the beginning of the 1980s, Koriak villages on the northeastern shore were the sites of resettlement programs designed to amalgamate smaller, independent settlements into larger economic units (*ukrupnenie*). Today, Tymlat houses five different subgroups: the original families from Tymlat; families who moved in the 1950s from the village of Karaga; and the resettled residents from the villages of Kichiga, Anapka, and Rekinniki. The people of Rekinniki were resettled in 1980, later than anyone else.

□ □ □

Although one important consequence of *ukrupnenie* and resettlement was that a considerable number of the "private" reindeer that Koriak herders had still thus far been able to herd were brought under state sponsorship, a second consequence was that resettlement gave rise to an interethnic community differentiation. Tymlat is not a culturally balanced community. The Koriak women and men I knew there expressed themselves strongly about forms of cultural difference and their feelings of uneasiness about "being stuck together" with others. Members of each subgroup quickly took offense at remarks they perceived as directed against them by individuals from other groups. Non-Rekinniki Koriak women and men frequently say that the *Rekinnikskie* are uncultured and do not attend to their houses and gardens. Because they prefer a livelihood in the tundra to one in the settlement, they are sometimes associated with a "backward" way of living, a way of living with dirt and in "undeveloped," mean conditions. Yet instead of appearing bowed down by these insinuations, women and men from Rekinniki turn the charges around. Their strategy is one that involves turning the rhetoric of primitiveness into the rhetoric of knowledge. Koriak women and men from Rekinniki are proud to maintain their traditional herding practices and beliefs by observing the rules and rituals revolving around the reindeer.

Claims to traditional and spiritual knowledge emerge as an important site of Rekinniki identity formation. Although many, in particular, young, Koriak women and men in Tymlat have come to associate this way of life with backwardness, dirt, and mean conditions, most young men from Rekinniki still look at reindeer herding as the proper way to make a living. Women and men from Rekinniki emphasize their performance of rituals in connection with the reindeer, along with their herding knowledge. In part, they explain, this knowledge is due to the fact that they represent the only subgroup in Tymlat that was moved from the western coast of the Okhotsk Sea to the northeastern shore. In contrast to groups from the eastern regions, *Rekinnikskie* say, they always observed rituals in connection with the reindeer, sang and danced for them, and talked to them. They also offered food, beads, fat, and *lauteng* to the animals and land to express their gratitude and respect.

The following story, told to me by a Rekinniki woman, succinctly illustrates Rekinniki identifications with reindeer-focused knowledge and tradition as an important means of community differentiation:

Last year [November 1993] Natasha [a woman from Rekinniki] put on a celebration for the animals of the land and the sea. One of her

□ □ □

sons lived as a herder in the tundra, and another one had just killed his first seal. We [the men and women from Rekinniki] do this to thank the animals that they give themselves to us and to make sure that their souls reach the Other World. Natasha invited all families from Rekinniki, and she also invited all her neighbors. There was fish, seal fat, reindeer meat, and even some frozen reindeer brain and marrow.[1] We played the drum, sang, and danced all night long. The other people from Tymlat also came, ate, and enjoyed the feast. But when Dariia [an elderly Koriak woman born and raised in Tymlat] held a celebration to thank the animals, she did not invite the people from Rekinniki. We also heard that she did not have enough to eat for everybody who came. The *Rekinnikskie* always give to everybody. We have enough to eat for everybody so that the animals recognize our thankfulness and good will. But many other villagers here are stingy. They do not like to give, and they do not want to give to us.

The way in which Rekinniki women and men frame cultural differences directs attention to the realm of tradition. Tradition, indeed, is one context in which reindeer-focused knowledge and the observance of ritual rules play an especially important role. Yet as the examples and story related above show, tradition is not a neutral concept but involves Koriak community members in Tymlat in different ways. The tradition produced and claimed in the performance of rituals for animals and cultural ways of living involves markers of culturally specific identities. It also shows that this knowledge forms a point of connection between women and men from Rekinniki and animals.

## The Conditions of Romantic Production

Although the majority of men from Rekinniki are engaged in the onerous work of reindeer herding, it is mainly women from Rekinniki who work in the local *masterskaia* where they skin, slice, and sew what their brothers, husbands, and fathers bring back from the tundra. As part of Tymlat's former collective farm,[2] the *masterskaia* is a small shack, its back clinging to the local pharmacy that carries mosquito repellents, pharmaceuticals for head- and stomach aches, ointments, and cotton. In winter, one must walk over heaps of snow to reach the entrance, and in summer, banks of dirt and mud hide the door. The first of the three rooms that form the *masterskaia* is long and narrow;

□ □ □

windows line the outer wall, and wooden benches face this only source of light. Teacups stand in an undefined order on a small wooden table below the windows, and a samovar ensures a daily morning break. This perennially cold room accommodates all utensils necessary to tan, darn, and color the hides stored under the benches. Rusty buckets filled with reindeer feces and bowls of minced elder tree branches stirred into human urine are placed beside the hides. Reindeer feces are used to smooth the skin; elder tree leaves release dyes of reddish or ocher color, depending on the thickness and length of their smearing. A pungent smell fills this antechamber and the two following rooms where women tan and sew. The floor here is covered with fur segments of differing shapes; china cups with decorative motifs such as shaded patterns and flowers hold beads of different sizes and colors. Long wooden benches line the walls; tanning utensils are tucked away in each corner; boards to stretch the hides are placed beside each woman's seat.

Women's tanning and sewing is strenuous work, involving physical strength, skill, and painstaking care. The daily labor routine of manufacturing clothes includes tanning, cutting, stitching, dyeing, and embroidering. I was impressed by the skill with which women I knew in the *masterskaia* treated the raw hides; they took pains to bring out the beauty of the shade and texture of each piece. Reindeer skin is delicate. Bristles easily fall out if the fur is kept in the light for several hours, and each unintentional cut can result in long, irreparable tears, thus reducing the worth of the hide and the value of a woman's work. For these reasons, women take great pains not to damage the skins. Immediately after the animal's death, the fur is cleansed of fiber and subcutaneous tissue. The raw hides are stretched out on the ground to dry in a warm place and are constantly moved and turned to prevent vermin from damaging them. They are then stored in a dark corner area until further work is done on them. Koriak women prefer to tan hides in the summer outdoors when the wind blows away offensive odors, which then easily evaporate.

The aesthetic transformation of the raw hides into soft, malleable skin demands the skillful handling of various utensils, differing in function and shape. Koriak women use both blunt and sharp instruments to clean off scabrous fiber and flesh; they apply crescent-shaped and razor-sharp copper blades to remove the first dense layer of fat. Only when this process is finished do they use wooden bars 50–60 cm long, which have inserted round stones, to soften and relax the skin. Every dried or tainted spot is carefully worked until the hide is without blemish and flaw, or, as a woman from Rekinniki said, "it shines like reindeer fat in the sun." An acrid mixture of reindeer feces and human urine makes an excellent solvent and is repeatedly smeared on the hide to speed up the tanning process. Rolled into a bundle with the hair outside, the soaked hide is carefully stored in a dark, cool place overnight. If on examination the following morning the skin is deemed soft and dry enough, the drudging labor of removing sinews and connective tissue begins again. The tanning process usually lasts for approximately five to six days. It is not considered complete unless all hard and tainted spots are removed.

Each part of reindeer skin is used for the creation of clothing. Body fur is generally sewn into *kukhlianki* (parkas), *kombizony* (women's overalls), pants, and shirts. Forehead skin and limbs are used to produce mittens, hoods, and boots. To make reindeer clothing last for several years, garments need to be relaxed either by wringing or by softening them by biting them several times a week.

If women wish to accentuate and enhance the quality of their work, they may dye the now-pliable hides and attach tufts of animal fur as decorative trims. Colors ranging from crimson to brown bring out the softness of the skin and enrich the allure of women's work. Many of the Koriak women and men I knew especially appreciated the dense texture of fox, wolverine, and white hare furs. The rareness of the latter underscores its preciousness in the production of clothing, and wolverine pelt has a radiant shine. Far from being the only means seamstresses used to embellish animal skins and to stress the skillfulness of their art, complex patterns of beadwork may outline seams and other features. Zigzags, ovals, circles, simple lines, and symmetrical motifs, lobes, and loops may decorate hoods and coats, and broad panels of intricate beadwork run along boot legs.

Women seamstresses from Rekinniki understand the coloration and embellishment of animal skin as a significant way to express aesthetic and sensual faculties of themselves. Through tanning, stitching, and dyeing, the embroiderer communicates aspects of herself precisely because tanned and embroidered skins bear traces of her labor and aesthetic sense. By means of dyeing, needlework, and beads, reindeer skin becomes the medium of self-expression. The styles and the motifs the women design can be called a form of "writing" in the genre of beadwork and sewing. The originality and individuality of their "writing" is key to understanding the work of tanning and embroidering as part of female projects to craft beauty and allure. Koriak women express this point particularly well when they say that "sewing is like stitching writing on the skin." Koriak women draw this analogy from their own experience in the boarding schools or from the school education of

□ □ □

their children. Writing or using a pen is not a meaningful form of creative expression in Koriak villages at the northeastern shore, yet tanning and embroidering are. In describing embroidering as a form of writing, Koriak women draw on a form of expression they learned at school to situate their own artistry in a familiar genre of creativity. The way in which they draw parallels between sewing and writing is one context in understanding their creativity, as I show next.

It is this "transfer of self into substance" (Seremetakis 1994, 15) that enables us to read tanned and embroidered fur as an embodied metaphor of a portraying and portrayed self. The feel of soft skin, the way in which embroidery pleases the eye, and the pleasure one can take in colors and shades turn the material into a sensory experience of the skin. Transformed hides open a venue for understanding the ambitions and desires of women from Rekinniki. They speak from the perspective of the intentional and sensual subject and the "perceptible, talking object" (Seremetakis 1994, 11). Beautiful reindeer skins reflect a beautiful human self by opening a passageway that reveals the contents of that very self. Let me explain this claim by providing more detail in the form of two love stories involving Rekinniki women and men in Tymlat.

## Two Love Stories

Shortly after I first met Larissa (in spring 1992), she told me that she had been in love with Volodia for a long time, but he barely paid attention to her. This, she explained, was not because he was a cool and indifferent person but because he was always so absent-minded and preoccupied with his work. The key to winning his attention, Larissa told me, was to offer him something that could capture and hold his attention. And the best way to attract his attention, she said, was to engage him with something he liked and could use: clothes of fur.

When I first met Larrissa, she was a young woman in her mid-twenties. Living as a single mother with her two children, one six years old and one nine years old, in a one-room apartment at the fringes of the village, she was looking for a trustworthy husband. A few years earlier, she had decided to leave her husband because, as she explained, "he did not help with the children and he had been drinking too much." Larissa's comment resonated with the difficulties many young Koriak women experience in raising children.

□ □ □

Such commentary, indeed, is one arena that many young Koriak woman use to articulate their dissatisfaction with the irresponsibility of young men. Many young women mother children from two or three different men; they spurn the prodigious alcohol consumption by young men that easily leads to death. And they frequently express themselves about how hard it is to find dependable men.

Koriak elders state that the recent tensions in gender relationships are a consequence of government education. In northern Kamchatka, as elsewhere in the Russian North, the process of turning autonomous reindeer herders into a dependent citizenry of the state was—in tandem with resettlement and collectivization—made possible by creating an educational system that alienated children from their parents. Boarding schools were introduced to have children grow up in educational environments, supportive of state-endorsed models of ideology. Today Koriaks frequently express themselves about the destructive effects of this education. In particular, elders mourn the fact that many of their children never learned how to tend reindeer, how to tan and sew. But they tried to teach their children as well as they could.

As an orphaned child, Larissa grew up under the care of one of her maternal uncles and his wife. Her uncle worked as a reindeer herder in the tundra, and her aunt lived with him; with both of them Larissa shared one small tent. Although her aunt was blind, Larissa explained, she was able to teach the child how to tan. Holding Larissa's hands with her own hands, her aunt guided them across the surface of the fur. She showed Larissa how to hold the wooden bar she needed to tan, letting her know by touch how much pressure to exert and how heavy the layer of reindeer feces paste should be. Larissa said that her aunt could feel the quality of her work so well that she was always able to show Larissa how to improve.

When she was six years old, Larissa, like all the other children from Rekinniki, left the camp to attend the boarding school in the village of Il'pyr'. Now she was able to visit her uncle and aunt only in the two summer months of her school vacation. Dissatisfied with the little time they were able to spend with Larissa, however, her foster parents decided to leave the camp and move into the village. They wanted to be closer to their niece. From then on, Larissa was able to walk home when her school lessons were over. And Larissa's aunt continued to teach her.

In the boarding school, Larissa met Volodia. Like her, he had spent the first six years of his life in a camp in the tundra. I knew Volodia well, and he told me that his father had taught him how to tend to the reindeer; how to

□ □ □

drive them through deep chasms and over cracking snow without losing them; how to train them as draft animals to pull cargo and sleds; and how to coil a lasso from lengthways-cut sealskin to catch them. He liked living in the tundra so much and was so impressed by his father's knowledge, Volodia explained, that he decided to spend his life as a herder. Rather than merely admire his father's skills, Volodia decided to learn from this tradition-based knowledge.

Larissa explained that she had always liked him. When they were both children in the boarding school, she used to follow him around, always wanting to play with him and his friends. Later, as a teenage girl, she gave him surreptitious looks, but he did not respond. Her girlfriends laughed and began to tease her. Why wouldn't she give up, they asked? Didn't she notice that Volodia remained indifferent and cool? His lack of interest and regard was easy even for Larissa to see. But she was not prepared to lose hope.

When Larissa and Volodia were approximately sixteen years old, all families from Rekinniki were resettled in Tymlat. Larissa's uncle and aunt moved there to join their relatives and friends. About that time, Larissa and Volodia were leaving the boarding school, and they lost touch. Larissa lived in Tymlat and worked in the *masterskaia;* Volodia worked as a reindeer herder in the tundra. Larissa's conduct expressed how much she missed him. In the evenings when I visited her, she would frequently interrupt her work to playfully mime his movements and style. Mockingly yet tenderly, she parodied his walk by stomping her feet especially loud, emulated his way of drinking tea, and echoed his facial expressions when either angered or surprised. Imitating his ways brought him closer to her, she said. And her tone was always gentle, never harsh.

In the village, Volodia was known as a responsible and charming young man. He was not handsome, but this was trivial in comparison to his other more substantial qualities. The young women I knew told me that they liked his patience, wit, and skill in fixing broken equipment such as engines or dogsleds. Unlike many of his male peers, Volodia neither drank nor smoked, nor was he known to flirt or pursue uncommitted sexual relationships. Although he was convivial and friendly to most people he met, he also kept quietly to himself and offered little opportunity for village gossip. He would, Larissa said, surely be a faithful husband and a reliable father. The problem she faced, however, was a delicate one. How could she manage to attract his attention? Given that Volodia lived his life in the tundra, she knew that one of the most likely ways was doing what she did best, namely to tan and sew. "This will also supply him with the clothes he needs," she said.

□ □ □

An opportunity offered itself. One day in early spring, when the snow had barely started to melt, Volodia came into the *masterskaia* with hands red and roughened from working barehanded in the cold. He had lost his warm and protective fur mittens while repairing a sled and was now in dire need of a new pair. He asked whether one of the women could sew him a new pair, and Larissa eagerly volunteered. But before she sat down to work, she searched for light-gray fur segments, a color that, as she knew, Volodia liked. She tanned the forelegs with care and even attached a strip of red-colored seal fur at the wrist. The tassel, she said, bounced comically. It fit the way in which he joked.

And indeed, Volodia received the mittens with a smile, noticing the tassel at the wrist. He also commented on the fineness of the stitches and complimented her by saying that few young women could match her mastery. Larissa beamed but said nothing and went quietly back to work. She told the women who worked in the *masterskaia* that, given her success, she would sew Volodia a pair of *torpaza* (knee-high boots made from either reindeer or sealskin) to truly impress him. "He doesn't like women who are disorderly and loud," she explained. "He needs somebody who can take care of him in the tundra. I'll show him what I can do." And she sat down to work. Again, she scraped and tanned the hide with care, making the leather wonderfully malleable. She chose to embroider the uppers of the boots with multicolored stripes of beads, in dark and light shades. This was a fine combination for a beloved, one of Larissa's aunts remarked one evening as she passed by. That, Larissa replied, was quite right, and she could only hope that Volodia would notice all the love and care she put into those boots. And he did. When, several weeks later, Larissa gave the boots to him, he blushed and thanked her. When he stayed in the village, he began to stop at Larissa's place, visiting her and drinking tea. Emboldened by his response, Larissa began thinking about another garment she could make. And the idea came to her soon.

At that time, summer was slowly approaching, and white deer fleece was finally available. Larissa asked her elder sister's husband to bring a white hide from the tundra when he visited his wife, and obligingly he did. Resolutely Larissa cut off the four legs to put them aside, tanned the hide, and commenced to sew a *malakhai,* a hood-like head cover, for Volodia. The careful manner in which she worked the blades, covered the fur with the reindeer feces paste, and chose the beads attested to the fact that she put more deliberation and care into the *malakhai* than into anything else she had sewn for Volodia so far. Instead of choosing regular brownish shades, she selected precious and

□ □ □

rare white hides. She even attached some beads she had received from her deceased mother and embellished the fringes of the hood with a lavish piece of raccoon fur. Raccoon fur radiates prismatic colors when held against the sun; Koriak women in Tymlat store away raccoon and red fox furs to use for special occasions.

On one of the several day trips that Volodia made to visit the village, Larissa gave the cover to him. He blushed again. The *malakhai,* he acknowledged, was a stunning piece, beautifully done. The artfulness of the hat indicated that it was more just ordinary protection against the tundra winds. Volodia clearly felt flattered. His whole behavior indicated that he felt touched by the beauty that she had created. "She is a beautiful seamstress," he said. "She is a woman with whom a man could live in the tundra."

He began to visit Larissa more frequently when he was in the village. He took her two children to fish, and in the evenings he would borrow a motorcycle and drive with her through the tundra. Villagers began to comment on the fact that they often saw them together. Their romance developed slowly; Volodia still spent much time away from the village in the tundra, and Larissa continued to work in the *masterskaia.* Yet increasingly Volodia found time to spend in Tymlat. By the end of the summer, they were a couple.[3]

Many of the salient features that form Larissa's story are also present in the story of another woman from Rekinniki. Liuba, too, draws on the work of tanning and sewing to capture the attention of the man she loves. And like Larissa, she locates her project in a tradition of cultural knowledge and female creativity.

In Tymlat, Liuba was known as an extraordinary seamstress, especially for the range and artistry of her arrangement of different fur shades. The artistic ability with which she combined furs of a palette of deep, somber gray to silvery white, of dark brown to copper color, of ashen, tawny, and bluish hues, was known throughout the region. Her reputation was so grand, indeed, that nearly everybody I spoke to in the village recommended that I learn from her. At that time, I had begun, under the guidance of some women who worked in the *masterskaia,* learning how to tan and sew. Liuba received me with extraordinary warmth; she also gave me some skins so that I could gain some practice in my own efforts to tan.

When I met Liuba, she was a middle-aged woman who loathed the life in the village and liked to spend as much time as possible in the tundra. "In the village," she firmly explained, like Ekaterina Chechulina, "there is never enough air to breathe," and she continued to tell me that "the air in the village stinks." Since her husband's death several years ago, she had not lived in the tundra but supported herself as a seamstress in Tymlat's *masterskaia*. Each of her six grown-up sons worked as a reindeer herder in the tundra; each of her four daughters was married to a man who pursued a livelihood as a reindeer herder. Liuba's daughters lived in the village and worked in the *masterskaia;* they tried to join their husbands as often as they could. When Liuba told me that she would travel with one of her daughters to spend several months in the tundra, she invited me to travel with her.

For some time in the village, furs had been in short supply. The seamstresses in the *masterskaia* began to stay away, complaining that material was so scarce that they could not work. Liuba also felt unsatisfied with the little work she had and decided to spend some time in the tundra. "In the camp of Igor," she said, "there are enough reindeer. There is also enough fur." More important even, she added, was that Igor was widowed and looking for a second wife. In the village I had heard women murmur that ever since the death of his wife Liuba had expressed a strong interest in him. Liuba herself explained that Igor was a masterful herder and trustworthy man. He would, she said, be an excellent husband and a good teacher for her sons. What widowed woman in the village would not be looking for a man like him, she asked?

In Tymlat, Igor enjoyed a great reputation as a masterly herder and hardworking man. But he was also known, and somewhat feared, for his obstinacy and violent temper. Like many men from Rekinniki, he loathed the life in the village, much preferring the onerous yet gratifying life in the tundra. And like many men from Rekinniki, Igor admired the skill and artistry of women tanners and seamstresses. Liuba told me that she wanted to find something special she could sew for him, for example, a particularly beautiful coat or a pair of boots. This item should be so excellent, she said, that he could not help but openly appreciate it. And during our travel she did not stop talking about this.

Our two-day journey to the camp was difficult and fatiguing, although we traveled with a very light load. When we arrived in the camp, Liuba immediately kindled a fire. Living in Koriak villages at the northeastern shore, I was often reminded of the extraordinary power of fire. The strength and warmth of flames are directly associated with a person's health and well-being. The Koriak women and men I knew "fed," as they said, a fire by tossing pieces of seal fat, dried meat, tea leaves, and small-sized beads into the flames. They

□ □ □

told stories to the flames and never damped the embers. In lighting a fire, Liuba was asking for physical and emotional health for the whole camp, and throughout my stay (two months) she never once allowed the fire to die out. Igor seemed pleased by Liuba's action, and his welcoming facial expression showed that he approved. He invited us to move into his tent where he lived together with three other herders.

In the first weeks after our arrival, Liuba began to work on the heap of skins piled close to the tent entrance. They were "stiff like frozen wood in the cold," she said, and worked hard to clean each fur of scabrous fiber and flesh. She scraped the skins until they were free of blemish or hard spots; she worked until the skins felt velvety and soft. Igor obviously noticed her work, for he commented to the residents of the tent on the softness of the only recently tanned furs. But he did not offer compliments to her.

Yet Liuba was not discouraged. Since our arrival, she had darned the holes in Igor's fur garment, had repaired the holes in the thick undersides of his boots, and had sewed smaller items such as mittens for him. She had also crafted a hat for him that stood out by virtue of its fine seams and fine alternation of various grayish tones. She had even attached what Koriak elders call "American beads," that is, beads originating from the extensive trade relationships between Koriak herders and American merchants at the turn of the century. Koriak women and men consider these beads particularly valuable. They are highly esteemed not because they are so rare but because they are markers of social distinction that identify Koriaks as successful and wide-trading people. She expressed affectionate interest in Igor, but she was not directly offering him with special attention. For Liuba also mended the garments of other herders and repaired their boots. Our tent companions said that she was always doing a bit more for Igor than for them, but they did not complain. To this, Liuba reacted with repose and calm. Secretly she said that she was still thinking of sewing something extraordinary for Igor. And she soon was able to seize such an opportunity.

This moment offered itself nearly by chance. In the early summer, one of Liuba's cousins visited the camp, bringing a sizable piece of sealskin with him. Sealskin is one of the most highly esteemed fur products among reindeer herders who work in the tundra. Warm and impervious to any wetness, it leaks no water during the snow thaws in spring. All the herders I knew favored sealskin boots over the widely worn rubber boots. "In rubber boots, feet turn quickly cold," herders said, and continued to explain that the rheumatism from which many Koriak women and men suffer today is a consequence

□ □ □

FIG. 10 | Fur work in the tundra (photo: author 1992).

of the fact that rubber does not keep their joints warm. Moreover, sealskin offers some aesthetic qualities that, most Koriaks agree, are hard to match, for example, the haphazardly spread, dark brown flecks that are set against the yellowish-brown hide of spotted seal. But because of its resistance and ability to withstand physical pressure, sealskin is also extremely hard to tan. Only a few women in Tymlat possessed the technical skill and physical strength to transform hard seal hides into malleable skin. Liuba was one of them. Contentedly she explained that this was the moment she had been waiting for. And she began to work.

She wanted the boots to be perfect, Liuba said. She wanted the hide so smoothly shaven that no hard spot would bother Igor's feet; the soles should be so firm that no hole would easily tear them apart; the seaming between underside and leg so small and dense that no drop of water would ever dare

□ □ □

to seep through; and the legs so long that they would reach beyond the knee, to be tied up with red-colored sealskin cording. The final product should be so beautiful that Igor would be very much impressed. It should highlight her superb mastery and skill. And, she added, it should stand as a sign that she wanted to live with him.

Much to Liuba's delight, Igor received the boots with much appreciation. He turned them in his hands, gently stroked the short-haired fur, and immediately tried them on for size. He appeared so moved that he proudly showed the boots to the other men who also greatly admired them. In the following days, he frequently hung about the tent, fetching water, collecting wood, bantering with Liuba. She was radiant and at ease. In a quiet moment, she told me that she "was glad that the boots had done the trick," and Igor was so impressed by them. Shortly after Liuba had handed the boots to him, we all found Igor preparing a separate bedstead in the tent. While he fastened some blankets to a wooden branch at the top of the tent, the blankets falling down to form a cylindrical tent within the tent, he explained to the men and to me that this bedstead was meant for Liuba and him.

The stories of Larissa and Liuba, as they are discussed here, suggest that beautifully crafted and embroidered gifts of fur help to entice men into sexual relationships. They show how women actively and purposefully work to forge worthwhile futures. Yet it is important to note that the men that women choose are not negligent or shiftless but men known for their hard work, temperance, and reliability. I mentioned before that Koriak women in Tymlat express themselves about the irresponsibility of men and the strains of single mothering. Many of the Koriak women I knew were not interested in exciting or short-lived flings; they were not out for adventure or passion in ardent love affairs. Instead, they were interested in men who appeared serious and trustworthy enough to support and help them. Volodia appears as a reliable man. He neither smokes nor drinks, and he is not known for outbursts of violent furies. Neither is Igor known for loosely flirting, bragging, laziness, or incaution. Because they are staunch, nondrinking, and dependable, such men are desirable; because women are reluctant to take chances, they actively work to entice those men.

The skillful transformation of raw hides into supple skins is a key element in traditional women's knowledge. It is also part of a labor process formed around the animals, involving concern for a larger human-animal community and usually—but not always—centering around a conjugal couple. The responsibility for tanning and sewing usually rests with women and not men,

□ □ □

although to a large extent reindeer herders are able to perform each of these labors, albeit in provisional ways. Women, then, engage in the tasks of tanning and sewing not only as part of a gendered labor process but also to maintain and secure animal–human relationships, as well as conjugal partnerships. Men appreciate, respect, and praise women's tanning and sewing as a necessary and quintessential part of animal-based work; indeed, they say that the products of tanning and sewing partly make life in the tundra possible. Although in contemporary Koriak everyday life, fur clothes are no longer a necessary part of living, young men still frequently express the wish to marry women who know how to tan and sew. Here I do not wish to imply that the embroidery and artistic enhancement of fur garments remove people's appreciation of their more practical aspects. In a climate marked by icy blights, freezing cold, and bitter, unceasing northwest winds, the Koriak women and men I knew would certainly agree that such an implication would be absurd. But the functional aspect of clothes does not take precedence over their more aesthetic qualities.

In recent years, a new aspect has emerged in connection with the tanning and embroidering of skin. The transition from state socialism to a market economy encouraged women to produce fur items such as hats and mittens for economic trade. While I lived in Tymlat, women frequently discussed the question of how to embroider hats with flowers in lieu of traditional forms such as reindeer antlers. Japanese entrepreneurs particularly asked for fur hats with stitched flowers. Yet flowers do not grow in abundance in the tundra, and Koriak women were wondering about the numerous shapes flowers can take. And they were working to craft items that responded to the tastes of others.

Russian entrepreneurs, too, are interested in the fur products Koriak women can offer. But instead of demanding items such as mittens or hats, they expressed a particular interest in slippers made from sealskin. In the summer of 1994, slippers were in such high demand that several Koriak women were able to run a small business. In fact, their slippers were so popular in the region that they were able to extend their trade relations to larger cities such as Petropavlovsk-Kamchatskii, Vladivostok, and Khabarovsk. As the former Soviet, and Koriak, world changes, new forms of artistic expression emerge.

## The Poetry of the Skin

Larissa's and Liuba's stories relate how Koriak women from Rekinniki portray and produce themselves as desirable and alluring. They invest artifacts with their content and yet allow them to speak for themselves. Fur artifacts work as metaphors because they resonate with a world in which desire is engendered through the fusion of animal bodies and human selves at the boundary of the skin. Examining Larissa's and Liuba's stories, I believe it may not be too far-fetched to say that they speak as poets—sewing the poetry of the skin.[4] But their poetry is not encapsulated in words or versification but dispersed on the surface of animal skin. With the help of beads, dye, and pelt tufts as lyric means, these women write the very physical poetry of fur, of cleaved animal body parts, of feces and urine, of odor and waste. This poetry draws on material and sensorial experience of everyday life, in turn contributing in its physicality to the excitement and vitalization of that very life (Fernandez 1986). Here poesis as a component of everyday life involves the making and imagining of routine labor products as inimitable and unusual. This process connects customary practices and emotions through material tissues of dailyness and their sensorial experience. Dyeing and embroidering are part of Rekinniki women's performances that evince the particular in the extraordinary. Women's poetry aims not to expose the extraordinary for the sake of its beauty and admiration; rather, the ordinary contains the extraordinary as a surplus of women's work, thought, and imagination.

For Rekinniki women in Tymlat, tanning and sewing are ordinary and usual practices. Every day, seamstresses meet in the *masterskaia* to tan, sew, and embroider fur pieces or designs. Their labor is embedded in a cultural world of signification in which animals and their products are of crucial importance for a life in the tundra. The reindeer enable the humans to be human: Without their meat and skins, herders would have little to subsist on. Thus, far from being material of only functional significance, skins become the nexus of meaning as they bring together humans and animals through the tactile qualities of fur and self. Fur is a material of cultural resonance: what Angela Zito (1994, 119) calls an "interfacing membrane," creating desire by means of optic pleasure and touch. The affective and aesthetic converge on the bodily surface of sewn and embroidered animal skin. This speaks of a cultural poetry and a cultural aesthetics that make use of skin to expose and represent individual aspects of its makers. Poetry is elicited through externality, at the boundary of the skin, but produced to disclose passages into the self. It is the skillfulness of women's work, or, as allegory, the idiosyncrasy of their poetry, that sets them apart from the context of ordinariness by projecting difference as an effect of their skill, creativity, and imagination (see Herzfeld 1985, 10–11). Beautifully sewn skin reflects a beautiful and desirable self. Larissa's and

□ □ □

Liuba's poetry produces an opening for the other to witness the self. Their work provides an arena in which a person's being for herself can be being for the other.

## Desire in the Gift

Here the exchange of gifts as mediums of selfhood and desire takes on the crucial significance of forging and maintaining lasting sexual relationships. The question both Larissa and Liuba face is how to entice the passion and desire of those men they have chosen for husbands and fathers. What can they offer to capture the attention of Igor and Volodia? How can they convince these men to enter into love relationships with them? In their project, they draw on meanings of reindeer as markers of cultural identity. In using tanning, dyeing, and skin embroidery as cultural means to "write" themselves onto skins, Rekinniki women "write" a cultural poetry that reflects sensual and aesthetic selves. As vehicles of cultural expression and desire, fur gifts initiate and mediate relationships.

In this way, gifts are agents, joining together "the different life trajectories of donor and recipient while creating new points of orientation from which to develop their relationships" (Battaglia 1992, 5). The beautiful material object generates an alluring and aesthetic self by inciting love and desire, an affectionate association that carries its participants into a new and shared future. We can thus say that gifts operate on two significatory levels. At the first level, an emotive one, the women from Rekinniki materialize elements of themselves by expressing aspects of themselves on the surface of the skin. At the second level, the connotative plateau of persuasion, the men from Rekinniki read the gift as what is meant, as an arena of opening and performance, an opening up and being for the other (Munn 1986, 102). If, following Mauss (1967), gifts represent social relationships objectified through things and other artifacts, the gift objectifies the person, or, as Strathern (1988, 176) says, "makes people appear." But people always appear in specific ways, and it is the particular design of each gift that engenders the person, shaping her or his idiosyncratic identity.

Correspondingly—to be successful and to be recognized as such—desire, or the gift, needs to assume culturally specific forms. The gift is triumphant when it persuades, and it persuades when it successfully mediates what it stands for, in this case an alluring self. Thus to persuade is to move, and to move is to

□ □ □

affect, to feel, and to touch, in short, to unsettle the boundaries of any given emotional order. Therefore, for the gift to be one of successful movement and persuasion, it needs to be read as what is meant: as an expression of affection and desire. To be effective, gifts rely on the enactment of cultural memory or cultural genealogies of meaning that endow the gift with the ability to materialize this very memory and turn it into practice. Exploiting the past to forge the future, it is precisely this paradoxical character of the gift that enables those involved in its exchange to enter into possible relationships.[5]

In other words, cultural memory, as it is stored in the gift, creates what Battaglia (1992, 9) terms "new points of orientation" that draw giver and receiver into a common future. Both Volodia and Igor put cultural memory to use when they accept women's gifts as vehicles of desire and seduction. They are skilled readers or recipients of a poetry written on the surface of the skin. It is their competence in understanding fur gifts as memory and vehicles of social aesthetics encoding personal desires that facilitates the decoding of the gift to interpret its phatic force. As competent readers of fur and skin, they draw on cultural memory as an arena of knowledge and recognition. Koriak women from Rekinniki *extract* aspects of themselves by presenting the gift, yet simultaneously they *extend* themselves by what they give away. This is what I call the "coincidental movement of the gift": Extraction and extension do not engender the ostensibly paradoxical quality of the gift but form an effective alliance to enrich both donor and receiver. The gift amalgamates presence and absence into a single identity; the gift embodies the donor as presence by hinting at the sensual and aesthetic qualities of the self, yet it ignites desire by relating this presence as absence.

In this chapter, I have attempted to show a form of cultural poesis that, written on the surface of animal skin, is generative of intimate, romantic relationships. I have argued that the cultural techniques of tanning, sewing, dyeing, and embroidering create an alluring and aesthetic self, shaping and being shaped by the sensual qualities of animal skin and the human ability of their modification. Larissa's and Liuba's stories show how reindeer skin turns into a "social skin" (Turner 1980) that signifies and mediates the intentions and longings of their makers. To create desire as a successful discourse of affection and persuasion, Rekinniki women make use of the cultural and material significance of reindeer to invest their skins with the symbolic content of work. Through the exchange of fur gifts and animal skin, women engage in a cultural discourse of meaning, endowing clothes and animal skin with the

□ □ □

powers of creating relationships, and thus contributing to a particular shape of the world. What I termed the "coincidental movement of the gift" is then the effect of fusing animal body parts and women's practices by bringing together cultural meaning and female desire at the boundary of the skin.

The form of agency I have described here requires an appreciation of women's creative expression and work. Anthropological accounts of animal skinning have tended to focus on distinct male practices in which women did not have much to say. Yet the stories I have told show that Koriak women raise significant points. Liuba and Larissa sew desire into the skin, yet they also sew an agenda of cultural boundedness and affirmation. Whether their particular practices actually represent reindeer-herding tradition was less important to this analysis than the understanding of how fur as a cultural idiom and powerful link to reindeer and the past offers symbolic positions of cultural affirmation and self-representation. It is the performance, the action itself, that comes to bear so much meaning in a world divested of appreciation and affirmation.

The configuration of surface-self that I have described outlines how Koriak women from Rekinniki mediate affection and desire by writing poetry of and on the skin. Larissa's and Liuba's stories show how the successful performance of self and desire is contingent on the ability to fuse the self with larger categories of cultural identity. By choosing a discourse of cultural knowledge that pivots on the meaning of animals and the land, they affirm a cultural script of selfhood and desire. Rekinniki women's practices of tanning, embroidering, and sewing show that what circulates through gifts is not only liability and bondage but also an aesthetic world of eroticism and desire, a world of significant pleasure.

□ □ □

# 8 | □ □ □

## And Tradition

Koriak women and men at Kamchatka's northeastern shore have no choice about dealing with tradition. As indigenous peoples, they are defined and made recognizable by their traditional markings—economy, religion, food, language, to name only a few and the most obvious. In this book, the issue of tradition has cropped up in various ethnographic representations and tropes: for example, the poetry offered in Chapter 2; the narratives of Koriak women elders; state disapproval of unregulated Koriak mobility that led to settlement; the outlawing of spiritual practices; and cultural representations of my own. At those times, I chose to let the issue of tradition pass so as not to confuse the inquiries I pursued then. In this chapter, I change the direction of my inquiry to ask explicitly about the power and particular shape of tradition. In this effort, I am particularly indebted to one Koriak woman, Kira, who has helped me to think about a set of issues involving the relationship of tradition, social commitment, and healing. In telling Kira's story, I tell of a particular Koriak woman's understanding of cure and healing as an unusual example of the shamanic tradition; of her struggle against gendered social conventions and expectations of love; and of her vision of social promise and betterment

The question of tradition and healing is intricately intertwined at the northeastern shore. Because Koriak women and men understand healing as part of the shamanic tradition, and because they see vital parts of this tradition as forgotten or lost, Koriak healers at the northeastern shore sometimes find it hard to establish themselves as expert healers. But in this context of difficulty and loss, Kira is a woman who dares to call herself a healer, at least, some of the time. Sometimes she describes herself as an apprentice, as somebody who "still doesn't have enough knowledge," and still needs to learn. Kira says, that she has a particular obligation to heal and learn.

Kira derives her own capacities for healing from her mother. Throughout the region, Kira's mother was known as a particularly talented and powerful healer. Indeed, her reputation was so great that women and men traveled from far away to her parents' camp to seek her mother's advice. She also had found a cure when her six-year-old daughter was struck by severe pneumonia and her father feared that she would die. Together with the help of her spirit guides, Kira said, her mother was able to heal the disease and release her into well being. It was at this point that Kira began to wonder whether she could also become a healer. Kira said that she remembers her mother frequently squatting in front of the fireplace, tossing bones and pieces of reindeer flesh into the flames, singing with a coarse voice to Raven, her mother's chief spiritual guide. Elders in the village called Kira's mother *anangnapal*; younger people called her a shaman.

Part of the problem of her own healing, Kira said, was that she had inherited the spirit of her mother but not the kind of knowledge a spirit might provide. When she was still a child, she put questions about healing to her mother, but she rarely received an answer. In fact, her mother told her that this kind of knowledge was to be treated carefully and was too fraught with perils and unforeseeable harm for a child to know. Harm-seeking spirits might attack Kira again. Kira heeded her mother's warning and remained cautious. But a sense of dejection and bitterness remained.

That Kira did not know about a body of traditional knowledge, and experienced this as loss, was not unusual at the northeastern shore. Many Koriak women and men I knew made the terms of this loss explicit as they attempted alternative interpretations and forged new models. But nobody I knew at the northeastern shore was more insistent than Kira in crossing the borders of cultural difference to actively search for new models of social alliance and connections. Nobody I knew went further than her to imagine communities not rooted in cultural membership and participation but mutual concern and reciprocity. Some of the Koriak women and men I knew questioned her interpretations of tradition or thought of her as naive and ignorant. But nobody I knew questioned her calling to be healer. What impressed me in Kira were her committed efforts to find new kinds of knowledge and interpretations for an infirm world. I begin by discussing the importance of debates about tradition for Koriak women and men, then move to Kira's own struggle to establish herself as a healer. In telling the story

□ □ □

of her difficulties as a woman healer, I stress many elements extraneous to the main argument yet key for understanding her own personal efforts and struggle. I offer this chapter in the spirit of her endeavors.

In the context of traditional loss, tradition is also a site for community differentiations. Various intersecting discourses circulate around the importance of tradition at the northeastern shore. This is material for further explorations of tradition in wider regional interests, struggles, and histories. It is precisely this aspect that allows me to pay attention to the issue of cultural loss and to ask both about its political meaning and the arguments involved in it. In this chapter, I show tradition not from the perspective of time-honored cultural practices or socially agreed-on conventions, but from the perspective of idiosyncratic struggle and interpretation.

## The Struggle for Tradition

The recent years have seen the emergence of a historical self-critical consciousness that asks about the purpose, function, and creation of tradition. In this debate, a Manichean division about true (and thus authentic) or invented (hence corrupted) traditions divides the debate. One agenda attends to the continuity of tradition (see, for example, Thomas 1992). This work explores the strategies and styles of tradition, arguing that even colonized peoples have always maintained certain traditions. The other agenda pursues the construction or invention of these traditions through the ways in which people envision their past (see, for example, Hobsbawm and Ranger 1983; Linnekin 1991; Handler 1988; Friedman 1992; Keesing 1989; Clifford 1988). This agenda has received much critical attention, arguing that traditions exist only in the fields of power and knowledge that make them imaginable and give rise to them in the first place. In recent years, advocates of each approach have criticized the other. Together, they have set the challenge of retaining a focus on the conditions for the perpetuity of traditions while refusing to treat the construction and invention of traditions as self-evident.

From a vantage point in the tundra, the stakes in this debate are high. Part of what is at issue is the recognition and affirmation of particular cultural identities. Indigenous peoples who see the traditions that are being discussed as their own often respond in critical and angry ways to studies of the invention of tradition (for example, Trask 1991). Central to these responses is the critique of scholarly assertions that claim that traditions are invented and not

□ □ □

rooted in permanent cultural practices and history. Such claims, critics charge, can debase native claims to sovereignty and land and can easily undermine testimonies to cultural continuity that may be important for supporting such claims. In cultural contexts marked by struggles and claims for cultural rights, then, the perspective of lost traditions can assume an insidious power. For example, a Russian construction worker who had lived in Tymlat for more than thirty years told me in the mid-1990s that when "they [Koriaks] began to live in settlements, they stopped being Koriak. They began to change. They gave up their tradition; they changed their language and their names. People stopped wearing fur clothes only to wear rubber boots." Another incident happened when in the first days of my arrival I met two Russian dog breeders from Palana, the chief administrative village of the district, while attending a dogsled race. They resolutely approached me, inquiring about my reasons for being in northern Kamchatka, wondering what had brought me to the peninsula. When I explained to them that my interest in the Russian Far East and in the region in particular had been sparked by earlier ethnographic descriptions of ritual and tundra use, they laughed. "You won't find anything interesting here," they opined. "Look around. Koriaks have lost their culture. You need to go farther north; there you will still find traditions in place. You've come to the wrong place"—and they left. In such commentaries as offered by the construction worker and dog breeders, the "loss" of tradition seems to turn Koriak women and men into questionable subjects in their own culture and thus makes them vulnerable to accusations of inauthenticity and loss.

The "culture" that emerges in these commentaries is tied to an under-standing of culture as homogenous and tradition bound. Yet most academics now accept an understanding of indigenous traditions as hybrid, syncretic, and firmly rooted in the histories and social and political conditions that give rise to them. Attention has shifted from examining the processes of assimilation or stable identities toward the fashioning of more open, plural, and eclectically composed identity positionings (for example, Tsing 1993). These understandings acknowledge the often-disempowering political effects of the transforming structures of domination while working to recognize the individual and collective interests and identities that are at stake in particu-lar traditional compositions and decompositions. These insights provide the context from which I can turn to Kira's own struggle for healing. They are also key in understanding and appreciating both idiosyncratic and collective involvements in, and contestations of, tradition at Kamchatka's northeast-ern shore.

□ □ □

## Kira's Struggle for Healing

I knew Kira well because in Tymlat she was a neighbor of the family with whom I lived, and she visited Grandmother frequently. She was a married woman in her late thirties, the mother of three children, and married once. Her apartment, in which she lived alone, was at the northeastern end of the village, only a few steps from the small airfield where helicopters could land. Together with her husband Tolik, her oldest son lived away from home to work as a reindeer herder throughout the year in the tundra. The two younger children, a daughter and a son, spent the largest part of the year in a special school about a four-hour flight from home. Diagnosed by medical specialists as mentally handicapped, they were not allowed, like their peers, to attend Tymlat's boarding school. Kira saw them only rarely and took this situation much to heart. Although she lamented the absence of her children, she barely cared that her husband was never around. "Who needs him anyway?" she asked. When he was in the village, she felt uneasy and troubled by his presence.

In the summer of 1992, one of Kira's biggest concerns was to realize herself as a healer. She had already ordered a drum from a herder known as learned in such a matter, asking for the appropriate wood and a fine-sounding reindeer membrane. But as long as she was married to Tolik, she said, she would not be able to refine her skills as a healer. She frequently talked about leaving her husband to live on her own; her ultimate goal was a divorce. Several years ago, she had discovered that two powerful women in the village had put her under a spell.

How did she find out? Soon after my first arrival in Tymlat, a close relative of Kira's died. Her aunt had been seriously ill for some time and shortly before her death called on Kira to visit her. It was during this visit that Kira discovered that together with Tolik's mother, Dasha, her aunt had cast a spell on her when she was a teen. Kira's future mother-in-law wished a wife for her son who could live in the tundra, knew how to cut reindeer meat, knew how to tan and sew, knew how to ride a reindeer sled, and who, most of all, was not afraid of isolation, wild animals, and the bitter cold. There were not many young women around who would want to live in such conditions, but Dasha knew that Kira was different. Kira would be a fitting wife for her son. In the end, Kira's aunt told her niece that the spell was so powerful that only Tolik's death could break it.

Kira had several close friends who knew about the spell and agreed that there was "no love between the couple" and that the marriage was not a real

□ □ □

match. They also knew Kira's mother-in-law and feared her as a powerful and dangerous person who was not afraid to "have many spirits in her house." In Tymlat, Dasha was reputed to be a woman of extraordinary command in matters of evil spirit craft and sorcery. But she was also said to be aided by the spirits of some rocks, both sagacious and powerful. Dasha was not shy to openly display in her apartment stone incarnations of some of the spirits with whom she worked. This is a rare practice and not endorsed by many of the Koriak women and men I knew, who spoke of the terrible dangers associated with such a routine. They warned me to stay away from Kira's mother-in-law, saying that her powers could make me sick and impair my research. I, in contrast, had found myself increasingly appreciative of Dasha's willingness to spend time with me and to show me certain tanning techniques (she was an excellent seamstress). I also liked listening to her stories. As my relation with both Kira and Dasha intensified, I found myself juggling different and contradictory expectations about my loyalties.

To share the nuances of Kira's situation of being under a spell, I must stress that Kira and her husband's kin did not get along well. She accused them of selfishness and greed; her sisters-in-law charged her with simplicity and naïveté. Because these kin relations were unstable and uneasy, the relatives rarely visited one another.

I had not known Kira's aunt, but I was present at her funeral. As an exceptionally large number of people gathered in the small room where her body lay, rumors spread through the crowd that the spell was nothing more than a cleverly thought-up strategy on Kira's part for abandoning her husband more easily. Some people said they could remember a time when the marriage was fine. At first the couple lived happily together in the tundra, they said. Kira mended Tolik's clothes, and she cooked and sewed for other herders, too. Just as their parents had done, Tolik and Kira worked hard together to create a living

The rifts occurred, some of the women I knew explained, when Kira was pregnant with their first child and still working in the tundra. Kira was not thinking about complications, they said, and "why should there be any?" But the morning when Kira went unexpectedly into labor, complications took place. During her delivery, a uterine breach occurred. Terrified Tolik called via a hand-cranked telephone (the only means of communication for camp members with the village administration) into the village; they quickly boarded a helicopter, and Kira was rushed to the hospital in Ossora. There, she said, the uterine breach was poorly sewn together. The doctors told her

□ □ □

that she could not have any more children and should think about giving up her life in the tundra to live in the village. Kira was willing to seriously contemplate the latter but unwilling to give up her hope for more children. After a long time of careful deliberation, the couple decided that Kira should return to the village. Tolik continued to work in the tundra.

Although she now lived in the village, Kira became pregnant two more times. The births were uncomplicated and went fast. At first, Tolik visited his wife as frequently as he could, but soon he spent more and more time in the tundra. His visits to Kira became infrequent, until they entirely ceased.

In the general context of economic hardship, Tolik became unemployed in the summer of 1994. He left the tundra and returned to the village, but in Tymlat there was nothing for him to do. Like many other herders around him, Tolik began to drink. Kira also said that he began to steal, taking some of the heirlooms her parents had passed on to her—beaded shirts, splendidly embroidered boots, their drums—to trade them for vodka or schnapps. She was growing scared, she said, and seriously began to think about some of the places she could go if she left. One night, Tolik pounded her into unconsciousness; the next morning, her sister came to pack up her things and bring her to a safe place. She was afraid of his fury, Kira said. He had even threatened to kill her.

In the end, Kira decided to leave Tymlat altogether to move to Ossora. There she hoped for a more undisturbed life. There, she also thought, she might become a healer.

The story of Kira and Tolik emphasizes a number of key problems in Koriak female-male relations. It draws attention to the difficulty of living arrangements when men work as herders for months without end in the tundra while their wives live and work in villages. It points to the violence that can beset relations when unemployment, frustration, and drinking set in. And it describes how women often see little chance for themselves except to separate or leave. These are problems that I have intimated or described before, and they are some of the most incessant and obstinate at the northeastern shore.

But, then, the story suggests even more. In describing the need for separation from her husband, Kira's explanation, in which a spell takes center stage, also recognizes the power of forces more gruesome than the conditions of living. In having her relationship to Tolik created and shaped by a spell, Kira is aware of the force that fences her in her marriage. The only power left to her is to destroy the power of the spell by destroying the connection that keeps her and Tolik together. The death of her marriage, and by extension

□ □ □

Tolik's social death, is the only means available for her self-affirmation.

The power of the spell is terrible because it leaves her with only little room for action while she resides in the midst of violence; it denotes terror because it presumes a frightening authority on the part of the person who can cast it and the deprivation of power for the one on whom it is cast. Such a situation contains only little social possibility. To be able to heal, her decision to leave is all that is available to her. Otherwise she would continue in the spell of the awful authority her husband's family possessed.

## Spirituality Versus Love

A woman like Kira who claims the right to heal must leave her husband to find her strength for healing. Only then can she begin to accomplish herself as a healer. But to assume that only frustrated love and violent men can thwart women's ambitions and aims would mean ignoring women's own dilemmas, at least in Kira's case. In the vicinity of Tymlat, many people knew that Kira had been in love with another man, Kirill, for a long time. Some of the people I knew even claimed that Kira had envisioned the fact of the spell as help in abandoning her husband more easily.

But at first, the chance for a match seemed slim. Kira was several years older than Kirill, married, and Kirill had never expressed much interest in any woman he knew. He liked to spend the largest part of the year in the tundra and sojourned in the village only occasionally to visit family and friends. There were times, though, when he talked about the kind of woman he wanted to marry. She doesn't need to be pretty, he said, but she should know how to live in the tundra. Most important to him, he said, was that she could tan and sew and was not afraid to spend time by herself in a tent. Few of the young women he knew were able to do so, he complained. He wondered if he would ever find a wife.

At this point, it might be useful to introduce my own involvements and form of friendship with Kirill. I came to know Kirill in one of the first weeks of my living in Tymlat. Because he thought ethnographic projects that concerned themselves with the collection of tradition were a good idea, he frequently came to visit me at Galina's house. He played his own collection of traditional songs to me and offered to introduce me to people he thought would be helpful for my project. It was in his stepfather's camp that I spent two months in the tundra, and Kirill visited frequently. Indeed, in this book

□ □ □

he already made an appearance in Chapter 3, when I introduced him as a fine herder and tradition-conscious hunter.

Because in the early summer of 1992 I began to visit Kira more frequently, Kirill often accompanied me to her house. He would sit in endless silence for hours on Kira's only chair, sip numberless cups of tea, and watch her work. Sometimes he would borrow a motorcycle from one of his friends, and together with Kira we would drive to the berry-yielding bogs that lay quite a distance from the village. I enjoyed the time, and so did they. Late in that summer I left; when I returned several months later in 1994 Kira and Kirill were known in the village as a couple.

But by then, the relationship already seemed at a breaking point. Several times Kirill had asked her to marry him, she said, but she had always declined. I was perplexed by her decision to reject the marriage offer of the man with whom she had been in love for such a long time. Wasn't a stable match what she had wanted, I asked? Yes, she replied, but she also reminded me that then she would also be obliged to take care of him like a wife. Her responsibilities would be many, and again, there would be no time to improve her skills as a healer. And besides, because they would live mostly in the tundra, perhaps there would be even less time to spend with her children.

Distressed by her argumentation, Kirill began to release some of his pressure, but he still continued in his insistence. By that time, Kira was already living in Ossora and ready to break off the affair altogether. But because she thought that it would be good idea for Kirill to find a suitable wife, she also began to think about several young women she knew. All of them were shy, but all could imagine a life away from the village in the tundra. With the cooperation of relatives and friends who supported her idea, she began to look for a fitting wife. At last, Kirill married, but rumors in the villages also had it that he began to drink. As far as I know, Kira never returned to Tymlat, where friends blamed his drinking on her.

Living in Ossora, Kira had barely enough to support herself. At first she lived with several other women in the damp bunker at the edge of the village, which I have briefly described in Chapter 6. But because she felt frequently sick while living there, she wondered if she could find another living arrangement. She was in luck. A relative of hers who owned a place but preferred to live at his mother's offered Kira his apartment. She didn't need to pay any rent, he said. She could stay for free.

To make a living for herself, she worked at odd jobs — doing laundry at the local hospital, cleaning fish during the fish run, sewing seal-fur slippers

□ □ □

for Russian clientele, and collecting berries and the nutty-tasting pine seeds to sell at a local store. But there were also days when Kira had no money and couldn't even afford to buy a loaf of bread. On those days, she hiked to a fishing camp run by relatives near the village to ask for some fish and tea.

In contrast to my description of the relationship between Kira and Tolik, my point in telling the story of Kira and Kirill is not to emphasize that Kirill also uses claims of a bold, threatening masculinity to establish gender authority and domineering. I knew Kirill as an exceptionally soft-spoken and compassionate man. Rather, my goal here is to emphasize that Kira prized her own aspirations for healing so highly that she was unwilling to barter her love for her independence. Kirill's marriage offer was frightening not only because he could then impose demands, but perhaps even more because her own love for him could thwart her ambition. From Kira's perspective, the power against which she struggles is perhaps just as fierce as the power of a spell. The pleasure of love, like the potentially harmful spell, wields the power to take her away from her own projects and aims. Marriage forces her to choose between her own ambitions and a life design that threatens to take her into directions she does not embrace.

## Reaching Out to Other Communities

Although in Ossora Kira lived in impoverished circumstances, she was not worn down by these conditions of her life. Finally, she said, she had the time to become a healer. And she did so with determination.

Kira had a friend in Ossora, Sasha, a Russian entrepreneur who enjoyed a great regional reputation as a faith healer, who healed with the force of his charismatic aura and the evocation of divine and time-honored Russian knowledge. In Ossora, he was part of the Russian faith-healing movement, which is partially connected to the Russian Orthodox Church and corresponds to the upsurge and renewal of religious beliefs and practices in post-Soviet Russia. As a result of the liberalization of state politics and the increasing recognition of spiritual needs, charismatic healers and prophets of the divine are able to attract large followings, and they are left undisturbed in their work. Particularly in remotes areas such as Ossora, away from urban centers and the institutions of the Orthodox Church, charismatic healers draw large crowds; their work is reminiscent of the Russian saints and holy people who once traveled throughout the country to bring the Christian gospels

□ □ □

and teaching to out-of-the-way places. Since 1991, small informal networks among faith healers exist, and patients are easy to find by word-of-mouth or personal contacts.

Their common interests, Kira explained, had made them friends. In the evenings, she would frequently visit him. She said that she was able to learn from his knowledge and skills; here was a way for her to create a healing repertoire of her own. Several times a year, Sasha traveled to Russian metropolitan centers such as Khabarovsk or Novosibirsk to cultivate the sacred aspect of his self in communion with other healers. At these congregations, faith healers participate in healing rituals to expand their therapeutic knowledge and converse with others. These are large and public meetings, which then branch out into smaller sessions. In each gathering, healers listen, talk, and pray, and they find out new techniques by observing and learning from the practices of their colleagues. On his return, he would teach Kira how to heal with the burning of scents, the speaking of prayers, the blessing of wounds, the laying on of hands, and the counseling of the sick. This was a kind of healing knowledge, Kira said, that she did not have. Nor was it the kind of knowledge that she recognized as customary or traditional. But it was certainly knowledge, she said, worth having.

Kira, indeed, traced part of her healing repertoire to Sasha's performances. As part of a small circle of disciples, she was sometimes allowed to be present and observe when Sasha healed or prayed. His invocation of holy words seemed powerful to her, and she was deeply moved when he collapsed on the ground and in an ecstasy-like state pronounced the names of God and Russian saints. His healing style, she commented, was truly powerful, for his possession not only showed that he was blessed but also that he was connected to a line of saintly people who communicated with him in hallowed language. This was a kind of spirituality she admired and from which she could learn.

## Kira's Healing

In Ossora, Kira managed to gather a small community of Koriak women and men around her who called on her when they felt sick and who praised her talents and expertise. Kira did not claim expert knowledge and readily told her patients so. Yet she always went to see her patients. But even though she freely admitted that her knowledge was limited, she felt she could manage to help, as in the case of a middle-aged man who was ill with a pain in his limbs.

□ □ □

All healing required here, Kira said, was white hare fur and *lauteng,* both of which she gently stroked across his arms. This procedure was repeated each morning and afternoon for several weeks. The man was thankful when the swellings ceased and promised to recommend Kira to his neighbors and kin.

In another healing ceremony about which Kira spoke a lot because it had posed great challenges to her, Kira spent days squatting in front of her stove, finding out from the spirits about the possible cause of the disease. Immediately after her divorce, a young woman had become sick and complained about a pain in her chest. Kira stipulated that the young woman was under the influence of a spell and was looking for an anti-spellbinding treatment. She assumed that somehow the young woman's ex-husband had managed to come too close to his former spouse, thus reminding her patients of the need for careful control of body boundaries through amulets and protection spells. The cure to be deployed was difficult to find because, as Kira made clear, she knew no spell-disrupting magic.

The cure Kira finally decided on was a concoction of Sasha's experience and her own style; she drew on Sasha's spiritual authority and contact with divine power, as well as her own intuitions and knowledge. Again, she used *lauteng* and hare fur, but she also decided to administer blessed water. She gave a list of the names of saints Sasha had dictated to her to the young woman and advised her patient to chant these names in small ceremonies in the presence of close kin. But she also ordered her patient to start a fire and feed it by tossing beads, tobacco, and, if at hand, small bones and meat pieces into it. As a ritual offering to the spirits, Kira advised her patient to burn incense as well. This, at least, might help to clean her. In the beginning of this therapy, I doubted its power and efficiency. At first, its mélange of Christianity-informed religious traditions and Koriak spiritual wisdom seemed rather incoherent to me, but Kira's patient spoke of the improvement she experienced because of this healing style. And after a few weeks, she seemed fine.

This is not the kind of story readers might want to be told about shamanic healing at Kamchatka's northeastern shore. The story offers no bounded knowledge to anchor Koriak tradition and defies classic ethnographic insight into proper cultural healing performances. For example, Koriak shamanic practices of curing and health maintenance involved many styles, including the management of night-long ceremonies in which a shaman chanted and danced to the accompaniment of a drum, the use of magic potions and spells, the killing of dogs and wild animals, and the use of divination techniques to find the distinct loci of pain. But Kira revises these expressive traditions as she

□ □ □

works hard to become a healer; she does not limit herself to one traditional domain. Although her work engages and builds on Koriak traditions, it also inserts itself into other traditions. In this way, her work is more transnational, more open to pluralism and dialogue, than many descriptions I have read. As she uses pieces from one tradition to enhance her own, she creates new products that are simultaneously sites of her own spiritual development and knowledge and open to local critical commentary and reproof. But because her healing was not out of line with regionally available assumptions about well-being and health, she managed.

The appreciation of Kira's efforts comes with an understanding of the personal and cultural circumstances in which she works. The most important context in which to situate her work is presumably the context of loss, both personal and in terms of tradition. Because her mother died when Kira was young, her daughter was not able to learn from her mother's gifts as a healer. Entrusted with her mother's spiritual gifts but not with spiritual tradition-rooted knowledge, Kira was forced to turn to a different tradition. Drawing on extralocal knowledge from a Russian faith healer may place Kira in an awkward relationship to local healing, but it also shows her creative and concerted efforts to build something out of the materials available to her. To Kira, Sasha's skills and erudition are important for devising a healing repertoire of her own. They are important because they enable her to fill the gap in her healing knowledge By drawing on an extralocal discourse of spirituality, she embeds her own tradition in a realm of sacred authority and thus crosses ethnic boundaries. In her own healing, she may stand on shaky traditional grounds, yet she persists in her work. In learning from Sasha, she can acquire something that brings her closer to her own project. "In any case, what is there to lose, if there is so little to begin with?" she once asked.

I never gathered more decisive evidence about shamanic healing at the northeastern shore. At least in 1992 and 1994, most people were more worried about managing their everyday lives then about shamanic traditions. In those years, too, Russian faith healers were far more popular than shamans. In Tymlat, I knew several women and men who had used all their savings to travel to Petropavlovsk to converse with some of these healers who promised they could keep them from drinking and alcohol. The presence of Seventh-Day Adventists and several forms of Pentecostalism grew palpable at the northeastern shore, and in 1994 Jehovah's Witnesses had attracted more than a handful of people. Even more recently, a spate of religious sects based on

□ □ □

Buddhist models and the Chinese Horoscope has competed with the shamanic tradition and Christian groups. Together they may indicate the beginning of a new era of spiritual thinking at the northeastern shore; some sects may win a place for themselves, and others may die because they cannot pass on their inspirations. It is difficult to clearly specify what will happen at the northeastern shore, yet the current resurgence of religion and spiritual movements indicates not only the disappearing power of national projects that thought of spirituality as harmful to state building and development, but also the fact of its current centrality in shaping forms of living in a Russia with a new spiritual face.

## Local Debates of Tradition

Tradition everywhere is a political matter. Not everybody I knew at the northeastern shore imagined tradition in the same unconventional way as Kira did. In fact, many Koriak women and men I knew emphasized the importance of the boundedness and homogeneity of tradition. Having analyzed Kira's own eclectic understanding of tradition, in the final sections of this chapter I represent different Koriak points of view about local customs and tradition and suggest interconnections of politically unlikely, yet mutually committed constituencies.

The question of how much original Koriak culture is or is not retained by present-day Koriak women and men in the Russian Far East simultaneously but variously concerned many people I met at the northeastern shore, including Koriak women and men, cultural rights activists, and anthropologists. Indigenous peoples who have lost their traditions are frequently seen as inauthentic and unreal, having lost what makes them indigenous, interesting, and real in the first place. The perspective of tradition as a series of uninterrupted cultural laws continuously, followed by a group of people from generation to generation, is interwoven with perspectives of indigeneity as a set of primordial identifications, harking back to some ancestral time. Such an understanding has its problems, as it ties the recognition of indigenous cultures and peoples to the problematic principles of historical continuity and uninterrupted cultural order. But what happens when, for example, in ethnographic representations or public understandings people are no longer bound to, and thus identify with, a cultural body of unbroken traditions? What happens when culture seems "lost," disconnected from, and thus unproductive

□ □ □

of Koriak (authentic) identities? Can Koriak women and men still claim to be real? Or do they lose such claims as a consequence of "having forgotten," as the dog breeders said, and thus no longer represent tradition-informed markings of indigenous identity?

These are questions of vital importance for Koriak women and men. In a liberalizing Russian context in which the recognition of tradition has become key for indigenous peoples and their insistence on cultural rights, traditions are important in supporting and giving legitimacy to demands for more political autonomy and ownership of native lands. In a significant contribution to indigenous understandings of tradition, Pika et al. (1994) argue that indigenous people should return to traditional occupations such as fishing and reindeer herding if they are to survive as a people. Although this argument offers an important antidote to descriptions of indigenous peoples in Russia as downbeat and open to loss, much of this work draws on models of culture that stress coherence over internal political dynamics. Such models make it difficult to talk about divisions, oppositions, and change. They offer scant insight into understanding the various cultural and political commitments of indigenous constituencies and individuals, except to see both as independent cultural units.

In practice, the politics of a tradition-embracing approach can be shaky. The Koriak women and men I knew were proud of their traditions and highlighted them whenever they could. Yet there was also considerable disagreement about their content and their form. Regional traditional styles ranged widely across Koriak settlements at the northeastern shore, and they brought community positions into view. Yet they also showed tradition from the perspective of Koriak idiosyncratic positionings in which traditional authority was frequently uncertain. To describe the ambiguity of such authority, I again tell a story, really a sketch, of a brief but sharp dispute, involving Kira and Tatiana, the woman who has already made an entrance in this book as Zoia's sister and a former party leader.

Kira may have embraced the fusion of various traditions, but Tatiana insisted on traditional coherence and order. To her relatives and friends, she talked much about the proper ways of "being Koriak," arguing that traditional logic and order were important for obtaining cultural rights. The political-economic context for this view was the fact the indigenous peoples in Russia have begun to ask pressing questions about cultural continuity and loss as they have begun to argue for their rights (see also Balzer 1999). At the northeastern shore, Tatiana saw herself as a community leader who openly disputed the political injustice and social wrongs that had shaped Koriak lives. Together with other local activists, she was prepared to speak to regional administrators or travel to Moscow and abroad to counter the conditions of political disfranchisement. Because like many other Koriak women and men she saw traditional knowledge best represented by individuals who still spoke several dialects and languages and were still familiar with traditional rituals and institutions, she had begun to record the stories of elders. Taping jokes, riddles, and songs; asking for stories about plants, animals, and the land; and learning how to dance and play drums marked her activities and those of many others.

But at least in 1992 and 1994, Tatiana was not a powerful political leader. In the eyes of several neighbors and community members, she was caught in the contradictions of her former political associations. As a politically ambitious woman and local administrator, she had once been legitimized by the political party and had invited state policies and intervention. Ironically, some said, the same interventions she had invited had helped to destroy some of the traditions she now wanted to embrace.

In the summer, Tatiana used to spend the days at the same lagoon where I collected Nina Ivanovna's story. Several times she had invited Kira to visit her, but Kira had always politely but firmly declined. She was, so she explained, very busy in the summer with her children, collecting mushrooms and pinecones and berries, which grow abundantly along the rocky fringes of cliffs and at the edges of bogs. So far it had been impossible for her to come to visit Tatiana, all the more because the hike was long and arduous. But after much insistence on Tatiana's part, Kira agreed to visit her for several days.

But there was another reason, too, for Kira's hesitation to pay a visit to Tatiana's place. In Ossora, Tatiana ran a small business in which several Koriak women, all widely known as excellent seamstresses, worked under Tatiana's management. Tatiana sold their works to Russian, Ukrainian, or foreign buyers who traveled through the region, or she sent them on commission to Petropavlovsk. She had long wanted Kira, also a fine seamstress, to participate in her business, but Kira objected to Tatiana's orders and demands. In particular, she opposed Tatiana's requirement that all embroidery and designs should show only traditional features and forms. "No flowers, no plants, nothing," Kira complained. Only "true Koriak style," as Tatiana used to say without any irony. In this respect, Kira said, her view was less ambitious than Tatiana's.

When we reached Tatiana's small cabin at the lagoon, Kira immediately set out to gather berries while Tatiana worked at the fishing net. Rain drove

□ □ □

us into the hut, and Tatiana prepared fish soup and *kiliki,* a customary dish combining cooked fish liver, soft roe, and seal fat. Kira, who had not tasted *kiliki* for a long time, ate prodigiously. Unfortunately, Tatiana apologized, seal fat was not at hand, so instead she had to take edible oil, which worked just like seal fat but lacked its pungent taste. Throwing a cautionary look at both of us, she continued: "This is not how Koriaks used to do this. Don't you forget." The next morning, Kira decided to leave, but not without, tongue-in-cheek, reproaching me: "What will happen when you write that we use cooking oil instead of seal fat? Will others then say that we are untraditional and poorly mannered people?" And chuckling, she left.

Although the comment was directed at me, the joke was aimed at Tatiana and had a point. In simultaneously copying and inverting Tatiana's understanding of tradition as part of hallowed custom, Kira 's ironic mocking pokes fun at the idea that traditions can really be lost—instead of, in keeping in tune with the view of tradition she promotes, being open to negotiation and shifting into novel forms. Tatiana never replied to Kira's joke, perhaps thinking that ignoring so much irreverence seemed best.

Yet there is also another context in which to read Kira's remark. In satirizing the elements that have helped to create the imagination of the "primitive" in the first place, Kira subjects them to their own inversion. The use of "primitive" foods such as seal fat, which not too long ago were seen by, for example, local administrators as an obstacle to progress and development (I also think here about some of the stories that Koriak women and men told about boarding school education), is now imbued with the power to turn Koriaks into "authentic" and bona fide Koriak beings. What a change in history, Kira seems to imply. Her comment offers an almost parodic glimpse into debates over tradition. And, of course, the titillation of the comment was such that an anthropologist, indeed, could not resist writing it down.

Both Kira and Tatiana drew from the same heritage of knowledge about tradition, but at the same time each chose a different interpretation. The divergence in both women's relationship to tradition is shaped by their different projects and goals. Kira's ambition was to become a healer, and she was ready to go along with whatever tradition was available to her. To create a reputation of her own, she did not limit herself to one cultural domain but drew eclectically from different traditional conventions. But Tatiana's concerns were more openly politically shaped, as she was involved in revivalist movements and local rights work. Because she knew that in the context of Koriak projects for more autonomy and greater social justice mixed traditions can be a difficult political basis on which to build authority and argue for cultural rights—and because traditional syncretism can easily be read as bogus and false by those not sympathetic to Koriak political dilemmas and claims—Tatiana considered Kira's kind of tradition as dangerous and not desirable.

The different opinions surrounding the struggle for tradition bring Koriak women's and men's stakes in this debate into clear focus. Assumed in Tatiana's talk about tradition is the compelling power of the inimitable nature of tradition to be Koriak women and men. And in a context of struggles for cultural rights, Kira's constructions are easy to ignore. They are too broken and fragmentary to assume authority. They are easy to ignore, too, because although they create a niche in which Kira can pursue her own project to distinguish herself as a healer, they offer no political solution to accusations of loss. And apart from addressing the specific needs of one individual in one place, they offer no platform for political empowerment or collective autonomy. Neither does fragmentation translate into political solidarity, a solidarity Koriak women and men may well need from other indigenous groups, scholars, and their neighbors.

Yet in spite of all these detractions, I believe there is something to be learned from Kira's own interpretation of tradition. Her story teaches something about the power and ambivalence of creative work in a context in which decisions—whether personal or social—are necessarily situated at the crossroads of tangled interests, ambitions, and choices.

## The Spirit of Tradition

This could be the end of the chapter; as a stopping place; however, it comes too soon. Kira's interpretation of tradition I have suggested here—as an eclectic and unconventional understanding of the shamanic tradition—is partially meant to serve as a defense against accusations that Koriak traditions are lost. Hence, it also involves a pledge for the future. In introducing Kira's work at the beginning of this chapter, I mentioned that Kira was looking for new forms of sociality in the face of controversy and amid the conditions of social desolation. Because Kira's interpretation of tradition was not locally bound, she was able to trespass cultural borders and imagine communities of broader constituencies, including Russian faith healers and an anthropologist.

□ □ □

When I approached the end of my first visit on Kamchatka's northeastern shore, Kira offered me the accompaniment of a spirit guardian. I needed protection, she said. Besides, my way home was long, and everybody should have a guardian. As neighbors and friends gathered late one afternoon in her small kitchen to stand by as Kira asked a spirit if she (spirits are gendered, as found I only out much later) could imagine traveling with me, I was offered the presence of a spirit guardian. I was also given careful instructions about how to talk to and provide for my protector.

I am not recounting this event to flirt with my own involvement in the shamanic tradition. It would be easy, too, to analyze this event as one of "ethnographic initiation," in which anthropologists are officially accepted by their hosts. I could tell more about my own involvements in everyday spiritual life at the northeastern shore and speak of sensitivity and compassion, as anthropologists have often done. But in contrast, I think, it is challenging to place this event in a wider context of sociality or community making. The choice of Koriak friends to entrust a spirit to my care, and, in turn, me to her care, directs attention to the emergence and building of new forms of sociality. Because Kira's interpretation of tradition—that is, of healing as an eclectic and unconventional understanding of the shamanic tradition—is not locally bound, she is able to trespass cultural borders and imagine communities of broader constituencies.

It is in this spirit, I believe, that Kira offered the guidance of a spirit to an anthropologist. And she reminded me that communities need to be carefully treated. Spirits protect, yet they are also in need of protection. To live, they need to be caressed, talked to, and fed. Spirits protect, but protection assumes responsibility. We, Kira said, have to take care of them.

Perhaps I found Kira's practices intriguing because in them I recognized some of the social community-building strategies I knew from Germany and North-America. I could follow Kira in her desire to build social and personal alliances on the grounds of affinity and mutual responsibility. I could also follow her desire to dare the static borders of cultural difference to think about alternative forms of sociality or to imagine possible new worlds. Perhaps I was so taken by Kira's efforts precisely because they reminded me of the necessity of thinking about new forms of social organizing in which cultural recognition and respect are not overshadowed by hallowed identities. Most likely, all of these reasons are true. I was certainly self-conscious when collecting tradition from so unusual a healer. But I could not help but be

□ □ □

impressed by Kira's own commitments and efforts to envision a world in which everybody can participate.

Recently, cultural rights activists and anthropologists alike have expressed a great deal of concern about the situation of indigenous peoples in the Russian North. Both indigenous peoples and scholars see cultural and physical survival as one of the most pressing issues indigenous people face. In some cultural rights arguments, political effectiveness is not gained through hybridity and mixing, but through establishing cultural autonomy through a group's claims to separate, culturally distinct, recognizable identities. When, as in indigenous politics in Russia, the stakes are high, tradition may be best based on a logics of safety—that is, on homogenous and dominant assumptions. Yet Kira's work raises questions about whether some of the most homogenous visions of identity politics can really lead to empowerment or liberation, as long as political effectiveness is based on the exclusion of others. It may be unfair on my part to put Kira's efforts in this political discourse; a person like Kira does not necessarily have the same agenda as, for example, anthropologists and indigenous leaders. But at the same time, her own agenda, however tentatively linked to the discourse of tradition and survival, evokes that world, albeit with a different interpretive practice. It is by acknowledging the dilemmas involved in Kira's story that one can appreciate her endeavors, perhaps not for everybody as a convincing example of the shamanic tradition, but as an alternative interpretation and creative intervention into a world Koriak women and men, along with other indigenous peoples in the Russian North, share.

□ □ □

# 9 | □ □ □

## Arrival?

My grandmother told me that we [Koriak
women and men] can walk on two paths. Today
I don't know which one we are on.

　　*—Ekaterina Chechulina, Ossora, August 1994*

The travel orientation of my project brings this book to an end. The stories I have told involved a considerable amount of traveling—in the tundra, between tundra and settlement, and between settlements—yet they did not center on traveling as a practice in and of itself. How can I speak of traveling as the organizing principle of this book if practices of traveling do not provide its analytical frame? There are relevant if tangential connections. Ethnographies are often expected to come to an end by way of a well-defined and concrete conclusion, but the life they are supposed to describe continues to move on. In my project, I wanted to retain a sense of this flux by allowing this book to keep the possibilities for living and vital futures open and alive. For this reason, I chose to entitle the final section of this book with a phrase that forestalls closure but references new ways of inquiry. The muted skepticism of *Arrival?* is not meant to show uncertainty; neither does it deny the possibilities for knowledge and learning. Rather, *Arrival?* is meant to signal openness and to invite new forms of thinking and learning about some of the issues I have explored in this book—administrative rule, the formation of regional and social inequalities, and gender differentiation. My goal here is to keep alive both the intellectual and social possibilities that have inspired Koriak projects and dreams.

In keeping the overall frame of this book in step with the travel practices of many Koriak women and men I knew, I chose movement as my guide. Yet European-influenced cultural theory frequently assumes lack of order and instability when people insist on changes of places and sites. How, then, can the (assumed) instability of movement provide a point of orientation? The travel-oriented cultural practices of many Koriak women and men I knew directed my thinking in this book because they shape local forms of understanding and living—from hunting trips in the tundra, to people's travels with animals, to seasonal changes in homes, to visits and communication between settlements, to the variance and changeability of opinions in settlements. Stories played an important role in following the "travel perspective" of Koriak women and men: They helped me to show Koriak interpretations and negotiations of political institutions and regional and administrative forms of authority from idiosyncratic points of view. The travel-orientation I pursued moved my project away from more classic ethnographic descriptions that seek out cultural principles underlying particular cultural instances and styles. In contrast, this book highlighted those perspectives that are most erased by more familiar, regionally oriented styles: the idiosyncratic perspectives of individual Koriak women and men.

As a form of analysis, stories disrupt the possibility of reading for certainty and fixed meanings. Because stories show social processes from the perspective of idiosyncratic alignments, they can be disputed by differently situated storytellers and observers. In arguing that the knowledge of an author, like that of the people about whom he or she writes, is situated and partial (Haraway 1991), I also argued for the recognition and respect for a variety of different Koriak political agendas. The difference and variance in social efforts and interpretations I saw at the northeastern shore challenge analysts to find new forms of descriptions.

Attention to the links between storytelling and travel-related Koriak forms of living requires attention to issues of ethnographic authority and representational styles. Although my choice to use stories as analytic passage-ways was stimulated by the cultural practice of the Koriak women and men I knew, it was also spurred by the works of many other anthropologists who have criticized the homogeneity-orientation of dominant representations. A number of recent ethnographic works have been experiments to the extent that they have thrown into relief disciplinary conventions that link scholarly authority and various forms of domination. To counter the key political problems reflected in earlier forms of cultural representation, anthropologists have

□ □ □

FIG. 11 | Northern Kamchatka camp (photo: author 1994).

suggested alternative ways of writing. Some have stressed the importance of abandoning fixed ethnographic categories and classifications (Rosaldo 1989; Clifford 1988) to expose cultural heterogeneity and the specificity of people's agendas. Others have argued for the use of collaborative projects (Ridington and Hastings 1997) or the creation of polyvocal texts (Pandolfo 1997). The textual strategies I pursued in the book were intended to find new forms of descriptions for—for example—Koriak involvements in and with regional power and social formations, their own projects of social betterment, and tradition. In this book, I have attempted a writing strategy in which respect for the people with whom I lived and worked was not overwhelmed by a generic ethnographic style that effaces the struggles, accomplishments, and dilemmas of many Koriak women and men I knew. Their careful aestheticism is part of the refusal to become dispirited by the current desperate conditions of living; it is part of the endeavor to recognize the creativity and beauty of living at the northeastern shore.

This book has turned attention from political centers to political peripheries; a perspective from the periphery can be a tool for destabilizing authority. Turning attention from centers to peripheries sheds light on the limitations and strengths of state rule and administrative agendas. Where many ethnographies

□ □ □

of the region locate themselves at a level in which state and administrative authority seems most certain, I have looked for places where these kinds of authority always seem to fall short of their full realization. This approach has helped me to understand how the authority of national policies was never as all-embracing as indicated in many studies I have read. The recognition that the interpretations and cultural practices of Koriak women and men subjected the dominion of state rule to its own displacement has also helped me to describe some cultural spaces that enabled Koriak women and women to pursue their own forms of living.

A starting point for my project was the recognition that cultural identities such as "the Koriak" are not a self-evident site for analysis but are created and maintained through various intersecting fields. For example, the homogeneity-orientation of ethnographic views of culture can be seen in the creation of poems and songs that relate visions of unified traditions. Yet the commentaries and stories of Koriak women and men reminded me not to assume stable and unified communities but to look for places in which tradition is uncertain or contested political terrain. Similarly, administrative models of stability and order have helped to shape official descriptions of bounded culture, but a variety of opinions and meanings forced me to pay attention to various sites of local and gender differentiation. Most of the time, the multiple, diverging perspectives of Koriak women and men took my interpretations beyond the terrain of official stories and explanations as they pointed to the complexity and specificity of cultural agendas. And through the particularistic connections I was able to make with Koriak women and men, I gained a sense about the individual experience of current predicaments and dilemmas, while recognizing overlapping agendas in dealing with them.

In particular through my associations with Koriak women, I learned something about the gendered features of power, history, and the experience of everyday living at Kamchatka's northeastern shore. But instead of looking at gender as an isolated cultural domain that can be studied in disconnection from power, regional inequalities, and community differentiations, I have tried to show the mutual embeddedness of these formations. As women challenged male claims to authority, addressed problems of raising children, and expressed themselves about the hazards of male drinking, they directed attention to the gendered specificities and stakes in both regional and national webs of meaning and power. The analytic space created by this recognition—that regional authority and inequalities are gendered, rather than parallel to gender— has shaped much of the analysis in this book. Yet even as women struggled

□ □ □

with regional-to-national standards of gender authority and differentiation, they insisted on their own agendas and points of view. This multiformity reminded me to ask about the unifying as well as disruptive features of women's perspectives without assuming gender homogeneity. At the same time, women's projects pointed me to the creative possibilities as well as the constraints inherent in their lives.

My attention to the social projects and possibilities for living in this book derived from the committed creativity I saw in Koriak women and men. I have suggested that these forms of creativity hold a promise of social betterment. Yet other scholars may not agree. Many of the problems I have described in this book—national and political inequality, poverty, domestic violence, and chronic alcohol abuse—have not abated but continue to trouble indigenous peoples in the Russian North. To concentrate these various forms of social suffering around a common meaning, scholars and advocates have recently begun to talk about the importance of cultural survival (for example, Golovnev and Osherenko 1999). This discussion self-consciously draws on the atrocious social effects, and experience, of economic, political, and environmental devastation. Because the theme of cultural survival raises key questions about the social futures for indigenous peoples, it is worth some attention here

Ekaterina Chechulina's comment resonates with many of social difficulties that I have described in this book and that commonly but variously engage indigenous groups. Her remark reveals a sense of an uncertain "Koriak future"; it offers no unambiguous insight into local wisdom but relates vulnerability and doubt. It would be easy to place Ekaterina's remark in the context of survival; it would be easy to use the comment as one more piece of evidence for the desperation indigenous peoples experience in the face of economic uncertainty and social demise. Yet such an interpretation, I believe, would mean ignoring an alternative meaning of her comment altogether. Because Ekaterina Chechulina is able to imagine two ways, she can also make room for socially more promising interpretations.

The immediate context in which I heard Ekaterina Chechulina's mentioning two possible ways was one afternoon in August 1994, after a bitter fight had ensured between her and her eldest son. For some time, Ekaterina's son had been trying hard to refrain from alcohol. Sometimes he managed to keep dry for several weeks, but eventually he always lapsed. He explained that he found it hard to turn down his friends' invitations to share one bottle of vodka, or two. He said that he found it hard to stop drinking because,

□ □ □

honestly, that would simply mean he would lose all of his friends. Ekaterina wanted nothing of this. She talked about her unwillingness to put up with her son's excuses any longer. She urged him to "get serious" about his life, she said. And she talked about a dream that I have described in Chapter 4. In this dream, two Russian men had told Ekaterina that her son would begin to heal soon, that is, she elaborated, if he chose to follow a path of personal strength and betterment. That was what it meant, Ekaterina reminded me, to talk about survival.

A comment like Ekaterina's can find itself in the middle of conflicting agendas and interpretations. Scholars and advocates see "survival" as a powerful political site from which social and human rights work can be launched. They care a great deal about the fate of indigenous peoples and often work in close and careful collaboration with activists from the groups they aim to help. Yet in popularizing the cause of the people they aim to help, scholars are frequently forced to highlight those aspects that base the legitimization of their work on images of indigenous peoples as downtrodden and dejected. Yet such an emphasis on survival runs the danger of placing indigenous peoples in a framework of endangerment that leaves only little room for recognizing their own creative efforts to define and manage their own situation (Rethmann 1998).

It is to the context of social possibility and promise, perhaps, that this book speaks most. In acknowledging Koriak women and men's refusal to entirely submit to the current atrocious conditions of living at the northeastern shore, one can appreciate their efforts and creativity. (And together with such appreciation, one might gain a sense of what it takes to stay alive.) But because there existed no social movement in the beginning of the 1990s at the northeastern shore, to a number of readers a number of the efforts I have described in this book may seem irrelevant—in particular, when compared with more organized collective struggles and campaigns. In a world, however, in which people have been confined to the margins of state rule and power, the possibilities for political articulation begin to flourish in the form of strategic refusals and back talk. These are forms of protest and demur that show Koriak women and men as autonomous subjects able to assess their own situation, rather than as victims in need of protection.

Writing this book at a time when indigenous organizing in Russia is well on its way, I wish to emphasize here that Koriak women and men have begun to speak against social disfranchisement and the misuse of power on official levels. As international support from foreign government agencies, human

□ □ □

rights organizations, and solidarity networks from other indigenous groups has been ushered into Russia, new political possibilities have opened up, and indigenous groups have been able to forge new connections for political cooperation and support. In northern Kamchatka, Koriak women and men have staged local protests against the encroachment of foreign corporations in search of natural resources and land, criticized local administrative corruption, and stressed the importance of their own political autonomy. Some of the people I knew best are in the process of rebuilding the destroyed village of Rekinniki at the northwestern shore. Others have chosen to revitalize tradition-oriented, livelihood-sustaining practices such as reindeer herding and hunting. In the course of all these activities, Koriak women and men may well bring about a cultural revival. Yet more important, perhaps, is that for all their own dreams, creativity, and efforts they have set new challenges for thinking and writing about indigenous living in the Russian North, as well as for opening up new horizons for re-imagining and formulating new forms of political and social commitment.

□ □ □

## Preface

1. At the current moment, as Russia vacillates between a shaky democracy and entrenched corruption, issues of democracy and civil society have moved to the fore (Hann and Dunn 1996). As social and political thinkers from Slavoj Žižek (1993) to Katherine Verdery (1996) explain, Western scholars have reasons of their own for revising these concepts. Increasingly, the recognition that culture is an irreducible and constitutive aspect of democracy and the liberal nation-state seems at risk. In addition, indigenous social movements in Russia have begun to argue for differentiated citizenship rights, involving both constitutional and legal recognition of their particular histories and the rights that follow from them.

2. Nerkagi (1996) and Abriutina (1997) give particularly passionate examples of the suffering experienced by indigenous peoples in Siberia and the Russian Far East. I have described the agonizing conditions of living in Koriak settlements by calling attention to the linked formations of violence and healing (Rethmann 1999).

3. In recent philosophical, cultural, and literary studies, scholars have increasingly turned their attention to issues of travel and traveling (for example, Clifford 1997; Kaplan 1996; Deleuze and Guattari 1987). There is also a growing body of anthropological literature in which issues and descriptions of traveling play a pivotal role (for example, Abu-Lughod 1986; Brody 1981; Boddy 1989; Leiris 1981; Tsing 1993).

4. Some of the material in Chapter 6 was published in "A Hopeless Life?: The Story of a Koriak Woman in the Russian Far East," *Anthropologica* 42 (1): 29–42. Part of the material treated in Chapter 7 appeared in different form in an article titled "Skins of Desire: Poetry and Identity in Koriak Women's Gift Exchange," in *American Ethnologist* 27(1) (2000): 52–71; used with permission of the American Authropological Association.

## Chapter 1

1. For an in-depth critique of Soviet social science narratives of economic advancement and progress, see Yuri Slezkine (1994, 323–35) and Bruce Grant (1995).

2. For a critique of Soviet anthropology, see, for example, Nikolai Vakhtin (1994). For critical analysis of Soviet-oriented ethnographic representations, see, for example, Elena Batia'nova (1998).

3. My generalizations here, however, overlook important exceptions. See, for example, Marjorie Mandelstam Balzer (1993), David Anderson (2000), Anna Kerttula (1997), and Gail Fondahl (1998).

4. See also Il'ich S. Gurvich and Kuz'ma G. Kuzakov (1960); Laurel Kendall, Barbara Mathé, and Thomas R. Miller (1997, 13–17).

*Chapter 2*

1. The historian Yuri Slezkine (1994, 316–46) analyzes the development of, and political distinction between, the use of the respective terms *natsii* (nation) and *narodnost'* (people). In an evolutionary scheme in which every cultural group was neatly segregated and placed in accordance with the Marxist-influenced view of the progression of history, on a certain evolutionary scale Koriaks did not fit in the category of "nation." A *natsii* was a clearly definable group with its own language, territory, and cultural membership; a *narodnost'* possessed such criteria as well, yet the crucial element of class antagonism was lacking and needed to be first introduced.

2. The fungi in the region of the village of Khailino seem to have been particularly powerful (Beretti 1929, 25). Il'ich Gurvich and Kuz'ma G. Kuzakov (1960, 100) affirm this; they also report that missionaries used these mushrooms in trade.

3. See, for example, James Forsyth (1992), Dennis Bartels and Alice Bartels (1995), Kerstin Kuoljok (1985), Adele Weiser (1989), Mikhail A. Sergeev (1955), and Yuri Slezkine (1994).

4. The Russian ethnographer Valentina Antropova (1971, 15) records the slogan that announces the administrative seizure of this rule:

> To you, the inhabitants of the Taiga and Tundra, turns the revolutionary committee of Kamchatka. There were bad people in Russia. They killed and robbed many other people; they wanted to become rich that way. We also had such people in Kamchatka. Then the poor people got together, took up weapons, and started driving out the bad people. A terrible war began. The people suffered. There was a shortage of goods—tea, tobacco, flour, guns. The ships stopped bringing goods. Many people lost their lives at that time. But the poor people defeated the bad ones. The people ended the war. All workers gathered and created a strong Soviet republic.
>
> Goods appeared again—flour, tea, very much money, guns. The ships were running often. The Russian people now hold meetings and talk about their needs. They have begun to build schools and hospitals. Now they want to help you, so that you, the nomadic people who live in the mountains and the tundra, can come together often at clan gatherings and speak about what you need. The clan will apply Soviet laws to improve your situation. Elect into the clan soviet the best people, people who will fight for you. The government of the Soviet Republic now consists of the best people chosen by the whole nation. It will be to you like a father to a son, but you too must obey its laws and obligations.
>
> If somebody hurts you—go to your clan soviet and tell them about it. The clan soviet then tells the district soviet, and this soviet will help you, and, if necessary, discuss your concern in the city.
>
> If you do not know what you should do and what you should not do—go to the clan or district soviet, and they will tell you everything. You will find out when you may hunt fur animals and when you must not, so that the animals will multiply. If you need a school or a hospital—go to your soviets and tell them. One of the most extraordinary people, comrade Lenin, has said: let Lamut or Koriak or Chukchi gain knowledge, let them study. The person returns to his people and works with them. He tells them about everything in their language. He will find out what they need, and then tell us. Then we come and help you.
>
> The Soviet Republic fights so that all people will have a good life; and you should understand that only the Republic can guarantee the protection of all workers, people like you, the inhabitants of the harsh North.

□ □ □

5. For detailed descriptions of Koriak celebrations for animals and the land, see, for example, N. Noianov (1932), Valentina Gorbacheva (1985), Il'ia S. Gurvich (1962), Vladimir N. Maliukovich (1974), Elizaveta P. Orlova (1926), N. B. Shnakenburg (1939), and Innokentii St. Vdovin (1971).

## Chapter 3

1. There are also some indications that wolves and not only bears played an important role in the Koriak universe (see Jochelson 1908, 89). Wolves were supposed to enjoy direct kinship relationships with humans. While I sojourned in Tymlat, I heard some women mentioning intimate relationships between wolves and human twins; however, the information was scant and full of gaps.

2. There are other discourses, albeit earlier ones, as well. In a world of moral debauchery—for example, the Chukchi, the Koriaks' neighbors to the north, practiced a loathsome form of women's exchange—Koriaks were a pillar of chastity and sexual propriety (Jochelson 1908, 733). There was also much speculation about the question of whether and how the levirate was a survival of particular forms of group marriage or whether it related to long-standing ritual practices for the protection of the family hearth (ibid., 749).

3. Raven is the founder of the Koriak world.

4. There is an extensive literature on Siberian shamanism. The following titles are important ethnographic examples. They have also been influential in bringing works on Siberian shamanism to the attention of Western audiences. See, for example, Marie A. Czaplicka (1914); Arkadii Anisimov (1958); S. M. Shirokogoroff (1935); and Vilmos Diószegi and Mihaly Hoppál (1978). For more recent works, see Anne-Victoire Charrin (1984); Dmitrii Funk (1995); Olga A. Murashko (1999).

5. There are a few by Waldemar Jochelson (1908) and N. N. Beretti (1929).

## Chapter 4

1. Thus, for example, anthropologists have used positioned storytelling as one kind of discursive practice to tap the power of homogenizing analytical styles (see, for example, Lila Abu-Lughod 1993; Anna Tsing 1993). Robin Ridington (1990) and Jean-Guy Goulet (1998) have shown the relevance of this discussion for northern anthropology. In a somewhat different vein, Julie Cruikshank (1998) has also shown that storytelling is an important means of calling attention to the linked formations of identity and community organizations.

## Chapter 5

1. My generalizations, however, miss important exceptions. See Lydia Black (1972) and Marjorie Mandelstam Balzer (1981).

2. Important volumes on issues of gender in the post-Soviet context include Mary Buckley, ed., *Perestroika and Soviet Women* (1992); Rosalind March, ed., *Women in Russia and Ukraine* (1996); and Mary Buckley, ed., *Post-Soviet Women: From the Baltic to Central Asia* (1997).

3. In anthropological research, the concept of agency has emerged as a key site of concern because it brings previously neglected cultural and human expressions of protest and resistance to our attention, thus restoring respect for those traditionally seen as powerless and downcast. The works of E. P. Thompson (1963) and Raymond Williams (1977) have been particularly influential in theorizing about agency. The writings of Michel Foucault (1978) and, albeit in a different vein, James Scott (1985), Lila Abu-Lughod (1990), Timothy Mitchell (1990), and Sherry Ortner (1995)

□ □ □

have been crucial in formulating ideas about agency in social science scholarship. As Talal Asad reminds us, "The doctrine of action has become essential to our recognition of people's humanity" (cited in Webb Keane 1997, 674). But although anthropologists and other social science scholars are in agreement that the concept is of fundamental significance, the question of what is or is not agency is highly contested. In recent years, two key agendas have emerged that situate agency in different political and discursive practices. On the one hand, scholars of political movements and resistance studies argue that we can speak of agency only if the actions of social actors involve a form of political consciousness or to some extent a form of intentionality. On the other hand, scholars hold that the intentionalities of social actors are not an inherent part of agency but rather emerge in and through people's everyday practices and actions; agency is visible precisely in the meanings these practices produce. Advocates of each approach tend to criticize the other for either de-emphasizing the importance of political transformations or dismissing the forms of agency that arise in subject-producing discursive practices as too ineffective. To wit, agency is perhaps best understood as an ambiguous concept, shaped as much by tension in scholarship as by the varied intellectual commitments out of which such tensions arise.

Questions of agency are especially slippery and frail with regard to gender. As feminist anthropologists have long remarked (for example, Abu-Lughod 1990; Tsing 1993), scholarship on agency often tends to neglect the interests and aspirations of women, along with the social and cultural conflicts out of which such interests arise. The anthropologist Sherry Ortner (1995, 179), for example, argues that in resistance studies the conspicuous absence of female-male relations emerges most problematically when gender conflicts are disavowed as part of the "impulse to sanitize the internal politics of the dominated," thus furthering false political homogeneities. There are, of course, important works that show that cultural gender differentiations shape issues of agency for women and men in different ways. Anna Tsing (1993), for instance, describes how in South Kalimantan, Indonesia, Meratus women and men are positioned unequally in relation to local and national authorities, so that women must work harder than men to craft an agency of their own. In a somewhat different vein, Janice Boddy (1989) shows how the *zar* possession cult of the northern Sudan helps women to articulate concerns by stressing their womanhood through the dramatization of gender conflicts. These works open up important venues for understanding the gendered formations of agency.

4. I must thank Alona Yerofima for reminding me of the importance of this point.

## Chapter 6

1. Videotapes, especially pirated videotapes, arrived in Russia at the beginning of the 1990s. Hollywood-style romances are particularly successful; Ossora's market is flooded with horror films and pornography.

2. The idea of the "Heroine Mother" was also part of this rhetoric, but it was never allowed to take precedence over toughness and bravery as female values.

3. Lidiia and Oleg adopted their son from a young Koriak woman who had had an affair with a Russian man.

4. Issues of birth control are important community concerns at the northeastern shore. In particular, young women and teenage girls suffer from and express themselves about the problems unwanted pregnancies can bring.

5. As new economic institutions and business practices develop in Russia, entrepreneurship has become an attractive economic means for women who find it difficult to obtain wage labor or to set up their own companies. If they succeed in becoming entrepreneurs, they are usually limited to the service sector or to textile and fashion businesses.

□ □ □

6. Except—perhaps and only sometimes—for bears. But that is a different story.

7. There is a rich literature on this issue. For issues of domesticity and the "double burden" in Russia, see, for example, Helena Goscilo (1993); Vitalina Koval (1995); Lynne Attwood, (1996); and Rebecca Kay (1997). For historical analyses, see Barbara Clements (1994) and Vera Dunham (1976).

8. A *dom kul'tury* (house of culture) is a place in which people conducted political meetings and engaged in social activities. The house of culture was a widespread institution in Soviet Russia; indeed, every village I visited on the northeastern shore had one.

9. Alla Pugacheva rose to stardom in the Soviet Union in the 1970s. In the Brezhnev era, she was the single female cult figure, and her recording sales were among the largest. Scorned by the party *nomenklatura* and *intelligentsia* alike, she was and is tremendously popular with, as Zoia said, "ordinary folks."

10. This exhaustion has been described as an essential part of Soviet and post-Soviet life. See, for example, Nancy Ries's (1997) wonderful descriptions of the tiredness that accompanies life in the era of perestroika.

## Chapter 7

1. Koriak women and men consider the fleshy parts of a reindeer head (in particular, brain, eyes, tongue, and lips) as particularly delectable.

2. The collective farm in Tymlat dissolved in March 1992. It was split into two private reindeer-herding enterprises, "Rekinniki" and "Shamanka," both of which continue to operate to this day.

3. Larissa and Volodia were a couple for two years. They separated because Larissa, whose mother had been a powerful healer, wanted to undertake an apprenticeship as a shaman. Volodia disapproved of her decision; the relationship began to crumble. In the end, Larissa left Tymlat. Volodia is now married to another woman.

4. By evoking the term *poetry* in this context, I am inspired by Michael Herzfeld's (1985) work on the construction and performance of masculinity in Glendiot, a mountain village in Crete. His use of poetry differs from its use in literary theory in that he pays attention to the sphere of social relationships. In describing customary male Glendiot practices such as card playing, dance, and—although less frequently—sheep theft, he elucidates the poetry of everyday life by highlighting the performative qualities of habitual actions. What counts, as Herzfeld (1985, 16) remarks, is "effective *movement:* a sense of shifting the ordinary and everyday into a context where the very change of context itself serves to invest it with sudden significance."

5. In a critical reading of Mauss's notion of the gift, Derrida (1992) seeks to challenge the economy of reciprocity, which, as he says, shapes our understanding of the gift. In *Given Time,* he criticizes the circular economy of gift exchange as violent because it enslaves the receiver as soon as she or he accepts the gift. According to Derrida, the gift establishes an oxymoron or paradox: It is the recognition of the gift that annuls it at the very moment that it is recognized as such. Hence gifts are possible as gifts only when they are not recognized as such by either donor or recipient; it is their self-referential character that cancels their significance as gifts. Following from this train of thought, one might argue that Derrida understands the gift as "autoerotic": Through the circulation of gifts, subjects demand the return of their own identity by reappropriating it as a property of the object. Thus, the exchange of gifts mirrors qualities of her- or himself to the giver.

□ □ □

# bibliography | ▫▫▫

Abriutina, Larissa.
    1997  "Narody Severa: Problemy, analiz prichin i perspektivy ikh preodoleniia" (Peoples of the North: Problems, analyses of their causes, and perspectives toward a solution). *Zhivaia Arktika* 2–4 (6–8): 16–23.

Abu-Lughod, Lila.
    1995  "Movie Stars and Islamic Moralism in Egypt." *Social Text* 42: 53–69.
    1993  *Writing Women's Worlds: Bedouin Stories.* Berkeley and Los Angeles: University of California Press.
    1990  "The Romance of Resistance: Tracing Transformations of Power Through Bedouin Women." *American Ethnologist* 17 (1): 41–55.
    1986  *Veiled Sentiments: Honor and Poetry in a Bedouin Society.* Berkeley and Los Angeles: University of California Press.

Allen, Paula Gunn.
    1998  "Special Problems in Teaching Leslie Marmon Silko's *Ceremony.*" In *Natives and Academics: Researching and Writing About American Indians,* ed. Devon A. Mihesuah, 55–65. Lincoln: University of Nebraska Press.

Anderson, Benedict.
    1983  *Imagined Communities: Reflections on the Origin and Spread of Nationalism.* London: Verso.

Anderson, David.
    2000  *Identity and Ecology in Arctic Siberia.* Oxford: Oxford University Press.

Anisimov, Arkadii F.
    1958  *Religiia Evenkov v istoriko-geneticheskom izuchenii i problemy proizkhozhdeniia pervobytnykh verovanii* (The religion of the Evenks as a historical-genetic study and problems of the origins of primitive beliefs). Moscow and Leningrad: Akademiia Nauk.

Antropova, Valentina V.
    1971  *Kul'tura i byt Koriakov* (Culture and life among the Koriaks). Leningrad: Nauka.

Aretxaga, Begona.
1997    *Shattering Silence: Women, Nationalism, and Political Subjectivity in Northern Ireland.* Princeton: Princeton University Press.


Arutiunov, S. A.
1988    "Koryak and Itelmen: Dwellers of the Smoking Coast." In *Crossroads of Continents: Cultures of Siberia and Alaska,* ed. William W. Fitzhugh and Aron Crowell, 31–35. Washington, D.C.: Smithsonian Institution Press.


Attwood, Lynne.
1996    "The Post-Soviet Woman in the Move to the Market: A Return to Domesticity and Dependence?" In *Women in Russia and Ukraine,* ed. Rosalind Marsh, 255–69. Cambridge: Cambridge University Press.


Balzer, Marjorie Mandelstam.
1999    *The Tenacity of Ethnicity: A Siberian Saga in Global Perspective.* Princeton: Princeton University Press.
1993    "Two Urban Shamans: Unmasking Leadership in Fin-de-Soviet Siberia." In *Perilous States: Conversations on Culture, Politics, and Nation,* ed. George Marcus, 131–64. Chicago: University of Chicago Press.
1981    "Rituals of Gender Identity: Markers of Siberian Khanty Ethnicity, Status, and Belief." *American Anthropologist* 83 (4): 850–67.


Bartels, Dennis A., and Alice L. Bartels.
1995    *When the North Was Red: Aboriginal Education in Soviet Siberia.* Montreal: McGill-Queen's University Press.


Bat'ianova, Elena Petrovna.
1998    "Russkie i russkoe glazami Koriakov" (Russians and Russian-ness through the eyes of Koriaks). In *Etnicheskie sterotipy v meniaiushchemsia mire,* ed. Elena P. Bat'ianova and Aleksandr N. Kalabanov, 41–51. Moscow: Akademiia Nauk.
1995    "Koriaki rasskazyvaiut o sebe (po materialam polevykh issledovanii na Kamchatke v 1995 gody)" (Koriaks talk about themselves [according to the data of the field expedition in Kamchatka in 1995]). In *Sotsial'no-ekonomicheskoe i kul'turnoe razvitie narodov Severa i Sibiri: Traditsii i sovremennost',* ed. Zoia P. Sokolva, 203–22. Moscow: Akademiia Nauk.
1991    "Koriakskii avtonomnyi okrug" (Koriak autonomous district). In *Narody Sovetskogo Severa (1960–1980 gg.),* ed. Il'ia S. Gurvich and Zoia P. Sokolova, 230–47. Moscow: Nauka.


Battaglia, Debbora.
1992    "The Body in the Gift: Memory and Forgetting in Sabarl Mortuary Exchange." *American Ethnologist* 19 (1): 3–18.

□ □ □

Bauerman, K.
1934 "Sledy totemicheskogo rodovogo ustroistva u parenskikh Koriakov" (Traces of totem-clan organization among the Parenski Koriaks). *Sovetskii Sever* 2: 70–78.

Behar, Ruth.
1993 *Translated Woman: Crossing the Border with Esperanza's Story.* Boston: Beacon Press.

Bell, Diane.
1983 *Daughters of the Dreaming.* Melbourne, Australia: McPhee Gribble.

Bentz, Marilyn.
1997 "Beyond Ethics: Science, Friendship, and Privacy." In *Indians and Anthropologists: Vine Deloria Jr. and the Critique of Anthropology,* ed. Thomas Biolsi and Larry. Z. Zimmerman, 120–33. Tucson: University of Arizona Press.

Bercovitch, Eytan.
1994 "The Agent in the Gift: Hidden Exchange in New Guinea." *Cultural Anthropology* 9 (4): 498–536.

Beretti, N. N.
1929 *Na Krainem Severo-Vostoke* (In the extreme North). Vladivostok: Izdanie Vladivostokskogo Otdela Gosudarstvennogo Russkogo Geograficheskogo Obshchestva.

Bergman, Sten.
1927 *Through Kamchatka by Dog-Sled and Skis: A Vivid Description of Adventurous Journeys Amongst the Interesting and Almost Unknown Peoples of the Most Inaccessible Parts of This Remote Siberian Peninsula.* London: Seeley, Service & Co. Limited.

Bilibin, N. N.
1934 *Obmen u Koriakov* (Exchange among the Koriaks). Leningrad: Izdatel'stvo Instituta Narodov Severa.
1933a *Klassovoe rassloenie kochevykh Koriakov* (Class stratification among the Koriaks). Khabarovsk: Dal'giz.
1933b "Batratskii trud v kochevom khozaistve Koriakov" (Farm work in the nomadic economy of the Koriaks). *Sovetskii Sever* 1: 36–46.
1933c "Sredi Koriakov" (Among the Koriaks). *Sovetskii Sever* 3: 91–97.
1933d "Zhenshchina u Koriakov" ([The position of] the woman among the Koriaks). *Sovetskii Sever* 4: 92–96.

Black, Lydia.
1972 "Relative Status of Wife Givers and Wife Takers in Gilyak Society." *American Anthropologist* 74 (5): 1244–48.

Bloch, Alexia.
1996 "Between Socialism and the Market: Indigenous Siberian Evenki Grapple with Change." Ph.D. diss., University of Pittsburgh.

□ □ □

Boddy, Janice.
  1989  *Wombs and Alien Spirits.* Madison: University of Wisconsin Press.

Bogoras [Bogoraz (-Tan)], Waldemar [Vladimir] Germanovich.
  1932  "Religiia, kak tormoz sootsstroitel'stva sredi malykh narodnostei Severa" (Religion as a brake among the small peoples of the North). *Sovetskii Sever* 1–2: 142–57.
  1930  "Prezhde na Severe" (Previously in the North). *Sovetskii Sever* 1: 59–75.
  1917  *Koriak Texts,* ed. Franz Boas. Publication of the American Ethnological Society v. New York-Leiden: E. J. Brill & G .E. Stechert.

Bogoyavlensky [Bogoiavlenskii], Dmitrii D.
  1997  "Native Peoples of Kamchatka: Epidemiological Transition and Violent Death." *Arctic Anthropology* 34 (1): 57–67.

Bonch-Osmolovskii, Gleb Anatolevich.
  1925  "Kamchatsko-Chukotskii krai" (In the far north of Kamchatka and Chukotka). *Severnaia Aziia* 1–2: 77–99.

Bridger, Sue, Rebecca Kay, and Kathryn Pinnick.
  1996  *No More Heroines? Russia, Women, and the Market.* New York: Routledge.

Brody, Hugh.
  1981  *Maps and Dreams: Indians and the British Columbia Frontier.* Vancouver: Douglas & McIntyre.

Buckley, Mary, ed.
  1997  *Post-Soviet Women: From the Baltic to Central Asia.* Cambridge: Cambridge University Press.
  1992  *Perestroika and Soviet Women.* Cambridge: Cambridge University Press.

Burch, Ernest S., Jr.
  1988  "War and Trade." In *Crossroads of Continents: Cultures of Siberia and Alaska,* ed. William W. Fitzhugh and Aron Crowell, 227–41. Washington, D.C.: Smithsonian Institution Press.

Butler, Judith.
  1995  "Contingent Foundations: Feminism and the Question of Postmodernism." In *Feminist Contentions: A Philosophical Exchange,* ed. Seyla Benhabib, Judith Butler, Drucilla Cornell, and Nancy Fraser, 35–57. New York: Routledge.
  1989  *Gender Trouble: Feminism and the Subversion of Identity.* New York: Routledge.

Charrin, Anne-Victoire.
  1984  "The Discovery of the Koryaks and Their Perceptions of the World." *Arctic* 37 (4): 441–45.

□ □ □

Chaussonnet, Valerie.
    1988  "Needles and Animals: Women's Magic." In *Crossroads of Continents: Cultures of Siberia and Alaska,* ed. William W. Fitzhugh and Aron Crowell, 209–27. Washington, D.C.: Smithsonian Institution Press.

Chichlo, Boris.
    1985  "The Cult of the Bear and Soviet Ideology in Siberia." *Religion in Communist Lands* 13 (2): 166–81.

Clark, Gracia.
    1994  *Onions Are My Husband: Survival and Accumulation by West African Market Women.* Chicago: University of Chicago Press.

Clark, Katerina.
    1981  *The Soviet Novel: History as Ritual.* Chicago: University of Chicago Press.

Clements, Barbara Evans.
    1994  *Daughters of the Revolution: A History of Women in the U.S.S.R.* Arlington Heights, Ill.: Harlan Davidson, Inc.
    1985  "The Birth of the New Soviet Woman." In *Bolshevik Culture: Experiment and Order in the Russian Revolution,* ed. Abbot Gleason, Peter Kenez, and Richard Stites, 220–38. Bloomington: Indiana University Press.

Clifford, James.
    1997  *Routes: Travel and Translation in the Late Twentieth Century.* Cambridge, Mass.: Harvard University Press.
    1988  *The Predicament of Culture: Twentieth-Century Ethnography, Literature, and Art.* Cambridge, Mass.: Harvard University Press.

Cole, Sally.
    1991  *Women of the Praia: Work and Lives in a Portuguese Coastal Community.* Princeton: Princeton University Press.

Comaroff, John, and Jean Comaroff.
    1992  *Ethnography and the Historical Imagination.* Boulder: Westview Press.

Cook-Lynn, Elizabeth.
    1998  "American Indian Intellectualism and the New Indian Story." In *Natives and Academics: Researching and Writing about American Indians,* ed. Devon A. Mihesuah, 111–39. Lincoln: University of Nebraska Press.

Cruikshank, Julie.
    1998  *The Social Life of Stories: Narrative and Knowledge in the Yukon Territory.* Lincoln: University of Nebraska Press.

□ □ □

Cruikshank, Julie, with Angela Sidney, Kitty Smith, and Annie Ned.
  1990   *Life Lived like a Story: Life Stories of Three Yukon Native Elders.* Lincoln: University of Nebraska Press.

Csordas, Thomas.
  1995   *The Sacred Self: A Cultural Phenomenology of Charismatic Healing.* Berkeley and Los Angeles: University of California Press.

Czaplicka, Marie A.
  1914   *Aboriginal Siberia: A Study in Social Anthropology.* Oxford: Clarendon Press.

Darnell, Regna.
  1977   "Hallowell's Bear Ceremonialism and the Emergence of Boasian Anthropology." *Ethos* 5 (4): 13–30.

DeLauretis, Teresa.
  1987   "The Technology of Gender." In *Technologies of Gender: Essays on Theory, Film, and Fiction,* 1–30. Bloomington and Indianapolis: Indiana University Press.

Deleuze, Gilles, and Félix Guattari.
  1987   *A Thousand Plateaus: Capitalism and Schizophrenia,* trans. Brian Massumi. Minneapolis: University of Minnesota Press.

Derrida, Jacques.
  1992   *Given Time, 1: Counterfeit Money,* trans. Peggy Kamuf. Chicago: University of Chicago Press.

Diószegi, Vilmos, and Mihály Hoppál, eds.
  1978   *Shamanism in Siberia.* Budapest: Akadémiai Kiadó.

Dit[t]mar, Karl v.
  1855   *O Koriakakh i ves'ma blizkikh k nim po proiskhozhdeniia Chukchakh* (About the Koriaks and the Chukchi closely related to them). Saint Petersburg: Vestnik Imperatorskogo Russkogo Geograficheskogo Obshchestva.

Dunham, Vera.
  1976   *In Stalin's Time: Middle Class Values in Soviet Fiction.* Cambridge: Cambridge University Press.

Elias, Norbert.
  1982   *The Civilizing Process, 1: The History of Manners,* trans. E. Jephcott. New York: Pantheon. 1st German ed. 1939.

Fabian, Johannes.
  1983   *Time and the Other: How Anthropology Makes Its Object.* New York: Columbia University Press.

□ □ □

Fernandez, James W.
    1986   *Persuasions and Performances: The Play of Tropes in Culture.* Bloomington: Indiana University Press.

Flax, Jane.
    1990   *Thinking Fragments: Psychoanalysis, Feminism, and Postmodernism in the Contemporary West.* Berkeley and Los Angeles: University of California Press.

Fondahl, Gail.
    1998   *Gaining Ground? Evenkis, Land, and Reform in Southeastern Siberia.* Boston: Allyn & Bacon.

Forsyth, James.
    1992   *A History of the Peoples of Siberia: Russia's North Asian Colony, 1581–1990.* Cambridge: Cambridge University Press.

Foucault, Michel.
    1978   *The History of Sexuality,* 1: *An Introduction,* trans. Robert Hurley. New York: Pantheon Books.

Freidin, Gregory.
    1994   "From Under The Rubble: Meaning, National Identity, and Social Justice in Russia After Communism's Collapse." *Yale Journal of Criticism* 7 (1): 229–38.

Friedman, Jonathan.
    1992   "The Past in the Future: History and the Politics of Identity." *American Anthropologist* 94: 837–59.

Funk, Dmitrii A., ed.
    1995   *Shamanizm i rannie religioznye predstavleniia* (Shamanism and primordial religious understandings). Moscow: Akademiia Nauk.

Gapanovich, N. N.
    1925   "Kamchatskoe tyzemnoe naselenie, kak kul'turno-ekonomicheskii faktor" (The native population of Kamchatka as a cultural-economic factor). *Severnaia Aziia* (5–6): 40–52.

Ginzburg, Carlo.
    1983   *The Night Battles: Witchcraft and Agrarian Cults in the Sixteenth and Seventeenth Centuries,* trans. John and Anne Tedeschi. Baltimore: Johns Hopkins University Press.

Golovnev, Andrei Vladimirovich, and Gail Osherenko.
    1999   *Siberian Survival: The Nenets and Their Story.* Ithaca: Cornell University Press.

□ □ □

Gorbacheva, Valentina V.
1985 "Sovremennyi byt Achaivaimskikh olennykh Koriakov" (Contemporary life among the Achaivaiam Reindeer Koriaks). In *Istoricheskaia Etnografiia: Problemy arkheologii i etnografii*, ed. K. V. Chistov, 3:12–17. Leningrad: Leningradskii Universitet.

Goscilo, Helena.
1993 "*Domostroika* or *Perestroika?* The Construction of Womanhood in Soviet Culture Under Glasnost." In *Late Soviet Culture: From Perestroika to Novostroika*, ed. Thomas Lahusen and Gene Kuperman, 233–57. Durham: Duke University Press.

Goulet, Jean-Guy.
1998 *Ways of Knowing: Experience, Knowledge, and Power Among the Dene Tha*. Lincoln: University of Nebraska Press.

Grant, Bruce.
1995 *In the Soviet House of Culture: A Century of Perestroika*. Princeton: Princeton University Press.

Grosz, Elizabeth A.
1994 *Volatile Bodies: Toward a Corporeal Feminism*. Bloomington: Indiana University Press.

Gurvich, Il'ich Samoilovich.
1962 "Koriakskie promyslovye prazdniki" (Koriak hunting celebrations). In *Trudy Instituta Etnografii Imeni N. N. Miklukho-Maklaia*, ed. B. O. Dolgikh, 78:238–58. Moscow: Akademiia Nauk.
1957 "Etnograficheskaia poezdka v Koriakskii natsional'nyi okrug" (An ethnographic journey through the Koriak national district). *Sovetskaia Etnografiia* 6: 43–58.

Gurvich, Il'ich Samoilovich, and Kuz'ma Grigorevich Kuzakov.
1960 *Koriakskii natsional'nyi okrug* (The Koriak national district). Moscow: Akademiia Nauk.

Hallowell, Irving.
1926 "Bear Ceremonialism in the Northern Hemisphere." *American Anthropologist*.

Handler, Richard.
1988 *Nationalism and the Politics of Culture in Quebec*. Madison: University of Wisconsin Press.

Hann, Chris, and Elizabeth Dunn, eds.
1996 *Civil Society: Challenging Western Models*. London: Routledge.

Haraway, Donna.
1991 *Simians, Cyborgs, and Women: The Reinvention of Nature*. New York: Routledge.

□ □ □

Herzfeld, Michael.
  1985  *The Poetics of Manhood: Contest and Identity in a Cretan Mountain Village.* Princeton: Princeton University Press.

Hobsbawm, Eric, and Terence Ranger, eds.
  1983  *The Invention of Tradition.* Cambridge: Cambridge University Press.

hooks, bell.
  1990  *Yearning: Race, Gender, and Cultural Politics.* Boston: South End Press.

Humphrey, Caroline.
  1983  *Karl Marx Collective: Economy, Society, and Religion in a Siberian Collective Farm.* Cambridge: Cambridge University Press.

Jochelson [Iokhel'son], Waldemar [Vladmir] Il'ich.
  1908  *The Koryak.* Jesup North Pacific Expedition, Memoirs of the American Museum of Natural History New York, vol. 6., ed. Franz Boas. Leiden: E. J. Brill & G. E. Stechert.

John, Mary E.
  1996  *Discrepant Dislocations: Feminism, Theory, and Postcolonial Histories.* Berkeley and Los Angeles: University of California Press.

Kantorovich, V. I.
  1931  *Po sovetskoi Kamchatke* (About Soviet Kamchatka). Moscow: Molodaia Gvardiia.

Kaplan, Caren.
  1996  *Questions of Travel: Postmodern Discourses of Displacement.* Durham: Duke University Press.

Kay, Rebecca.
  1997  "Images of an Ideal Woman: Perceptions of Russian Womanhood Through the Media, Education, and Women's Own Eyes." In *Post-Soviet Women from the Baltic to Central Asia*, ed. Mary Buckley, 77–89. Cambridge: Cambridge University Press.

Keane, Webb.
  1997  "From Fetishism to Sincerity: On Agency, the Speaking Subject, and Their Historicity in the Context of Religious Conversion." *Comparative Studies in Society and History* 39 (4): 674–93.

Keesing, Roger.
  1989  "Creating the Past: Custom and Identity in the Contemporary Pacific." *Contemporary Pacific* 1: 19–42.

□ □ □

Kendall, Laurel; Barbara Mathé, and Thomas Ross Miller.

   1997   *Drawing Shadows to Stone: The Photography of the Jesup North Pacific Expedition, 1897–1902.* New York: American Museum of History, in association with University of Washington Press, Seattle.

Kennan, George.

   1871   *Tent Life in Siberia, and Adventures Among the Koryaks and Other Tribes in Kamchatka and Northern Asia.* London: Low and Marston.

Kerttula, Anna M.

   1997   "Antler on the Sea: Creating and Maintaining Cultural Group Boundaries Among the Chukchi, Yupik, and Newcomers of Sireniki." *Arctic Anthropology* 34 (1): 212–26.

Klokov, Konstantin B.

   1996   *Nekotorye problemy razvitiia khoziaistva korennykh naradov Severa* (Some problems in the economic development of northern indigenous peoples). Saint Petersburg: Nauchno-Issledovatel'skii Institut Geografii St.-Petersburgskogo Gosudarstvennogo Universiteta.

Koester, David.

   1997   "Childhood in National Consciousness and National Consciousness in Childhood." *Childhood* 4 (1): 125–42.

Kopytoff, Igor.

   1986   "The Cultural Biography of Things: Commoditization as Process." In *The Social Life of Things: Commodities in Cultural Perspective,* ed. Arjun Appadurai, 64–91. Cambridge: Cambridge University Press.

Korobova, E. S., ed.

   1991   *Narodov Malykh ne Byvaet* (Small peoples do not exist). Moscow: Molodaia Gvardiia.

Kosygin, F. N.

   1990   *Doch' Severa: Biobibliograficheskii spisok (Tat'iana Petrovna Lukashkina)* (Daughter of the north: A bibliographical list, Tat'iana Petrovna Lukashkina). Palana.

Koval, Vitalina V.

   1995   "Women and Work in Russia." In *Women in Contemporary Russia,* ed. Vitalina V. Koval, 17–33. Oxford: Berghahn Books.

Krasheninnikov, Stepan Petrovich.

   1972   [1755]*Explorations of Kamchatka: Report of a Journey Made to Explore Eastern Siberia in 1735–1741, by Order of the Russian Imperial Government,* trans. and intro. E. A. P. Crownhart-Vaughan. Portland: Oregon Historical Society.

□ □ □

Kreinovich, E. A.
  1969  "Medvezhii prazdnik u Ketov" (The bear celebration among the Kets). In *Ketskii sbornik: Mifologiia, etnografiia, teksty,* ed. V. Vs. Ivanov, V. N. Toporov, and B. A. Uspenski. Moscow: Nauka.

Krupnik, Igor.
  1998  "Jesup Genealogy: Intellectual Partnership and Russian-American Cooperation in Arctic/North Pacific Anthropology Part I: From the Jesup Expedition to the Cold War, 1897–1948." *Arctic Anthropology* 35 (2): 199–227.

Kuoljok, Kerstin Eidlitz.
  1985  *The Revolution in the North: Soviet Ethnography and Nationality Policy,* trans. T. M. Gray and N. Tomkinson. Stockholm: Almquist and Wiksell International.

Kuz'mina, E.
  1932  "Koriakskaia zhenshchina" (The Koriak woman). *Prosveshchenie Natsional'nostei* 7: 93–99.

"L."
  1990  *60 Let Koriakskomu Avtonomnomu Okrugu* (Sixty years of the Koriak autonomous region).

Leacock, Eleanor.
  1981  *Myths of Male Dominance.* New York: Monthly Review Press.

Leiris, Michel.
  1981  *L'Afrique fantome.* Paris: Gallimard.

Lemon, Alaina.
  1996  "'Your Eyes Are Green like Dollars': Counterfeit Cash, National Substance, and Currency Apartheid in 1990s Russia." *Cultural Anthropology* 13 (1): 22–56.

Lévi-Strauss, Claude.
  1966  *The Savage Mind.* London: Weidenfeld & Nicholson.

Levin, M.
  1936  "Nymylany (Koriaki)" (Nymylans, Koriaks). *Sovetskoe Kraevedenie* 6: 45–53.

Linnekin, Jocelyn.
  1991  "Cultural Invention and the Dilemma of Authenticity." *American Anthropologist* 93: 446–49.

L'vov, V.
  1932  "Zhenshchina Severa" (Women of the North). *Prosveshchenie Natsional'nostei* 1: 39–44.

Maliukovich, Vladimir N.
  1974  "Letnaia chast'ia: Koriakskie prazdniki." *Kraevedecheskie Zapiski* 5.

Mani, Lata.
  1987  "Contentious Traditions: The Debate on SATI in Colonial India." *Cultural Critique* 7: 119–56.

Marsh, Rosalind, ed.
  1996  *Women in Russia and Ukraine.* Cambridge: Cambridge University Press.

Mauss, Marcel.
  1967  *The Gift: Forms and Functions of Exchange in Archaic Societies,* trans. I. Cunnison. New York: W. W. Norton.

McClellan, Catharine.
  1970  *The Girl Who Married the Bear.* Ottawa: National Museum of Man, Publications in Ethnology no. 2.

McClintock, Anne.
  1995  *Imperial Leather: Race, Gender, and Sexuality in the Colonial Contest.* New York: Routledge.

Mitchell, Timothy.
  1990  "Everyday Metaphors of Power." *Theory and Society* 19: 545–77.

Mohanty, Chandra Talpade.
  1984  "Under Western Eyes: Feminist Scholarship and Colonial Discourses." *Boundary 2* 12 (3): 333–58.

Morris, Rosalind C.
  1995  "All Made Up: Performance Theory and the New Anthropology of Sex and Gender." *Annual Review* 24: 256–92.

Munn, Nancy.
  1986  *The Fame of Gawa: A Study of Value Transformation in a Massim (Papua New Guinea) Society.* Cambridge: Cambridge University Press.

Murashko, Ol'ga A.
  1999  "Shamanstvo i traditsionnoe mirovozrenie Itel'menov" (Shamanism and the traditional worldview of the Itel'men). In *Izbravskie dukhov: Traditsionnoe shamanstvo i neoshamanism,* ed. K. I. Kharitonova, 160–83. Moscow: Akademiia Nauk.

Murashko, Ol'ga A., Alexander I. Pika, and Dimitrii Bogoiavlenskii.
  1993  *Sotsial'no-demograficheskie transformatsii na Kamchatke* (Social-demographic transformations in Kamchatka), vol. 2, no. 1. Moscow: Institut Narodnokhoziaistvennogo Prognozirovaniia.

□ □ □

Nerkagi, Anna.
   1996  "About That for Which There Is No Name." In *Anxious North: Indigenous Peoples in Soviet and Post Soviet Russia,* comp. and ed. Alexander Pika, Jens Dahl, and Inge Larsen, 273–91. Copenhagen: IWGIA Document no. 82.

Noianov, N.
   1932  "Koriakskii prazdnik" (A Koriak celebration). *Taiga i Tundra* 4(1): 241–53.

Orlova, Elizaveta Porfirev'na.
   1927  "Koriaki poluostrova Kamchatki" (Koriaks of the Kamchatka peninsula). *Severnaia Aziia* 3: 83–114.

Ortner, Sherry.
   1995  "Resistance and the Problem of Ethnographic Refusal." *Comparative Studies in Society and History* 37(1): 173–93.

Pandolfo, Stefania.
   1997  *The Impasse of Angels: Scenes from a Moroccan Space of Memory.* Chicago: University of Chicago Press.

Pesmen, Dale.
   1995  "Standing Bottles, Washing Deals, and Drinking 'for the Soul' in a Siberian City." *Anthropology of East Europe Review* 13(2): 65–75.

Pika, Alexander [Aleksandr].
   1993  "The Spatial-Temporal Dynamic of Violent Death Among the Native Peoples of Northern Russia." *Arctic Anthropology* 30(2): 61–76.

Pika, Alexander [Aleksandr] I., and Boris B. Prokhorov, eds.
   1994  *Neotraditionalism na Rossiskom Severe* (trans. Bruce Grant et al., as *Neotraditionalism in the Russian North: Indigenous People and the Legacy of Perestroika* [Seattle-London: University of Washington Press and Canadian Circumpolar Institute, Edmonton, 1999]). Moscow: Institut Narodnokhoziaistvennogo Prognozirovaniia.

Pika, Alexander; Jens Dahl, and Inge Larsen, eds.
   1995  *Anxious North: Indigenous Peoples in Soviet and Post-Soviet Russia.* Copenhagen: IWGIA Document no. 82.

Pilkington, Hilary, ed.
   1996  *Gender, Generation, and Identity in Contemporary Russia.* New York: Routledge.

Reiter, Rayna Rapp.
   1975  *Toward an Anthropology of Women.* New York: Monthly Review Press.

Rethmann, Petra.

  1999   "Deadly Dis-Ease: Medical Knowledge and Healing in Northern Kamchatka, Russia." *Culture, Medicine, and Psychiatry* 23: 197–217.

  1998   "In the Time of the Lizard: On Indigenous Problems, Post-Colonialism, and Democracy." *Anthropology of East Europe Review* 16 (2): 91–95.

  1997   " 'Chto Delat'? Ethnography in the Post-Soviet Cultural Context." *American Anthropologist* 99 (4): 770–74.

Ridington, Robin.

  1990   *Little Bit Know Something: Stories in a Language of Anthropology.* Iowa City: University of Iowa Press.

Ridington, Robin, and Dennis Hastings.

  1997   *Blessing for a Long Time: The Sacred Pole of the Omaha Tribe.* Lincoln: University of Nebraska Press.

Ries, Nancy.

  1997   *Russian Talk: Culture and Conversation During Perestroika.* Ithaca: Cornell University Press.

Rosaldo, Renato.

  1989   *Culture and Truth: The Remaking of Social Analysis.* Boston: Beacon Press.

Roudakova, Natalia, and Deborah S. Ballard-Reisch.

  1999   "Femininity and the Double Burden: Dialogues on the Socialization of Russian Daughters into Womanhood." *Anthropology of East Europe Review* 17(1): 21–34.

Schindler, Deborah L.

  1991   "Theory, Policy, and the Narody Severa." *Anthropological Quarterly* 64 (2): 68–79.

Schweitzer, Peter.

  1989   "Spouse Exchange in Northeastern Siberia: On Kinship and Sexual Relations and Their Transformations." In *Kinship, Social Change, and Evolution, Proceedings of a Symposium Held in Honor of Walter Dostal,* ed. André Gingrich, Siegfried Haas, Sylvia Haas, and Gabriele Paleczek. *Vienna Contributions to Ethnology and Anthropology* 5: 17–38.

Scott, James.

  1986   *Weapons of the Weak: Everyday Forms of Peasant Resistance.* New Haven: Yale University Press.

Scott, Joan Wallach.

  1992   "Experience." In *Feminists Theorize the Political,* ed. Judith Butler and Joan Scott, 22–40. New York: Routledge.

  1988   *Gender and the Politics of History.* New York: Columbia University Press.

□ □ □

Seremetakis, Nadia C.
  1994  "The Memory of the Senses, Part I: Marks of the Transitory." In *The Senses Still: Perception and Memory as Material Culture in Modernity,* ed. Nadia C. Seremetakis, 1–19. Chicago: University of Chicago Press.

Sergeev, Mikhail Alekseevich.
  1955  *Nekapitalisticheskii put razvitiia malykh narodov Severa* (The noncapitalist road of the small peoples of the North). Moscow-Leningrad: Akademiia Nauk.
  1933  *Koriakskii natsional'nyi okrug* (Koriak autonomous district). Leningrad: Institut Narodov Severa.

Shirokogoroff, S. M.
  1935  *Psychomental Complex of the Tungus.* New York: AMS Press.

Shnakenburg, N. B.
  1939  "Nymylany-Kereki" (Kereki-Nymylans). *Sovetskii Sever* 3: 85–104.

Silverblatt, Irene.
  1987  *Moon, Sun, and Witches: Gender Ideologies and Class in Inca and Colonial Peru.* Princeton: Princeton University Press.

Slepzova, M.
  1912  *Ostanovka (iz zhizni Koriakov).* Saint Petersburg: M. N. Slepzova.

Slezkine, Yuri.
  1994  *Arctic Mirrors: Russia and the Small Peoples of the North.* Ithaca and London: Cornell University Press.

Sliunin, Nikolai Vasil'evich.
  1900  *Okhotsko-Kamchatskii krai* (Okhotsk-Kamchatka region), vols. 1 and 2. Saint Petersburg: Ministerstvo Finansov.

Spivak, Gayatri Chakravorty.
  1991  *In Other Worlds: Essays in Cultural Politics.* New York: Routledge.
  1985  "Can the Subaltern Speak?" In *Marxism and the Interpretation of Literature,* ed. Cary Nelson and Lawrence Grossberg, 271–313. Urbana and Chicago: University of Illinois Press.

Stebnitskii, Sergei Nikolaevich.
  1938  "Nymylany-Aliutortsy" (Aliutor Nymylans). *Sovetskaia Etnografiia* 1: 129–44.
  1933  "Koriakskie deti" (Koriak children). *Sovetskii Sever* 4: 39–47.
  1932  *Nasha kniga: Perevod iz Koriakskogo iazyka* (Our book: Translation from the Koriak language). Moscow and Leningrad.
  1931  *U Koriakov na Kamchatke* (Among the Koriaks in Kamchatka). Moscow: Izdatel'stvo Krest'ianskaia Gazeta.

□ □ □

Steller, Georg Wilhelm.
    1974  [1774]*Beschreibung von dem Lande Kamchatka.* Stuttgart: F. A. Brockhaus Geschichte GmbH, Abteilung Antiquarium.

Stoler, Ann.
    1985  *Capitalism and Confrontation in Sumatra's Plantation Belt: 1870–1979.* New Haven: Yale University Press.

Strathern, Marilyn.
    1992  "Qualified Value: The Perspective of Gift Exchange." In *Barter, Exchange, and Value: An Anthropological Perspective,* ed. Caroline Humphrey and Stephen Hugh Jones, 169–91. Cambridge: Cambridge University Press.
    1988  *The Gender of the Gift: Problems with Women and Problems with Society in Melanesia.* Berkeley and Los Angeles: University of California Press.
    1987  "An Awkward Relationship: The Case of Feminism and Anthropology." *Signs* 12 (2): 276–92.

Thomas, Nicholas J.
    1992  "The Inversion of Tradition." *American Ethnologist* 19 (2): 13–32.
    1991  *Entangled Objects: Exchange, Material Culture, and Colonialism in the Pacific.* Cambridge, Mass.: Harvard University Press.

Thompson, Edward P.
    1963  *The Making of the English Working Class.* New York: Vintage.

Trask, Haunai-Kay.
    1991  "Natives and Anthropologists: The Colonial Struggle." *Contemporary Pacific* 3: 159–77.

Trinh T. Minh-ha.
    1989  *Woman, Native, Other: Writing Postcoloniality and Feminism.* Bloomington: Indiana University Press.

Tsing, Anna Lowenhaupt.
    1993  *In the Realm of the Diamond Queen: Marginality in an Out-of-the-Way Place.* Princeton: Princeton University Press.

Turner, Terence.
    1980  "The Social Skin." In *Not Work Alone: A Cross-Cultural View of Activities Superfluous to Survival,* ed. J. Cherfs and R. Levin, 113–40. Beverly Hills, Calif.: Sage.

Vakhtin, Nikolai.
    1994  *Native Peoples of the Russian Far North.* Minority Rights Group International Report 92/5. London: Manchester Free Press.

□ □ □

Vasilevich, G. M.
1971 "O kul'te medvedia u Evenkov" (About the bear cult among the Evenks). In *Religionznye predstavleniia i obriady narodov Sibiri v xix—nachalo xx veka: Sbornik muzeia antropologii i etnografii,* ed. A. P. Potapov and S. V. Ivanov, 27:150–170. Leningrad: Nauka.

Vdovin, Innokentii Stepanovich.
1979 "Vliianie khristianstva na religioznye verovaniia" (The influence of Christianity on religious beliefs). In *Khristianstvo i lamaizm u korennogo naseleniia Sibiri (s vtoraia polovina xix—nachalo xx v.),* ed. I. S. Vdovin, 88–115. Leningrad: Nauka.
1973 *Ocherki etnicheskoi istorii Koriakov* (Essays on the ethnic history of the Koriaks). Leningrad: Nauka.
1971 "Zhertvennye mesta Koriakov i ikh istoriko-etnograficheskoe znachenie" (Sacrificial places of the Koriaks and their historic-ethnographic meaning). In *Religioznye predstavleniia i obriady narodov Sibiri v xix—nachale xx veka,* ed. A. P. Potapov and S. V. Ivanov, 3:275–99. Leningrad: Nauka.

Verdery, Katherine.
1996 *What Was Socialism and What Comes Next?* Princeton: Princeton University Press.

Weiner, Annette.
1992 *Inalienable Possessions: The Paradox of Keeping While Giving.* Berkeley and Los Angeles: University of California Press.

Weiser, Adele.
1989 *Die Völker Nordsibiriens: Unter Sowjetischer Herrschaft von 1917 bis 1936.* Munich: Klaus Renner.

West, Cornel.
1990 "The New Cultural Politics of Difference." In *Out There: Marginalization and Contemporary Cultures,* ed. R. Ferguson, M. Gever, Trinh T. Minh-ha, and Cornel West, 19–36. Cambridge, Mass.: MIT Press.

White, Stephen.
1996 *Russia Goes Dry: Alcohol, State, and Society.* Cambridge: Cambridge University Press.

Williams, Raymond.
1977 *Marxism and Literature.* Oxford: Oxford University Press.

Wolf, Eric P.
1982 *Europe and the People Without History.* Berkeley and Los Angeles: University of California Press.

Zito, Angela.
1994 "Silk and Skin: Significant Boundaries." In *Body, Subject, and Power in China,* ed .Angela Zito and Tani E. Barlow, 103–30. Chicago: University of Chicago Press.

Žižek, Slavoj.
1993 "Eastern Europe's Republics of Gilead." In *Dimensions of Radical Democracy: Pluralism, Citizenship, Community,* ed. Chantal Mouffe, 193–211. London: Verso.

Zolotarev, Alexander M.
1937 "The Bear Festival of the Olcha." *American Anthropologist* (39): 113–29.

# index □□□

Numbers in *italics* indicate maps or photographs.

□ □ □

□ □ □

□ □ □

□ □ □

□ □ □

□ □ □

□ □ □